SOCIO

NEW DIRECTIONS

Date label overleaf

Edited by Michael Haralambos

Written by Aidan Foster-Carter, Simon Frith,
David Glover, Nicky Hart, John Lambert, John
Richardson, Martin Slattery, Sheelagh Strawbridge

Causeway Books

British Library Cataloguing in Publication Data

Sociology: new directions.—(Themes & perspectives
in sociology)
    1. Sociology
    I. Haralambos, Michael   II. Series
    301   HM51

    ISBN 0–946183–17–1

Published 1985
Reprinted 1985, 1986, 1988, 1989, 1990,
1991, 1992, 1993, 1995

Causeway Press Ltd.
PO Box 13, Ormskirk, Lancashire L39 5HP
© Causeway Press Ltd., 1985

Typesetting by Bookform, Merseyside
Printed and bound by The Alden Press, Oxford

PAM JENOFF
KOMMANDANT'S
Girl

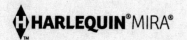

This edition published in Great Britain 2016.
Harlequin MIRA, an imprint of Harlequin (UK) Limited,
Eton House, 18-24 Paradise Road,
Richmond, Surrey, TW9 1SR

© 2007 Pam Jenoff

ISBN 978-1-848-45405-7

59-0415

Pam Jenoff is the author of several novels, including the international bestseller *Kommandant's Girl*, which also earned her a Quill Award nomination. Along with a bachelor degree in International Affairs from George Washington University and a Master's degree in History from Cambridge, she received her *Juris Doctor* from the University of Pennsylvania and previously served as a Foreign Service Officer for the US State Department in Europe, as the Special Assistant to the Secretary of the Army at the Pentagon and as a practising attorney. Pam lives with her husband and three children near Philadelphia where, in addition to writing, she teaches law school.

Visit Pam at www.pamjenoff.com

To my family

ACKNOWLEDGEMENTS

For several years after my return to the United States in 1998, I had wanted to write a novel that captured the experiences in Poland, and particularly with the Jewish community there, that had affected me so profoundly. I was captivated for some time by the vision of a young woman nervously guiding a child across Krakow's market square during the Nazi occupation. But it was not until early 2002, when I had the good fortune to ride a train from Washington, DC to Philadelphia with an elderly couple who were both Holocaust survivors, that I learned for the first time the extraordinary story of the Krakow resistance. And with that historical foundation, *Kommandant's Girl* was born.

There are so many people who have walked this path with me from concept to finished novel. I am eternally grateful to my family, friends and colleagues, including my mother and father, my brother Jay (yes, you can read it now), Phillip, Joanne, Stephanie, Barb and others too numerous to mention for their endless interest, patience and love. I would also like to thank my writing instructor, Janet Benton, and the other writers who have offered selfless guidance, fellowship and support every step of the way.

This book would not have been possible without the relentless efforts of my wonderful agent, Scott Hoffman of Folio Literary Management, who recognised the potential in this book before anyone else, worked tirelessly to refine it, and persevered long after most others would have quit. I would also like to salute my brilliant editor, Susan Pezzack, for her many insights in bringing this work to life and for making a dream come true.

Finally, I have come to realise through the writing of this book that the term "historical fiction" is somewhat of an oxymoron. While creating imaginary characters and events, I have endeavoured to remain true to the spirit of those who lived and died during World War II and the Holocaust, and to realistically depict the full range of human strengths, frailties and emotions brought out by this tragic and remarkable era. To this end, I would like to express my boundless admiration for the Jewish communities of Poland, and all of Central and Eastern Europe, past, present and future: your courageous struggle is an inspiration to us all.

CHAPTER 1

As we cut across the wide span of the market square, past the pigeons gathered around fetid puddles, I eye the sky warily and tighten my grip on Lukasz's hand, willing him to walk faster. But the child licks his ice-cream cone, oblivious to the darkening sky, a drop hanging from his blond curls. Thank God for his blond curls. A sharp March wind gusts across the square, and I fight the urge to let go of his hand and draw my threadbare coat closer around me.

We pass through the high center arch of the Sukennice, the massive yellow mercantile hall that bisects the square. It is still several blocks to Nowy Kleparz, the outdoor market on the far northern edge of Kraków's city center, and already I can feel Lukasz's gait slowing, his tiny, thin-soled shoes scuffing harder against the cobblestones with every step. I consider carrying him, but he is three years old and growing heavier by the day. Well fed, I might have managed it, but now I know that I would make it a few meters at most. If only he would go faster. *"Szybko, kochana,"* I plead with him under my breath. *"Chocz!"* His steps seem to lighten as we wind our way through the flower vendors peddling their wares in the shadow of the Mariacki Cathedral spires.

Moments later, we reach the far side of the square and I feel a familiar rumble under my feet. I pause. I have not been on a trolley in almost a year. I imagine lifting Lukasz onto the streetcar and sinking into a seat, watching the buildings and people walking below as we pass. We could be at the market in minutes. Then I stop, shake my head inwardly. The ink on our new papers is barely dry, and the wonder on Lukasz's face at his first trolley ride would surely arouse suspicion. I cannot trade our safety for convenience. We press onward.

Though I try to remind myself to keep my head low and avoid eye contact with the shoppers who line the streets this midweek morning, I cannot help but drink it all in. It has been more than a year since I was last in the city center. I inhale deeply. The air, damp from the last bits of melting snow, is perfumed with the smell of roasting chestnuts from the corner kiosk. Then the trumpeter in the cathedral tower begins to play the *hejnal,* the brief melody he sends across the square every hour on the hour to commemorate the Tartar invasion of Kraków centuries earlier. I resist the urge to turn back toward the sound, which greets me like an old friend.

As we approach the end of Florianska Street, Lukasz suddenly freezes, tightening his grip on my hand. I look down. He has dropped the last bit of his precious ice-cream cone on the pavement but does not seem to notice. His face, already pale from months of hiding indoors, has turned gray. "What is it?" I whisper, crouching beside him, but he does not respond. I follow his gaze to where it is riveted. Ten meters ahead, by the arched entrance to the medieval Florian Gate, stand two Nazis carrying machine guns. Lukasz shudders. "There, there, *kochana*. It's okay." I put my arms around his shoulders, but there is nothing I can do to soothe him. His eyes dart back and forth, and his mouth moves without sound. "Come." I lift him up and he buries his head in my neck. I look around for a side street to take, but there is none and turning around might attract attention. With a furtive glance to make sure no one is watching, I push the remnants of the ice-cream cone toward the gutter with my foot and proceed past the Nazis, who do not seem to notice us. A few minutes later, when I feel the child breathing calmly again, I set him down.

Soon we approach the Nowy Kleparz market. It is hard to contain my excitement at being out again, walking and shopping like a normal person. As we navigate the narrow walkways between the stalls, I hear people complaining. The cabbage is pale and wilted, the bread hard and dry; the meat, what there is of it, is from an unidentifiable source and already giving off a curious odor. To the townspeople and villagers, still accustomed to the prewar bounty of the Polish countryside, the food is an abomination. To me, it is paradise. My stomach tightens.

"Two loaves," I say to the baker, keeping my head low as I pass him my ration cards. A curious look crosses his face. It is your imagination, I tell myself. Stay calm. To a stranger, I know, I look like any other Pole. My coloring is fair, my accent flawless, my dress purposefully nondescript. Krysia chose this market in a working-class neighborhood on the northern edge of town deliberately, knowing that none of my former acquain-tances from the city would shop here. It is critical that no one recognize me.

I pass from stall to stall, reciting the groceries we need in my head: flour, some eggs, a chicken, if there is one to be had. I have never made lists, a fact that serves me well now that paper is so dear. The shopkeepers are kind, but businesslike. Six months into the war, food is in short supply; there is no generous cut of cheese for a smile, no sweet biscuit for the child with the large blue eyes. Soon I have used all of our ration cards, yet the basket remains half empty. We begin the long walk home.

Still feeling the chill from the wind on the market square, I lead Lukasz through side streets on our way back across town. A few minutes later, we turn onto Grodzka Street, a wide thoroughfare lined with elegant shops and houses. I hesitate. I had not meant to come here. My chest tightens, making it hard to breathe. Easy, I tell myself, you can do this. It is just another street. I walk a few meters farther, then stop. I am standing before a pale yellow house with a white door and wooden flower boxes in the windows. My eyes travel upward to the second floor. A lump forms in my throat, making it difficult to swallow. Don't, I think, but it is too late. This was Jacob's house. Our house.

I met Jacob eighteen months ago while I was working as a clerk in the university library. It was a Friday afternoon, I remember, because I was rushing to update the book catalog and get home in time for Shabbes. "Excuse me," a deep voice said. I looked up from my work, annoyed at the interruption. The speaker was of medium height and wore a small yarmulke and closely trimmed beard and mustache. His hair was brown with flecks of red. "Can you recommend a good book?"

"A good book?" I was caught off guard as much by the swimming darkness of his eyes as by the generic nature of his request.

"Yes, I would like something light to read over the weekend to take my mind off my studies. Perhaps the Iliad…?"

I could not help laughing. "You consider Homer light reading?"

"Relative to physics texts, yes." The corners of his eyes crinkled. I led him to the literature section, where he settled upon a volume of Shakespeare's comedies. Our knuckles brushed as I handed him the book, sending a chill down my spine. I checked out the book to him, but still he lingered. I learned that his name was Jacob and that he was twenty, two years my senior.

After that, he came to visit me daily. I quickly learned that even though he was a science major, his real passion was politics and that he was involved with many activist groups. He wrote pieces, published in student and local newspapers, that were critical not only of the Polish government, but of what he called "Germany's unfettered dominance" over its neighbors. I worried that it was dangerous to be so outspoken. While the Jews of my neighborhood argued heatedly on their front stoops, outside the synagogues and in the stores about current affairs and everything else, I was raised to believe that it was safer to keep one's voice low when dealing with the outside world. But Jacob, the son of prominent sociologist Maximillian Bau, had no such concerns, and as I listened to him speak, watched his eyes burn and his hands fly, I forgot to be afraid.

I was amazed that a student from a wealthy, secular family would be interested in me, the daughter of a poor Orthodox baker, but if he noticed the difference in our backgrounds, it did not seem to matter. We began spending our Sunday afternoons together, talking and strolling along the Wisla River. "I should be getting home," I remarked one Sunday afternoon in April as the sky grew dusky. Jacob and I had been walking along the river path where it wound around the base of Wawel Castle, talking so intensely I had lost track of time. "My parents will be wondering where I am."

"Yes, I should meet them soon," he replied matter-of-factly. I stopped in my tracks. "That's what one does, isn't it, when one wants to ask permission to court?" I was too surprised to answer. Though Jacob and I had spent much time together these recent months and I knew he enjoyed my company, I somehow never thought that he would seek permission to see me formally. He reached down and took my chin in his gloved fingers. Softly, he pressed his lips down on mine for the first time. Our mouths lingered together, lips slightly parted. The ground seemed to slide sideways, and I felt so dizzy I was afraid that I might faint.

Thinking now of Jacob's kiss, I feel my legs grow warm. Stop it, I tell myself, but it is no use. It has been nearly six months since I have seen my husband, been touched by him. My whole body aches with longing.

A sharp clicking noise jars me from my thoughts. My vision clears and I find myself still standing in front of the yellow house, staring upward. The front door opens and an older, well-dressed woman steps out. Noticing me and Lukasz, she hesitates. I can tell she is wondering who we are, why we have stopped in front of her house. Then she turns from us dismissively, locks the door and proceeds down the steps. This is her home now. Enough, I tell myself sharply. I cannot afford to do anything that will draw attention. I shake my head, trying to clear the image of Jacob from my mind.

"Come, Lukasz," I say aloud, tugging gently on the child's hand. We continue walking and soon cross the Planty, the broad swath of parkland that rings the city center. The trees are revealing the most premature of buds, which will surely be cut down by a late frost. Lukasz tightens his grip on my hand, staring wide-eyed at the few squirrels that play among the bushes as though it is already spring. As we push onward, I feel the city skyline receding behind us. Five minutes later we reach the Aleje, the wide boulevard that, if taken to the left, leads south across the river. I stop and look toward the bridge. Just on the other side, a half kilometer south, lies the ghetto. I start to turn in that direction, thinking of my parents. Perhaps if I go to the wall, I can see them, find a way to slip them some of the food I have just purchased. Krysia would not mind. Then I stop—I cannot risk it, not in broad daylight, not with the child. I feel shame at my stomach, which no longer twists with hunger, and at my freedom, at crossing the street as though the occupation and the war do not exist.

Half an hour later, Lukasz and I reach Chelmska, the rural neighborhood we have come to call home. My feet are sore from walking along the uneven dirt road and my arms ache from carrying the groceries, as well as the child, for the last several meters. As we round the corner where the main road divides in two, I inhale deeply; the air has grown colder now, its pureness broken only by an acrid hint of smoke from a farmer burning piles of dead winter brush. I can see the fires smoldering across the sloping farmland to my right, their thick smoke fanning out over the fields that roll like a gentle green lake into the horizon.

We turn left onto the road dotted with farmhouses that, if taken farther, winds upward into the tree-covered hills of Las Wolski. About fifty yards up the road stands Krysia's house, a dark wood, three-story chalet, nestled among the pine trees. A plume of smoke rises from the chimney to greet us. I set the child down and he runs ahead. Hearing his footsteps, Krysia appears from behind the house and walks to the front gate. With her silver hair piled high on her head, she looks as though she is attending the opera, except that her hands are clad in cracked leather gardening gloves, rather than silk or lace. The hem of her working dress, nicer than anything I could ever hope to own, is caked with dirt. At the sight of Lukasz, her lineless face folds into a smile. She breaks her perfect posture to stoop and lift him.

"Did everything go all right?" Krysia asks as I approach, still bouncing Lukasz on her hip and studying his face. She does not look at me. I am not offended by her preoccupation with the child. In the time he has been with us, he has yet to smile or speak, a fact that is a source of constant worry for both of us.

"More or less."

"Oh?" Her head snaps up. "What happened?"

I hesitate, not wanting to speak in front of the child. "We saw some, um, Germans." I tilt my head in Lukasz's direction. "And it was upsetting. But they didn't notice us."

"Good. Were you able to get everything at market?"

I shake my head. "Some things." I lift the basket slightly. "Not as much as I hoped, though."

"It's no matter, we'll manage. I was just turning over the

ground in the garden so that we can seed next month." Wordlessly, I follow Krysia into the house, amazed as ever at her grace and strength. There is a sense of purpose in the way she shifts her weight as she walks that reminds me of my husband.

Upstairs, Krysia takes the basket from me and begins to unpack the groceries. I wander into the parlor. After two weeks of living here, I am still awestruck by the plush furniture, the beautiful artwork that adorns every wall. I walk past the grand piano to the fireplace. On the mantel sit three framed photographs. One is of Marcin, Krysia's deceased husband, seated with his cello in front of him, wearing a tuxedo. Another is of Jacob as a child playing by a lake. I lift the third picture. It is a photograph of Jacob and me, taken on our wedding day. We are standing on the steps in front of the Baus' house on Grodzka Street, Jacob in a dark suit, me in the ankle-length white linen wedding dress that had been worn by my mother and grandmother before me. Though we were supposed to be looking at the camera, our heads are tilted toward each other, my lips parted with laughter at a joke he had just whispered to me.

Originally, we had intended to wait to marry until Jacob graduated the following year. But by late July 1939, Germany had swallowed the Sudetenland from Czechoslovakia, and the other countries of Western Europe had done nothing to stop him. Hitler stood poised on the Polish border, ready to pounce. We had heard stories of the Nazis' abysmal treatment of the Jews in Germany and Austria. If the Nazis came into Poland, who knew what our lives would be like? Better, we decided, to get married right away and face the uncertainties of the future together.

Jacob proposed on a humid afternoon during one of our

Sunday walks by the river. "Emma…" He stopped and turned to me, then dropped to one knee. I was not entirely surprised. Jacob had walked to synagogue with my father the previous morning, and I could tell from the pensive way my father looked at me as they returned to the apartment afterward that they had not been discussing politics or religion, but rather our future together. Still, my eyes watered. "Times are uncertain," Jacob began. Inwardly, I could not help but laugh. Only Jacob could turn a proposal into a political speech. "But I know that whatever is coming, I want to face it with you. Will you do me the honor of becoming my wife?"

"Yes," I whispered as he slipped a silver ring with a tiny diamond onto my left hand. He rose and kissed me, longer and harder than ever before.

We wed a few weeks later under a canopy in the Baus' elegant parlor, with only our immediate families in attendance. After the wedding, we moved my few belongings to the spare room in the Baus' home that Jacob and I were to share. Professor and Mrs. Bau departed shortly after we returned for a teaching sabbatical in Geneva, leaving Jacob and me on our own. Having been raised in a tiny, three-room apartment, I was unaccustomed to living in such splendor. The high ceilings and polished wood floors seemed better suited to a museum. At first, I felt awkward, like a perennial guest in the enormous house, but I soon came to love living in a grand home filled with music, art and books. Jacob and I would lie awake at night and whisper dreams of the following year after his graduation when we would be able to buy a home of our own.

One Friday afternoon about three weeks after the wedding, I decided to walk down to the Jewish quarter, Kazimierz, and pick up some challah bread from my parents' bakery for dinner. When I arrived at the shop, it was crowded with customers rushing to get ready for Shabbes so I stepped behind the counter to help my harried father fill the orders. I had just handed a customer her change when the door to the shop burst open and a young boy ran in. "The Germans have attacked!" he exclaimed.

I froze. The shop became instantly silent. Quickly, my father retrieved his radio from the back room, and the customers huddled around the counter to hear the news. The Germans had attacked the harbor of Westerplatte, near the northern city of Gdańsk; Poland and Germany were at war. Some of the women started crying. The radio announcer stopped speaking then and the Polish national anthem began to play. Several customers began to sing along. "The Polish army will defend us," I heard Pan Klopowitz, a wizened veteran of the Great War, say to another customer. But I knew the truth. The Polish army, consisting in large part of soldiers on horseback and on foot, would be no match for German tanks and machine guns. I looked to my father and our eyes met. One of his hands was fingering the edge of his prayer shawl, the other gripping the edge of the countertop, knuckles white. I could tell that he was imagining the worst.

"Go," my father said to me after the customers had departed hurriedly with their loaves of bread. I did not return to the library but rushed home. Jacob was already at the apartment when I arrived, his face ashen. Wordlessly, he drew me into his embrace.

Within two weeks of the German invasion, the Polish army was overrun. Suddenly the streets of Kraków were filled with tanks and large, square-jawed men in brown uniforms for whom the crowds parted as they passed. I was fired from my job at the library, and a few days later, Jacob was told by the head of his department that Jews were no longer permitted to attend the university. Our world as we had known it seemed to disappear overnight.

I had hoped that, once Jacob had been dismissed from the university, he would be home more often, but instead his political meetings took on a frenetic pace, held in secret now at apartments throughout the city at night. Though he did not say it, I became aware that these meetings were somehow related to opposing the Nazis. I wanted to ask him, beg him, to stop. I was terrified that he might be arrested, or worse. I knew, though, that my concerns would not squelch his passion.

One Tuesday night in late September, I dozed off while waiting for him to come home. Sometime later, I awoke. The clock on our nightstand told me that it was after midnight. He should have been home by now. I leapt from bed. The apartment was still, except for the sound of my bare feet on the hardwood floor. My mind raced. I paced the house like a mad- woman, returning to the window every five minutes to scan the street below.

Sometime after one-thirty, I heard a noise in the kitchen. Jacob had come up the back stairway. His hair and beard, usually so well-kept, were disheveled. A thin line of perspiration covered the area above his upper lip. I threw my arms around him, trembling. Wordlessly, Jacob took my hand and led me into our bedroom. I did not try to speak further as he pushed me down to the mattress and pressed his weight on top of me with an urgency I had never felt before.

"Emma, I have to leave," he said later that night, as we lay in the dark listening to the rumbling of the trolleys below. The sweat of our lovemaking had dried on my skin in the cool autumn air, leaving me with an inescapable chill.

My stomach tightened. "Because of your work?"

"Yes."

I knew he was not referring to his former university job. "When?" I asked, my voice trembling.

"Soon…days, I think." There was an uneasiness in his voice that told me he was not saying all that he knew. He rolled over to press his stomach against my back and curled his knees under mine. "I will leave money in case you need anything."

I waved my hand in the dark. "I don't want it." My eyes teared. Please, I wanted to say. I would have begged if I thought it would have done any good.

"Emma…" He paused. "You should go to your parents."

"I will." When you are gone, I thought.

"One other thing…" His warmth pulled away from me and he reached into the drawer of the nightstand. The paper he handed me felt new, the candle-wax seal raised. "Burn this." It was our *kittubah,* our Hebrew marriage certificate. In the rush of events, we had not had time to register our marriage with the civil authorities.

I pushed the paper back at him. "Never."

"You must take off your rings, pretend we were never married. Tell your family to say nothing." He continued, "It will be dangerous for you if anyone knows you are my wife once I am gone."

"*Dangerous?* Jacob, I am a Jew in a country occupied by Nazis. How much more dangerous can it get?"

"Just do it," he insisted.

"Okay," I lied, taking the paper from him and sliding it under the mattress. I would not burn the one thing that would always link me to him.

I lay awake after Jacob had begun to breathe his long, even sleep. Softly, I touched his hair where it reached his collar, burying my nose there and inhaling his scent. I traced his hand with mine, trying to etch the shape in my mind. He shifted and grunted, already fighting the enemy in his sleep. As my eyelids at last grew heavy, I struggled to stay awake. There would be plenty of time for sleeping later.

But eventually I lost to my exhaustion. I awoke hours later to the sounds of the street sweepers brushing the sidewalks, and the rhythmic hooves of the deliverymen's horses banging against the cobblestones. Outside, it was still dark. I ran my hand across the empty space in bed beside me, the sheets still warm and rumpled where my husband had lain. His musky scent hung heavily in the air above me. I did not have to look up to know that his rucksack and other belongings were gone.

Jacob had disappeared. We'd been married for six weeks.

"...hungry?" Krysia's voice jars me from my thoughts. I realize that she has come into the parlor and has been speaking to me, but I have not heard what she has said. I turn to her reluctantly, as though I have been woken from a pleasant dream. She holds out a plate of bread and cheese toward me.

"No, thank you." I shake my head, still half lost in memories.

Krysia sets down the plate on the coffee table and comes over to me. "That's a beautiful picture," she says, gesturing toward my wedding photo. I do not answer. She lifts up the photo of Jacob as a child. "But we should put these away so no one sees them."

"Who would see them?" I ask. "I mean, it's just the three of us here." Krysia let her maid and her gardener go before Lukasz and I arrived, and in the weeks we have lived with her, there has been no one else inside the house.

"You never know," she replies. Her voice sounds strange. "Better to be safe." She holds out her hand and I hesitate, not wanting to surrender one of the last ties I have to my husband. She's right, I realize. There's no other choice. With a sigh, I hand her the wedding photograph and watch numbly as she carries it from the room.

CHAPTER 2

The morning Jacob disappeared, not daring to leave a note, I sat in bed for several minutes, blinking and looking around the bedroom. "He's not coming back," I said aloud. I was too stunned to cry. I rose and dressed, my movements reflexive, as though I'd rehearsed for this moment a thousand times. I packed my small suitcase as quickly as I could. Reluctantly, I took off my engagement and wedding rings, and slipped them, along with our marriage certificate, into the bottom of my suitcase.

At the door of our bedroom, I hesitated. On the crowded bookshelf by the door, nearly buried beneath Jacob's physics textbooks and political treatises, lay a small stack of novels, *Ivanhoe, Pride and Prejudice* and a few others, mostly by foreign authors. I reached out to touch the bindings of the books, remembering. Jacob had given these to me shortly after we had met. He used to come visit me at the library every day, and often he brought me small gifts, such as an apple or a flower or, best of all, a book. I laughed the first time he did this. "Bringing books to a library?" I teased, examining the slim, leather-covered tome, a translation of Charles Dickens's *Great Expectations*.

"But I am sure you do not have this one!" he protested in earnest, holding out the book, his brown eyes smiling. And he was right, for although I had already read many books, I had not possessed a single one of my own until then. My parents had encouraged learning and had sent me to the Jewish girls' school as long as they could manage, but owning books, other than the family Bible and prayer book, was not a luxury we could afford. I treasured each of the half dozen or so books Jacob brought me, never telling him that I had read them all before from the library, some so many times I knew them almost by heart. I reread each one (the story was somehow different now that the book was my own) and then tucked it away safely in my dresser drawer. They had been among the few possessions I had brought with me from my parents' house to the Baus'.

Picturing Jacob as he gave me the first book, my eyes burned. Where are you, I wondered as I stared at the bookshelf, and when will you be back? I brushed away a tear and studied the books. I can't take them with me, I thought. They're too heavy. But I won't leave them all, either. Finally, I pulled two of the books from the shelf and squeezed them into my bag.

I walked to the front door of the Baus' house, bags in hand. My eyes lingered on the rose-colored silk curtains, held back gracefully from the high windows with bronze-colored rope, the gold-rimmed china in the glass-front cabinet along the foyer wall. With the house empty, what was to stop vagrants, or even the Nazis, from looting the place? For a moment I considered staying. Jacob had been right, though; it would not be safe for me alone. Searches by the Gestapo had become commonplace, and several fine apartments in the city center had already been expropriated from their Jewish owners and given to high-ranking Nazi officers. I thought fleetingly of taking a few of the Baus' belongings to protect them, perhaps a few small paintings or the silver candlesticks. But even if I had been able to transport these things to my parents' tiny home, they would hardly be any safer there. Pausing in the foyer, I looked around one last time before closing the door behind me.

I made my way down Grodzka Street, away from the city center toward the Jewish quarter. As I walked, the houses grew more dilapidated, the streets narrower. I could not help but remember the first time I had allowed Jacob to escort me home from the library. He had offered for months, but I had always refused, afraid that if he saw the poor, religious world I came from, he would realize the differences between us and disappear forever. I had watched his face as we reached the edge of the Jewish quarter. I could tell by the way he bit the inside of his cheek and tightened his arm protectively around me that he was taken aback by the naked poverty, by the cramped, run-down buildings, and shabbily dressed inhabitants of my neighborhood. He never said a word, though. If anything, his affection toward me seemed to grow after that day, and he seemed determined to take me away to his world. Until now, I thought, staring at the desolate street before me. Now he was gone and I was returning to Kazimierz, alone. I could feel the tears gathering in my eyes once more.

Soon I reached Szeroka Street, the main square at the heart of the Jewish quarter. I paused, taking in the synagogues and shops that lined the square. Something was different from when I'd last visited just weeks ago. Though it was a weekday morning, the streets were empty and eerily silent. Gone were the neighbors calling to one another through open windows, the men arguing in front of the shops, the shawl-covered women carrying bundles of food and kindling. It was as if the neighborhood had disappeared overnight.

I decided to stop in the bakery and say hello to my father before heading to the apartment. The bakery, which consisted of just a tiny shop with an adjacent kitchen, was my father's labor of love. He had opened it as a young man more than thirty years ago to support him and my mother, and had worked there every day since. Even after the occupation, he had stubbornly insisted upon keeping the store open with few supplies and even fewer paying customers in order to provide a source of food to our family, friends and neighbors, and to furtively produce small quantities of the Jewish breads, the challah loaves for the Sabbath and matzah for Passover that were now forbidden.

He would want me to stay, of course, to set my suitcases in the corner and put on one of his large aprons and bake with him. Helping my father was one of the things I missed most about not living in Kazimierz since I had gotten married. We used to talk for hours as we made and kneaded the dough together. Often he told me stories of his childhood, of my grandparents, whom I had never met, and the large general store they had owned, close to the German border. Sometimes he would grow quiet and I could hear him humming under his breath. I did not have to look over to know that he was smiling to himself, his dark beard white with flour.

I turned right at the corner of Jozefa Street and stopped in front of the bakery. I tried to open the front door, but it was locked. For a moment, I wondered if I had gotten my days wrong and the bakery was closed for Shabbes. The last time my father had not opened the bakery on a day other than Saturday or a Jewish holiday was the day I was born. I pressed my face against the window. The shop was dark inside. An uneasy feeling arose in me. It was after eight o'clock; my father should have been working for several hours already. I wondered if something was wrong, if he or my mother was sick. With a shiver, I hurried toward our apartment on Miodowa Street.

A few minutes later, I entered the dimly lit building where I had lived all of my life before marrying Jacob. Inside, the air was heavy with the odor of cabbage and onions. I made my way up the three flights of stairs. Breathing heavily, I set my bags down in the hallway, then turned the handle of the door to our apartment. "Hello?" I called, stepping into the living room. Morning sunlight streamed through the two large windows. I looked around. Growing up, I had not minded our tiny, cozy apartment, but after marrying Jacob and moving into the Baus' grand house, my childhood home seemed somehow changed. On my first visit back after our honeymoon, I had taken in our yellowed curtains and frayed chair cushions with distaste, as though seeing for the first time how small and disheveled our apartment really was. I felt guilty at leaving my parents behind here while I lived in comfort with Jacob. But they did not seem to notice; for them it was the only home they had ever known. Now I have to live here again, I thought, wishing I did not. I was immediately ashamed at my snobbery.

"Hello?" I said again, louder this time. There was no response. I looked at the clock over the mantelpiece. It was eight-thirty, which meant that my father should have long since departed for the bakery. My mother never left this early, though; she should have been home. Something was not right. I sniffed the air. The lingering scent of eggs and onions, the breakfast my mother always cooked, was missing. Alarmed, I raced into my parents' bedroom. Some of the dresser drawers were open, clothes hanging out. My mother never would have gone out with the apartment in such a state. My grandparents' gray wool blanket, which usually lay folded at the foot of my parents' bed, was gone.

"Mama…?" I called, panic seizing me. I ran back through the living room into the corridor and stared down the stairwell. The building was silent except for the echoing of my footsteps. I heard none of the early-morning noises that came through the paper-thin walls, sounds of people talking and pots banging and water running. My heart pounded. Everyone had disappeared. I froze, uncertain what to do.

Suddenly, I heard a creaking noise on the stairway above. "Hello?" I called, starting up the stairs. Through the railings, I could see a flash of blue clothing. "It's Emma Gershmann," I said, using my maiden name. "Who's there?" It did not occur to me to be afraid. I heard one footstep, then another. A small boy, no older than twelve, came into view. I recognized him as one of the many Rosenkrantz children from the fourth floor. "You're Jonas, aren't you?" I asked. He nodded. "Where is everyone?"

He did not speak for several minutes. "I was playing in the courtyard when they came," he began, his voice barely a whisper.

"Who came, Jonas?" I asked, dreading his answer.

"Men in uniforms," he replied softly. "Lots of them."

"Germans?" He nodded. Suddenly my knees felt weak. I leaned against the railing for support. "When?"

"Two days ago. They made everyone leave in a hurry. My family. Yours, too."

My stomach twisted. "Where did they go?"

He shrugged. "They walked south toward the river. Everyone had suitcases." The ghetto, I thought, sinking down to the bottom stair. Shortly after the start of the occupation, the Nazis had created a walled area in Podgorze, a district south of the river. They had ordered all of the Jews from the nearby villages to move there. It had never occurred to me that my family might have to relocate there, though; we already lived in the Jewish quarter. "I hid until they were gone," Jonas added. I did not reply, but leapt up and raced back down the stairs to our apartment. At the entrance, I stopped. The mezuzah was gone, ripped from the wooden door frame. I touched the faint shadow that remained where the small metal box had hung for decades. My father must have broken it off as they left. He knew they weren't coming back.

I had to find them. I grabbed my suitcase and closed the apartment door behind me, turning to Jonas, who had followed me down the steps. "Jonas, you can't stay here, it isn't safe," I said. "Do you have anyone to go to?" He shook his head. I paused. I couldn't take him with me. "Here," I continued, reaching into my bag and passing him a handful of the coins that Jacob had left me. "Use this for food."

He shoved the coins in his pocket. "Where are you going?"

I hesitated. "To find my parents."

"Are you going to the ghetto?"

I looked at him in surprise. I had not realized that he understood where his family had been taken. "Yes."

"You won't be able to leave," Jonas said with childlike logic. I hesitated. In my haste, it hadn't occurred to me that going to the ghetto meant I would be imprisoned, too.

"I have to go. You be careful. Stay out of sight." I put my hand on his shoulder. "I'll tell your mother you're okay if I see her." Not waiting for him to reply, I turned and raced down the stairs.

Outside I paused, looking in both directions down the deserted street. The Nazis must have cleared the entire neighborhood, I realized. I stood motionless, trying to figure out what to do. Jonas was right, of course. If I went to the ghetto, I would not be able to leave again. But what other choice did I have? I could not stay in our apartment. Even standing here on the street was probably not safe. I wished desperately that Jacob was here; he would surely know what to do. Of course, if he was here, I would still be safe in our bedroom in the Baus' apartment, instead of alone on the street corner with nowhere to go. I wondered how far away he was by now. Would he have left if he realized what would happen to me so soon after he was gone?

I will go to the ghetto, I decided. I had to know if my parents were there, if they were all right. Picking up my bags once more, I began walking swiftly through the empty streets of the Jewish quarter, making my way south toward the river. The scraping of the soles of my shoes and my suitcase against the pavement were the only sounds that broke the early morning silence. My skin grew moist under my clothes and my arms ached as I struggled to carry my overstuffed bags in the thick autumn morning.

Shortly, I reached the edge of the Wisla River, which separated our old world from our new one. I paused at the foot of the railway bridge, looking across to the far bank. Podgorze was a foreign neighborhood to me, commercial and crowded. Scanning the dirty, dilapidated buildings, I could just make out the top edge of the ghetto wall. A shiver ran through me. You will only be a few kilometers away, I told myself. The thought gave me no comfort. The ghetto was not Kazimierz, not our home. It might as well have been another planet.

For a moment, I considered turning around and running away. But where would I go? Taking a deep breath, I started walking across the bridge. My legs felt like lead. As I trudged silently across the railway bridge, I could hear the river rippling gently against the shore from which I had come. The smell of brackish water wafted up through the slats in the bridge. Don't look back, I thought. But as I reached the far bank, a starling cried out behind me and I turned, almost against my will. On the far shore, high atop an embankment overlooking the river, sat Wawel Castle, its roofs and cathedral spires bathed in sunrise gold. Its grandeur seemed a betrayal. For my entire life, I had worked and played, walked and lived in its shadows. I had felt protected by this fortress, which for centuries had been the seat of the Polish monarchy. Now it seemed I was being cast out. I was walking into a prison, and the castle seemed oblivious to my plight. Kraków, the City of Kings, was no longer mine. I had become a foreigner in the place I had always called home.

CHAPTER 3

From the foot of the bridge, I walked a few hundred meters along the granite wall of the ghetto. The top edge of the wall had been sculpted into arcs, each about two feet wide. Like tombstones, I thought, my stomach twisting. When I reached the entrance, an iron gate, I paused, inhaling deeply before approaching the Nazi guard. "Name?" he asked, before I could speak.

"I—I…" I stammered.

The guard looked up from his clipboard. "Name!" he barked.

"Gershmann, Emma," I managed to say.

The guard scanned his list. "Not here."

"No, but I think my parents are, Chaim and Reisa Gershmann."

He looked again, turned to another page. "Yes. Twenty-one Limanowa Street, apartment six."

"Then I want to be with them." A look of surprise flashed across his face and he opened his mouth. He's going to tell me I cannot come inside, I thought. For a moment, I felt almost relieved. But then, seeming to think better of it, the guard wrote my name beside my parents' on the list and moved aside to let me enter. I hesitated, looking down the street in both directions before stepping into the ghetto. The gate slammed shut behind me.

Inside, a wall of human stench assaulted me and I had to fight the urge not to gag. Trying to take only shallow breaths through my mouth, I asked directions from a man, who pointed me toward Limanowa Street. As I made my way through the ghetto, I tried not to look at the gaunt, bedraggled passersby who stared at me, a new arrival, with unabashed curiosity. I turned onto Limanowa Street, stopping before the address the guard had given me. The building looked as though it had already been condemned. I opened the front door and climbed the stairs. When I reached the top floor, I hesitated, wiping my sweaty palms on my skirt. Through the rotting wood door of one of the apartments I could hear my mother's voice. Tears sprang to my eyes. Until now, I hadn't wanted to believe they were really here. I took a deep breath and knocked. *"Nu?"* I heard my father call. His footsteps grew louder, then the door opened. At the sight of me, his eyes grew wide. "Emmala!" he cried, throwing his enormous arms around me and hugging me so hard I thought we would both fall over.

Behind him, my mother clutched her apron, her eyes dark. "What are you doing here?" she demanded. When my father finally released me, she pulled me into the apartment.

Looking around, I shuddered inwardly: did they really live here? Small and dark and smelling dankly of mold, the single room with its lone cracked window made our modest Kazimierz apartment look like a palace in comparison. I could tell that my mother had tried to make the place habitable, fashioning pale yellow curtains to hang over the cloudy, cracked window and hanging sheets to divide the room into two parts, a makeshift bedroom and a tiny communal living area, barely big enough to hold three chairs and a small table. But it was still horrible.

"I came back to stay with you, but you were gone." I could hear the accusing tone in my own voice: why hadn't you told me where you had gone, or at least left a note?

"They gave us thirty minutes to leave," my father said, pulling out two chairs for me and my mother to sit on. "There was no time to get word to you. Where's Jacob?"

"His work," I said simply. They nodded in unison, unsurprised. They were well aware of Jacob's political activities. Aside from the fact that he was not Orthodox, it was the one thing they did not like about him.

"You shouldn't be here," my father fretted, pacing the floor. "We are older people. Probably no one will bother us. But it is the young people…" He did not have to finish the sentence. The young people were the ones being deported from Kraków. Those who received deportation orders in the ghetto were trapped, unable to run.

"I had nowhere else to go," I replied.

"Well," my mother said, taking my hand, "at least we are all together. Let's get you settled."

The next morning, I reported to the Jewish Administration

Building to register with the Judenrat, the group of ghetto inhabitants designated by the Nazis to run the internal affairs of the ghetto. I was assigned to work in the ghetto orphanage. My parents had already received work assignments, and by some luck, they had also been given reasonable jobs, my father to the communal ghetto kitchen, where he could once again bake, my mother to the infirmary as a nurse's aide. We had all managed to escape the dreaded work details, where Jews were forced to perform heavy manual labor outside the ghetto walls under the eyes of brutal Nazi guards.

I began working that afternoon. The orphanage was a small, two-story facility that the Judenrat had established on Josefinska Street. The inside was dark and overcrowded, but a tiny grass enclosure behind the nursery gave the children, mostly toddlers, a place to play. It housed about thirty children, virtually all of whom had lost their parents since the start of the war. I enjoyed watching them. Aside from being woefully thin from the meager ghetto rations, they were still children, oblivious to the war, their abysmal surroundings and the dire situation of having no parents to care for them in an uncaring world.

Yet despite the small amount of pleasure I took in my job, I thought constantly of Jacob. Surrounded by children, I was often reminded of the family we might have started by then, if not for the war. At night I played back our moments together in my head, our courtship, our wedding, and after. The nights had been few and dear enough that I could remember every single one. Staring up at the low ceiling of our apartment, I thought guiltily, defiantly, of sex, of the silent, unexpected joys that Jacob had fleetingly taught me. Where was Jacob? I worried each night as I lay in bed, and whom he was with? There must be girls in the resistance, yet Jacob had not asked me to join him. I wondered with shame not if Jacob was hurt or warm enough, but whether he was faithful, or if some braver, bolder woman had stolen his heart.

I was lonely not just for Jacob but for other company, too. My parents, overwhelmed by the twelve-hour work shifts spent almost entirely on their feet, had little energy to do more than eat their rations and crawl into bed at day's end. The ghetto had taken a tremendous toll on both of my parents in the short time they had been there; it was as if they had aged overnight. My father, once hearty and strong, seemed to move with great effort. My mother moved more slowly, too, dark circles ringing her eyes. Her rich, chestnut mane of hair was now brittle and streaked with gray. I knew that she slept little. Some nights, as I lay in bed, I could hear her muffled sobs through the curtain that separated our sleep quarters. "Reisa, Reisa," my father repeated, trying unsuccessfully to reassure her. Her cries unsettled me. My mother had grown up in the small village of Przemysl in a region to the east known as the Pale, which had been under Russian control prior to the Great War and was subject to intense, sudden outbursts of violence against its Jewish inhabitants. She had seen houses burned, livestock taken, had witnessed the murder of those who offered a hint of resistance. It was the violence of the pogroms that had caused her to flee west to Kraków, after her parents had succumbed to illness brought on by the brutal living conditions. She had managed to survive, but she knew just how afraid we all ought to be.

The other women who worked in the orphanage were not much company, either. In their fifties and older, and mostly from the villages, they were not unkind, but the work of bathing, feeding and minding so many children left little room for conversation. The closest I came to a friend at the orphanage was Hadassa Nederman, a heavy-set widow from the nearby village of Bochnia. Round-faced and perpetually smiling, she always had time for a kind word or a joke. Most days, after the children had gone down for their afternoon naps, we would share a few moments of conversation over our watery afternoon tea, and though I could not tell her about Jacob, she seemed to sense my loneliness.

One day when I had been working in the nursery for about two months, Pani Nederman came to me, leading a dark-haired girl with her same thick-waisted build by the hand. "Emma, this is my daughter, Marta."

"Hello!" Marta cried exuberantly, drawing me into a bear hug as though we were old friends. I liked her instantly. A few years younger than me, she had bright eyes that leapt out from behind her improbably large spectacles and wild dark curls that sprung from her head in all directions. She smiled and talked nonstop. Marta's job in the ghetto was to serve as a messenger for the Judenrat, delivering notes and packages within and sometimes outside the ghetto.

"You must come to our Shabbes dinner," she declared after we had spoken for a few minutes.

"Your family's?" I asked, puzzled. People seldom admitted observing the Sabbath in the ghetto, much less invited guests to join them.

She shook her head. "My friends and I have a gathering every Friday night. It is just over there." She pointed to a building across the street from the orphanage. "I checked ahead of time, when my mother told me about you. They said it is all right for you to come."

I hesitated, thinking of my parents. Shabbes in the ghetto was just the three of us, but we observed it together every week. My father would smuggle a tiny loaf of forbidden challah out of the ghetto kitchen, and my mother would burn a small amount of our precious remaining candles on a saucer, the candlesticks having been left behind in Kazimierz. Though weary from their long, grueling workweeks, my parents always seemed renewed on Friday nights. Their backs would straighten and the color would return a bit to their cheeks as they chanted the Sabbath prayers in hushed but unwavering voices. We would sit together for hours, sharing the anecdotes we were too tired to relate on other days. I hated to think of leaving them alone, even for a single Friday.

"I'll try," I promised Marta, thinking that it was unlikely I would go. In truth, it was not just my parents that concerned me; I was shy, and the thought of walking into a room full of strangers made me nervous. But as the week progressed, I found myself wanting to go with Marta. Finally, on Thursday night, I mentioned it to my parents.

"Go," they replied at the same time, their faces lifting. "You need some company your own age."

The next afternoon, when my shift at the orphanage was ending and the children had all been fed, Marta appeared at the door unannounced. "Ready?" she asked, as though my attendance at the dinner had never been in question. Together we walked across the street to Josefinska 13.

Marta led me up a flight of dimly lit stairs and through an unlocked door. The room we entered was long and narrow, with a kitchen off to the right side and another door at the far end. The faded, frayed curtains were drawn. A long wooden table occupied most of the room, surrounded by mismatched chairs. Marta introduced me to the dozen or so young people already gathered in the room, some seated at the table, others milling around. I couldn't remember most of their names, but it didn't seem to matter. Newcomers, it appeared, were not unusual, and I forgot to be nervous among the friendly banter. I recognized a few of the people from around the ghetto, but they looked like entirely different people from the somber characters I had seen on the streets. Here, they were energized, talking and laughing with friends as though at a party a million miles from the ghetto.

A few minutes later, someone rang a small bell. As if on cue, everyone quieted and gathered around the table to find seats. Marta led me to two empty places at the end of the table by the front door. Looking around, I counted at least eighteen people. It seemed there would not be room for so many, but everyone jostled and squeezed in. We stood shoulder to shoulder with the others at our respective places in silence.

The door at the far end of the room opened and two men entered. One was stocky and appeared to be in his early twenties, the other slightly taller and older with a trim goatee. They stood at the places that had been left empty at the head of the table. A young woman standing beside the older man lit the candles. The gathering watched in silence as she circled the flames with her hands three times, reciting the Sabbath prayer.

"That's Alek Landesberg," Marta whispered, gesturing toward the older man. "He sort of leads this group."

"*Shalom aleichem,*" the man began to sing in a rich baritone, and the group all joined in the traditional welcome to the Sabbath. I looked around the table. The faces had been unknown to me an hour ago. Now, bathed in candlelight, they looked as familiar as family. As they sang, their voices rose and formed a tapestry that seemed to separate this place from the horrible, desolate world outside. Tears came to my eyes. Marta, noticing my reaction, squeezed my hand.

When the song was over, we sat down and Alek raised a rusted wineglass and said the kiddush blessing. He then said the *motze* over the challah before sprinkling salt on it, cutting it and passing it around. The bread was clearly not from the ghetto kitchen; it had a thick crust and a soft inside that reminded me of father's bakery. As soon as the plate had passed by, I regretted not managing to take an extra piece to take to my parents. Then several girls stood and went to the kitchen and emerged with steaming pots, from which they ladled generous spoonfuls of chicken stock, carrots and potatoes into our bowls. My stomach rumbled. This, too, was obviously not ghetto food.

Throughout the meal, people chattered nonstop. They were friendly, but self-absorbed, and there were many inside jokes, teasing and nicknames that no one bothered to explain to me. I listened with interest as Marta talked over me with the girl to my right about various boys, and then debated with two boys to her left whether the United States would enter the war. I did not mind that no one addressed me directly or asked me questions. At the head of the table, I could see the man who had chanted the prayers looking in my direction. He whispered something to the stocky, younger man on his left. I could feel my cheeks growing flushed in the crowded, too-hot room.

After dinner, as the girls served strong, black coffee in cracked cups with mismatched saucers, a young man produced a guitar and began to play. People pushed back from the table and reclined in their chairs, looking as happy and relaxed as though they were at a spa in Krynice for a summer holiday. We sang and listened for hours to the Yiddish and Hebrew songs, including some that I had not heard in years. Finally, when Marta and I dared stay no longer for fear of the curfew, we thanked the others and left.

From that night onward, I returned to the apartment on Josefinska Street every Friday. I tried to shrug off the guilt I felt at not spending the Sabbath with my parents. For those brief few hours each week, I could forget where I was and all that was going on around me. Shabbes dinner became the highlight of my week.

One Friday night, when I had been coming to Shabbes dinner at Josefinska 13 for about six weeks, Helga, the woman who cooked the dinner each week, approached Marta and me as the evening was ending and we were putting on our coats. "Alek would like to see you," she said, addressing me.

My stomach jumped. Marta flashed me a questioning look. I shrugged, trying to act nonchalant. "You don't have to wait for me," I told her. The woman gestured toward the door at the back of the room. I approached nervously, wondering if perhaps I had done something to offend Alek. But when I knocked on the half-open door, he waved me in affably.

The back room was less than half the size of the front, with a small table covered in papers, a few chairs and a cot. "Emma, I'm Alek," he said warmly, extending his hand. I shook it, surprised he knew my name. Alek introduced the man who had been seated beside him at dinner. "This is Marek." The other man nodded and, gathering a stack of papers from the table, excused himself from the room. "Have a seat." I perched on the edge of the chair Alek had indicated. Up close, I could see the dark circles and fine lines around his eyes. "I apologize for not introducing myself sooner, but I have had pressing business." I wondered what kind of business one could have in the ghetto. "Emma, let me be blunt." He lowered his voice. "We have a mutual friend." His eyebrows lifted. "A very close friend. From the university."

Alek knows Jacob, I realized, my heart leaping. I was unable to control the flash of recognition that crossed my face. Then, regaining my composure, I started to protest. "I...I don't know what you're..."

"Don't worry." He raised his hand to silence me. "I am the only one who knows." He continued, "I heard about you from him some time ago, saw your picture." I blushed. He was referring to our wedding photo, the same one that Krysia had hidden. I knew Jacob had a copy, but I didn't realize he had shown it to anyone. Did he still have it? I wondered. How long ago had he shown it to this man? "He asked me to keep an eye out in case you arrived here," Alex explained. "I didn't know who you were until you came here recently. We do the same work, you see, your friend and I." I realized then that Alek was also part of the resistance movement.

"Have you...?" I didn't dare to finish the question.

"We occasionally have word from him, usually through our messengers, since of course he cannot come to the ghetto. I will send word that we've made contact and that you are all right."

"Please, it would mean a great deal to me." He nodded. I hesitated before speaking again. "Can I help, too...with the work, I mean?"

Alek shook his head firmly. "I'm sorry, but no. Our friend thought that you might ask, and he made it very clear that you were not to become involved. He is concerned for your safety."

"I wish he was a little less concerned with my safety and a little more with his own." I was surprised at the forcefulness of my own words.

Alek eyed me sternly. "Your husband is a great fighter, Emma. You should be very proud."

"I am," I replied, chastised.

"Good. For the time being, I will respect his wishes and keep you uninvolved. But—" he paused, stroking his goatee "—you are your own person, and if you wish to help, the time may come when you can be of use to us. As you can see, many women are involved." He gestured to the larger room and I realized for the first time that the others at the Shabbes gathering, including Marta, were actually part of the resistance. "Meanwhile, you are always welcome here. Of course, the others cannot know who you are—your marriage must remain a secret. I just wanted to make contact and let you know about our connection."

"Thank you." I grasped Alek's arm, a wave of relief and gratitude washing over me. He nodded and smiled warmly, then turned back to his paperwork in a manner that, while not rude, told me that our conversation was over and it was time for me to go. I crossed back through the apartment and out the door, almost dancing. Alek knew Jacob and he knew about our marriage. For the first time since my husband had disappeared, I did not feel completely alone.

CHAPTER 4

The Monday after my conversation with Alek, Marta
appeared at the orphanage as my shift ended. I was not
surprised to see her; she had dropped by almost every
day in the time since we'd become friends. "I have to return the
kettle to the kitchen," I told her. Each morning, the central
kitchen in the ghetto delivered a large vat of soup to the orphanage for the children. The broth was always pale and watery, with
only tiny flecks of potato or cabbage. The meager cup that each
child was allotted as one of two meals each day was not nearly
enough; Pani Nederman and I and some of the other orphanage staff would share our own rations with the children whenever possible.

"I'll walk with you," Marta offered.

"Okay." I pulled my coat from the hook on the door. We
said goodbye to Marta's mother and headed out onto the

snow-covered street. The winter air was crisp, but the bitter wind that had been blowing when I'd arrived at work that morning had died down.

"What did you and Alek talk about Friday night, anyway?" she asked as we turned left onto Lwowska Street and walked along the inside perimeter of the ghetto wall. I could tell that she was a little jealous that he had singled me out for conversation.

"Just about a mutual acquaintance," I replied evenly, not looking at her.

"Oh." Seemingly placated by my answer, she did not speak for several minutes. "Did you have a boyfriend before the war?" she asked abruptly as we approached the brick warehouse that served as the central kitchen.

I hesitated, uncertain how to answer. I did not enjoy deceiving Marta about my marriage. I had never had a girlfriend to confide in before and I desperately wanted to tell her about Jacob, to share my memories and make them come alive. Perhaps she had even met him through the resistance. But I had promised Jacob I would tell no one of our marriage. He, and Alek, too, had said it would not be safe to do so. "No one special," I answered at last. My heart twisted at having to deny Jacob's existence, our love for each other.

"So there were several!" She giggled. I shook my head, suppressing a laugh at the notion of my having multiple suitors; before Jacob, there had been no one.

"I think Alek fancies you," she whispered, after I handed the empty kettle to the woman at the back door of the kitchen.

"Marta, he's married!" And so am I, I thought. If only she knew the truth. I liked Alek, but mostly because he was my one connection to Jacob. We began the walk back. "And you?"

I asked, eager to change the subject. "Have you met anyone in your travels as a messenger?" She looked away and did not answer, a faint blush creeping upward from her neck.

"There is someone," she confessed in a low voice.

"Aha!" I exclaimed. "I knew it. Tell me about him."

"He's one of us." I knew she meant the resistance movement. Her voice grew wistful. "But he doesn't notice me."

I squeezed her shoulder. "Perhaps he will someday. Give it time." It began to rain then, thick, heavy drops that signaled the coming of a larger storm. We ran for cover back to the orphanage and spoke no more about it.

I thought about my conversation with Marta several weeks later, as I stood in the kitchen of our apartment, trying to wash linens in the impossibly small sink. It was a Thursday afternoon and I was home alone, enjoying a rare moment of solitude. Normally I worked days at the orphanage, but I had swapped shifts with another girl, agreeing to work the following Sunday instead. I remembered Marta asking me if I had a boyfriend, if I had dated anyone special. Perhaps she knew about Jacob, I mused, and was trying to get me to admit it.

Suddenly, the silence was shattered by a loud knocking sound in the alleyway below. I jumped, splashing soapy water everywhere. Wiping the water from my dress, I leaned forward. Through the window over the sink, I heard a woman's voice, high pitched and desperate, a man's low and angry. I stepped to one side of the sink, pressing myself against the wall so I could look out the window without being seen. From this vantage point, I could just make out two figures below. I was alarmed to see a man in a Nazi uniform standing in the doorway of the apartment building across the alley. The Nazis, afraid of disease, seldom came inside the ghetto, preferring instead to let the Judenrat run internal, daily affairs. He was arguing with a blond woman I did not recognize. She was tiny but thick around the middle, and I could tell even from where I stood that she was several months pregnant. *"Prosze,"* I heard her plead.

The voices continued arguing. Though I could not make out most of their words, I surmised that she was trying to keep the soldier from entering the apartment. The woman is very brave, I thought. She must be hiding something important.

At last, the Nazi said something and shoved the woman aside harshly. She hit the door frame and fell to the ground with a thud, motionless. The Nazi stepped over her and into the building. Loud crashing noises arose from inside the apartment, as though furniture was being thrown. Moments later, the Nazi reemerged, grasping a small, religious-looking man by the collar.

The woman on the ground seemed to instantly revive. She wrapped her arms around the Nazi's ankles, seemingly oblivious to any danger to herself. "Don't take him!" she pled. The Nazi tried to shake the woman from his ankles, but she would not let go. As the woman continued to beg, the small man's eyes darted around, like a trapped animal looking for an escape. His gaze shot upward and I ducked back from the window, fearful that he might see me.

The voices rose louder. A shot rang out. I froze. It was the first time in my life I had heard that sound.

Now it was the man who cried out, his wail almost as high pitched as the woman's had been. Unable to keep from looking, I stepped in front of the window. The woman lay motionless on the ground, her eyes open, her head ringed by a halo of blood. One arm lay draped protectively over her full, round stomach. The Nazi dragged the screaming man from the alley.

I ducked my head and vomited into the sink, great heaving waves of hatred and despair. When at last my stomach spasms subsided, I wiped my mouth and looked back out the window.

The door of the apartment was still ajar. In the doorway, I saw something move. It was a child, not more than three years old, with the same blond hair as the woman's. The child stood motionless in the doorway, his blue eyes luminous as he stared at the woman's lifeless form.

A set of hands shot out of the doorway and snatched the child back inside. The door slammed shut, leaving the dead woman like unwanted refuse on the pavement.

I sank to the kitchen floor, trembling and weak, the taste of bile still heavy in my mouth. Until now, I realized, it had been easy to stick my head in the sand like an ostrich, to pretend that the ghetto was just another neighborhood and that the violence and killing were isolated incidents far away. Though we had heard rumors, stories of brutal executions in the forests and even in the street, we had wanted to believe these accounts were exaggerated. Now it was no longer just a rumor from Tarnów or Kielce. The killing had come home.

I spent the rest of the day trying to compose myself, to block out what I had seen. My parents had enough to worry about, and I did not intend to upset them with the news. But others in our apartment block had seen or heard the commotion, and the story spread quickly. When my parents arrived home that night, the shooting in the alleyway was all they could talk about. At dinner, I listened to them describe thirdhand accounts of the events that had taken place next door. Finally, I could hold back no longer. "I saw it!" I burst out, weeping. "I saw everything." Stunned, my parents looked at me in silence. My father came to my side then. My mother disappeared into the kitchen and returned a moment later with a cup of steaming tea. With shaking hands, I recounted for them exactly what I had seen earlier that day. "And the woman was with child, too," I added. My father blanched—that was the one detail that had not made it to the ghetto rumor mill. "What had she done to deserve that, Papa?" I asked, sniffling. "Just because she was a Jew?"

"Her husband, the man they took, was Aaron Izakowicz, a rabbi from Lublin," my father replied. "He is descended from a very great rabbinic family, dating back centuries. Pan Halkowski told me that he had arrived with his wife and child a few days ago. I had no idea they were staying so close by. The Nazis knew that his presence in the ghetto surely would have buoyed the spirit of our people here. That is probably why he was arrested." He shook his head. "Such a loss." My father spoke as though the man was already dead.

"Surely they would not kill such a respected and famous man." But even as I said this, I knew that nothing could be further from the truth.

"They killed his wife." It was my mother who spoke then, and there was a harshness to her voice that I had never heard before. They killed his wife. His pregnant wife, I added silently. The words echoed in my head as I lay awake that night, seeing the hollow eyes of the blond-haired child before me.

The next Friday afternoon, Marta did not come for me. "She has a cold," Pani Nederman had informed me a few hours earlier. As we bathed and fed the children that afternoon, I deliberated whether I would go to Shabbes dinner without her. The thought of walking into the gathering alone terrified me; even though I had been going for months, I still thought of myself largely as Marta's guest, rather than as someone who belonged. At five o'clock, I put on my coat and stepped out onto the street. Straining my head to the right, I could see the soft lights behind the yellow curtains at Josefinska 13. My heart twisted as I imagined not being there, going home to our cold, quiet apartment instead. Suddenly, my mind was made up. I crossed the street and entered the building. I climbed the steps and, inhaling deeply, knocked timidly on the door. When no one answered, I entered the apartment.

"*Dobry wieczor,* Emma," Helga greeted me from the kitchen as I entered.

"*Dobry wieczor,*" I replied. "Do you need help?"

She shook her head. "No, but it would be great if you could stay afterward and help clean up. Katya is sick with the flu."

"I can help. Marta is sick, too," I added. I turned from the kitchen to the main room. A dozen or so people were already there, the faces familiar to me after a few weeks of visits. "Emma, come join us," a boy named Piotrek called out, and I soon found myself listening to a story about a one-legged shoe salesman that I somehow doubted was true. It didn't matter; I was grateful just to be treated as one of them. A few minutes later, a bell rang, Alek and Marek came out, and the weekly ritual began. I enjoyed the dinner, surrounded by the people I had come to know, but it wasn't the same without Marta beside me to whisper and share confidences.

The crowd thinned out after dessert, with only a handful

of us remaining behind to clean up. Alek, Marek and a third man, whom I had noticed at dinner but did not recognize, retreated to the back room. As I cleared the dishes from the table, I noticed that the door to the room was ajar. Curious, I found myself lingering by the door as I cleared the end of the table nearest to it. Edging closer, I could hear the men arguing. "...the railway line outside Plaszow," I heard Marek say.

"It's too soon," Alek replied. "We need to build up the provisions first."

"We have two dozen guns, a hundred bullets, some grenades..." Marek protested.

"Not enough."

The stranger spoke then. "In Warsaw, they are organizing within the ghetto."

"Warsaw is different. The movement, the ghetto itself, everything is bigger," Alek said.

"If only Minka can get..."

"Emma," Helga said, coming up behind me and making me jump. "Do you need help with those plates?"

"N-no, thank you," I stammered, afraid she had caught me listening. I balanced a stack of plates on my forearm and made my way to the kitchen. As I placed the dishes in the sink and turned the tap on, I heard the door to the back room creak and the men still talking as they made their way to the front door. Alek paused at the kitchen entrance and whispered something to Helga. The three men exited the apartment.

A few minutes later, as I was drying the plates, Helga came over to the sink. "I'll finish this," she said, taking the towel from my hands. "Would you mind taking out the garbage on your way down?" She pointed to two bags by the kitchen door. I thanked her and bid the others good-night.

At the bottom of the stairs, I turned and found the back door leading out to the alley. Outside, it was pitch black. I blinked several times, trying to adjust my eyes to the light, before feeling for the step downward. It was a deeper step than I had thought, and icy. I stumbled, almost dropping the garbage bags in the process. "Oh, oh!" I cried.

"Careful," a deep voice said from the shadows.

I jumped, caught off guard. Then I recognized the voice. "Alek!" I gasped. "What are you doing here? You frightened me."

"Shhh," he whispered, taking the bags from me and setting them by the garbage cans. "Come here." He grabbed my sleeve. He must have asked Helga to have me bring down the garbage in order to speak with me, I realized, as he led me to the far corner of the alley where two buildings met. What did he want? Had I done something to make him mad? I wondered if he had seen me listening by the door. "I have a message." His voice did not sound angry. He pressed a tiny crumpled slip of paper into my hand.

My heart leapt. "From Jacob?" I asked, my voice rising.

"Shh!" he admonished. He lit a match. "Read it quickly." I unfolded the paper.

Dearest love,
I am well. I miss you more than you know. Take care of yourself, and do not give up. Help is coming.
Emmeth

There was no signature. *Emmeth* was the code word Jacob and I had chosen before his disappearance; it was Hebrew for *truth*. I read the note over and over, until the match threatened to burn Alek's fingers and he was forced to blow it out. "I don't understand. Is he near?"

"No, quite the opposite. That note traveled many hundreds of kilometers to reach you."

"Where is he?"

"Don't ask me that," Alek replied sharply. "He is safe, that is all you need to know."

"But…" A million questions raced through my mind.

"He is on a…procurement mission," he said. "Getting things that are very important to us. I can't tell you any more than that."

I suddenly realized that my husband was the man about whom they had been speaking in the back room. "Minka?" I asked, forgetting I was not supposed to have heard.

"Yes. Outside the ghetto, we refer to one another by our aliases for safety's sake. But you should not have been listening to our conversation. Believe me when I say that the less you know, the better."

"I understand." But I didn't really. My mind whirled. Where was Jacob? Was he okay? What did his note mean?

"Your husband has a talent for getting things, for finding what we need and persuading people to help us." I smiled at this, imagining Jacob's imploring expression and cajoling tone. I could never refuse him anything, or stay mad at him when he looked at me like that. Alek continued, "He also knows a great deal about guns and munitions." I realized then how very little I knew about the man I had married. "All right then." Alek reached over and took the paper from my hand. "You can't keep that. I'm sorry." I watched in dismay as he lit another match and held it to the corner of the note.

"But…" I started to protest. Then I stopped, knowing he was right. If the paper was somehow found and traced to Jacob, it could be dangerous. I thought of our marriage certificate and rings, hidden in a book underneath my mattress in our apartment. Nobody knew that I still had them.

"Emma, I know this is difficult for you," Alek said when the paper was gone and the flame extinguished. The air around us was dark and cold once more. "You must have faith. Jacob is okay, and you are not alone. At least you have your family." His voice sounded hollow as he said the last part.

"What about you, Alek?" I could not help but ask. I knew only from what Marta had told me that he had a wife and that she was not in the ghetto.

"My family lived in Tarnów before the war." His voice was flat. "My parents weren't fighters. They were terribly afraid. The night before the Nazis came for us, they lay down in bed, took something. The next morning they were dead."

"I'm so sorry," I said helplessly.

"And my wife is not in the ghetto," he added. I could not tell from his tone if he considered this a good thing.

"So you are alone here?"

"Yes, except for my cousin, Helga." Surprised, I pictured the round-faced cook in my mind. I had not known they were related. "So you see, I understand what you are feeling being away from Jacob. We have to be patient." I nodded. "Okay, hurry home now. I promise to let you know if I hear anything more about him."

If, I thought. Not when. "Thank you, Alek." I reached up and kissed him awkwardly on the cheek, then turned and walked quickly from the alley. On the way home, I puzzled over all I had learned. Jacob was traveling somewhere, getting weapons for the resistance. I shuddered. It sounded terribly dangerous. But at least he is alive, or was when he sent the note to me. My thoughts shifted to Alek. He, too, was separated from the person that he loved. And he was the head of the resistance, yet his own parents had given up, refused to fight. I considered my own parents, who kept going day after day. Suddenly, their simple acts of getting up each morning, of putting one foot in front of the other, seemed remarkably courageous. They did it, I knew, for me. As I reached the safety of our apartment, a wave of gratitude washed over me, and I had to fight the urge to go over to their mattress and hug them as they slept.

I undressed and lay awake in bed, thinking of Jacob and the note. Alek had been unwilling to tell me where he was, but I had seen the piece of envelope on which it was written. The postmark was from Warsaw. It didn't mean that he was there, but maybe…I shivered. The one place that was more dangerous than Kraków. And his message: help is coming. The words echoed in my head until my eyes grew heavy and I fell into a deep sleep.

That night I dreamed I was with Jacob in the mountains. It was bitterly cold and we were being chased by wolves through deep snow. My feet had gone numb. The harder I ran, the slower I moved, until at last I was several hundred meters behind but he did not notice. "Jacob!" I cried, but he was too far ahead to hear me. One of the wolves leapt at me and I fell, screaming.

I awoke with a start. A floorboard creaked. It was just a dream, I told myself, drawing the blankets closer. But I could not fall back to sleep. On the other side of the curtain, my mother snored. The floor creaked again, louder this time. A shadow appeared suddenly by my bed. I sat up, but before I could react, a hand clamped over my mouth.

"Quiet!" a strange voice whispered. "I'm not here to hurt you." Panicked, I struggled to break free, but the stranger's grip was too strong. "Stop it! Alek sent me." I could make out the stranger's face faintly in the darkness. He was the man who had been arguing with Alek and Marek in the back room after dinner. *"Emmeth,"* he said, his voice barely audible. *"Emmeth."* I relaxed slightly as the stranger repeated my and Jacob's code word. I realized then that it was Jacob, most likely through Alek, who had sent this stranger to me.

"Who...?" I started to ask as he released his hand from my mouth.

"Shh! There's no time. Get dressed." I leapt up. Maybe Alek had at last found a way for me to help, I thought as I hurriedly put on my work dress over my nightgown. Perhaps Jacob needed me. I climbed into my boots and coat, and followed the stranger toward the door of our apartment. A few feet before the door, I paused by the curtain that separated my parents' bed from mine. I drew back the curtain. My parents were sleeping soundly, my father's large arm wrapped protectively around my mother.

"Come," the stranger whispered harshly, tugging at my arm. I let the curtain drop and followed him from the apartment. The stairway was dark, and each step creaked beneath our feet. At last, we reached the ground and stepped out the back door of the apartment building.

Taking my hand, the stranger led me through the back alleyways of the ghetto. The streets, slick with frozen moisture, were empty except for several large rats scurrying between the gutters. A few minutes later, we reached a corner of the ghetto I had never before seen. There, a crack no more than twelve inches wide separated two sections of the outer wall. Looking furtively from side to side, the stranger pushed me ahead of him, and I realized he meant for me to fit through the hole. I sucked in my breath and held it, forcing myself into the hole. Halfway through, I could go no farther. "I'm stuck," I whispered, panicking. The Nazis would surely find me here, trapped. I felt the stranger's arms on me, pushing me hard from behind. The rough stone edges scraped my skin and threatened to tear my clothes. Finally, I broke free and found myself standing on the other side of the wall. Grunting, the stranger then squeezed through behind me.

Grabbing my arm, the stranger pulled me into an alleyway, then peered out onto the street in both directions. "Come," he mouthed silently, tilting his head to the right. He began to walk with small, swift steps, hugging the side of the building, remaining in the shadows. I obeyed, following as quickly and quietly as I could. At that moment, shocked and confused, I did not realize I had just escaped from the ghetto.

CHAPTER 5

Without speaking, the stranger led me through the empty back streets of Podgorze. I struggled to keep up and to mimic his swift, silent footsteps. My mind switched continuously between bewilderment, a sense of wonder of being outside and terror that we would be caught at any moment. Even our smoky breath threatened to betray us in the cold night air. Finally, the houses thinned and gave way to industrial warehouses. The paved road became dirt, then a crooked, snow-covered path leading into the forest.

Only when we had been enveloped by the trees did the stranger speak. "I'm a friend of Alek's." He paused. "And Jacob's." He did not slow or turn to face me. "They sent me to take you away."

"To Jacob?" My voice rose with excitement.

"Shh!" The stranger stopped and looked around. "Not to him. I'm sorry," he said, seeing my face fall. "He wanted to come himself but it would not be safe."

Not safe. Nothing was safe. "Then where?"

"No more questions. Trust me. *Emmeth*," he repeated, as though his knowledge of my and Jacob's secret word would magically invoke obedience within me. "I am sorry that we have to walk so far. To do otherwise would attract too much attention."

"It feels good to be out walking," I said, though in truth my toes were a bit numb. Then I froze in my tracks. "I'm not coming back, am I?"

"No."

My heart sank. "But my parents…"

"I will make sure word gets to them that you are safe. But it is better for them if they know little."

I pictured my parents as I had last seen them, sleeping peacefully. Then I imagined them waking up and finding me gone. I had not had the chance to say goodbye. I opened my mouth to say that I would not leave them, but the stranger had already begun walking once more and I had no choice but to follow him or be left behind. It was nearly dawn, I realized, as fine cracks of light began to appear in the eggshell night sky. Looking around at the seemingly unfamiliar route, I recognized then a small wooden church in a clearing. We were in Las Wolski, the forest to the west of the city. I knew then where I was going. "Pani Smok…?" I recalled that Jacob's aunt, Krysia Smok, lived on the far side of Las Wolski. The stranger, still moving, nodded. "But won't I put her in danger?"

"There are papers. You will not be the same person." My mind raced, overwhelmed by the flood of events and information, but there was little time to wonder. The stranger moved swiftly, and I fought to keep up and not trip on the stones and tree roots that littered our path.

As we cut through the forest, I pictured Jacob's aunt. I had first met Krysia at a dinner at the Baus' apartment a few weeks before Jacob and I were married. I remember dressing for the occasion as though I was to be introduced to royalty. Krysia was legendary in Kraków, both as the wife of the cellist, Marcin Smok, and as a social figure in her own right. But when we were introduced, Krysia proved to be as unpredictable as she was regal, skipping the traditional three airy kisses on the cheek and drawing me into a firm embrace. "I can see why you love her so," she exclaimed to a blushing Jacob.

Krysia's warm reception of me seemed ironic when I considered that she was not even a Jew, but a devout Catholic. Her marriage to Mrs. Bau's brother, Marcin, had been an enormous source of controversy and scandal—interfaith marriage was simply unheard of, even for the secular Bau family. Marcin and Krysia had eloped to Paris and the Baus shunned the couple for several years thereafter. Only when Jacob was born did Mrs. Bau, who had lost both of her parents to disease at an early age and had few other relatives, soften and decide to forgive Marcin for the sake of her son.

I quickly understood why Jacob adored Krysia—her mix of elegance and unpredictability was irresistible. The child of diplomats who had refused to consign her to boarding school, Krysia had grown up in places I had only read about: Rome, London, Paris. When she married Marcin, they settled in Kraków, and while he continued to travel and perform, Krysia made their home in the city. Their two-story apartment on Basztowa Street quickly became a hub for the city's cultural elite, with Krysia throwing lavish parties at which she introduced some of Poland's most promising artists and musicians to those who would become lifelong sponsors and patrons. Yet despite her prominent social role, Krysia shunned convention: she could just as easily be found in one of Kraków's many cavernous brick cellar taverns, drinking shots of ice-cold potato vodka and debating politics late into the night, as attending the opera or a charity ball.

Krysia and Marcin remained childless; Jacob once told me that he did not know whether this was by choice or by nature. Marcin had died in 1932 after a two-year struggle with cancer. After his death, Krysia sold their apartment in the city center and retreated permanently to their weekend home at Chelmska. There, Krysia mixed solitude with sociability, enjoying the quiet of her garden during the week while continuing to throw dinner parties for those who came to call on the weekends. It was to this house that the stranger was now taking me.

Soon the forest path began to slope downward and the trees grew thinner. A few minutes later, we emerged from the woods. Below us lay the farmhouses of the Chelmska neighborhood. As we started down the road, a rooster's crowing, then a dog's bark cut through the silence, threatening to betray our presence. The stranger placed a heavy hand on my shoulder and we froze behind a large bush until the noises subsided. Looking carefully to make sure the way was clear, the stranger led me across the road and around the back of one of the larger houses. He knocked on the door, almost inaudibly. A second later, the back door opened and there, in the dim light, stood Krysia Smok. Before her larger-than-life presence, I felt shamed by my worn clothes and unkempt hair, but she reached out and drew me through the door and into her arms. Her scent, a mix of cinnamon and apples, reminded me of Jacob.

"*Kochana,*" she said, stroking my hair softly. I stood in her embrace without moving for several moments. Then, remembering the stranger, I turned to thank him, but he was gone.

"Are you tired?" Krysia closed the door and drew me up the stairs into the parlor to a seat beside the fire. I shook my head. "I'll be right back." She disappeared and I could hear her footsteps as she climbed the stairs to the third floor, followed by the sound of running water overhead. I looked around the room in bewilderment. On the mantel over the fireplace, there were several framed photographs. I stood and walked toward them. Jacob as a child. Jacob and I on our wedding day. Jacob. It was so strange being there without him.

A few minutes later, Krysia reappeared. "You need a warm bath," she said, placing a large mug of tea on the low table in front of me. "I'm sorry we had to do it this way, there was no choice."

I buried my head in my hands. "My parents…"

"I know." She came to stand by my side, and her spicy scent wafted over me once more. "There was no way to get all of you out together. They will be happy to know that you are safe. And we will do what we can to help them from outside."

I began sobbing, the months of despair catching up with me at last. "I'm sorry," I whispered, ashamed. Krysia did not reply but simply put her arm around my shoulder and led me upstairs to the bathroom, where fresh nightclothes had been laid out beside the steaming water. When she left, I undressed and stepped into my first real bath in months. I scrubbed from head to toe, washing my hair twice, and lingered until the water had gone cold and brown with dirt.

When I emerged, relaxed and almost too exhausted to stand, Krysia led me to a bedroom. I stared in amazement at the vase of fresh gardenias on the nightstand: did such things really still exist in the world? "Sleep now," she said, turning back the duvet to reveal crisp white sheets. "I promise that in the morning, I'll explain everything."

After months on my straw ghetto pallet, the thick mattress and soft linens felt like a dream. Despite all that had happened that night, I fell quickly into a deep sleep.

I awoke the next morning, confused. Looking around the elegant bedroom, I wondered for a second if I was back in the room I had shared with Jacob at the Baus'. Suddenly, the events of the night before came rushing back to me. I'm at Krysia's, I remembered, looking out at the forest and wondering how long I had been asleep. The sun was already well across the sky. I went downstairs to the kitchen where Krysia stood at the stove. "I'm sorry to have slept so long," I apologized.

"Sleep was exactly what you needed. That, and a good meal." She gestured to a platter of freshly cut fruit on the table. "Sit down." I sat, hoping she could not hear the loud rumbling of my stomach. She placed a glass of orange juice, thick with pulp, before me. "I am told that your disappearance has already been explained to your parents, and that another girl is taking your place at the orphanage so you will not be missed." I was both relieved and intensely curious: how did Krysia know such things?

I hesitated, wanting to ask her about Jacob. "The Baus?" I inquired instead, when she had set a plate of eggs in front of me and sat down.

Krysia shook her head. "I heard from them about two months ago. Nothing since. They are fine, although living not in Fania's usual style." I detected a wry note in her voice. I nodded. Polish money, even a great deal of it, surely would not go that far in Switzerland, and I knew that much of the Baus' wealth was inaccessible to them because of the war. "They wanted to contact you themselves, but they were afraid to draw attention to the fact that you were related."

"Their home…" My stomach twisted at the thought of their grand home.

"It was occupied by a high-ranking Nazi official last spring. The Baus know, or have guessed." She placed her hand over mine. "There was nothing you could have done to stop it. Now eat." I obeyed, forgetting my manners and washing down enormous bites of eggs and fruit with mouthfuls of juice. But as I savored the meal, my stomach twisted at the thought of my parents, left behind with only ghetto rations.

"Your name," Krysia began when I had finished eating, "is Anna Lipowski. You were raised in the northern city of Gdańsk but your parents died in the early days of the war and you have come to live with me, your aunt Krysia."

I stared at her in astonishment. "I don't understand…"

"You are to live as a gentile, outwardly and openly," she replied matter-of-factly. "It is the only way. It is impossible to hide Jews in the city, and the countryside is even worse. You are fair-skinned and can easily pass for a Pole. And with the exception of your former coworkers at the university, whom you will avoid, anyone who would have known you as a Jew is gone from the city." Her last words rang in my ears. Kraków had so changed, I could pass as a stranger in the place I had lived all my life.

"Here are your papers." She pushed a brown folder across the table to me. Inside were an identity card and two birth certificates.

"Lukasz Lipowski," I read aloud from the second one. "A three-year-old?"

"Yes, I understand you've been eager to help in Jacob's work." She paused. "Now is your chance. There is a child who has been hidden in the ghetto for months. He has no parents. He will be brought here to live with us and...to the outside world, he will be your little brother. He arrives tonight." I nodded slightly, my head spinning. Twenty-four hours ago, I was living in the ghetto with my parents. Now I was free, living with Krysia as a gentile and caring for a child.

"One other thing." She pushed a smaller envelope across the table. I opened the clasp, and a gold chain with a small gold cross slithered out onto the table. My hand recoiled. "I understand," she said. "But it is a necessary precaution. There is no other way." She picked up the necklace and stepped behind me to fasten the clasp. And with that, my life as a non-Jew began.

After breakfast, I followed Krysia upstairs to her bedroom. She opened her closet and pushed back the dresses to reveal a set of stairs leading to the attic. She climbed the stairs and handed down to me several pieces of metal and a small mattress. We carried the parts to the guest room that was to be the child's. "This was Jacob's," she said as we assembled the crib. "I kept it here for his parents after he'd outgrown it, thinking perhaps I might use it for a child of my own." Her eyes had a hollow look, and I knew then that her childlessness was not by choice. When it was assembled, I stroked the chipped wooden rail of the bed, imagining my husband lying there as an infant.

At lunch, Krysia set out plates heaped with cold cuts, bread and cheese. I hesitated momentarily. Surely the meat was not kosher, and eating meat and cheese together was forbidden. "Oh," she said, noticing my hesitation and realizing. "I'm so sorry. I would have tried to get kosher meat, but…"

"There are no more kosher butchers," I finished for her. She nodded. "It's okay, really." The food had not been strictly kosher when I lived at the Baus', and in the ghetto, we ate whatever we could get when we could get it. I knew my parents would understand, and be glad I had good food to eat. As if on cue, my stomach rumbled then. A look of relief crossed over Krysia's face as I took generous helpings of the meat and cheese.

"You know, I've never cared for a child," Krysia confessed later that afternoon. We were standing on the balcony just off the parlor, hanging freshly washed children's clothing, which Krysia said had been given to her by a friend.

"Me, neither, until I worked at the ghetto orphanage." I looked at Krysia. She was staring at the damp blue children's shirt in her hand, a helpless expression on her face. I could tell that she was really worried. "But, Krysia, you have cared for a child. Jacob told me he was often here as a boy."

She shook her head. "Being an aunt for a few hours isn't the same."

I took the shirt from her, hung it on the line. "We'll figure it out. It will be okay. I promise."

The child, Krysia told me, would arrive late that night as I had done the night before. By early evening, Krysia looked exhausted. "Why don't you rest a bit?" I offered, but she shook her head. As the hands on the walnut grandfather clock in the hallway climbed well past midnight, she continued moving around the cottage without resting, cleaning and organizing dozens of little things. Krysia had turned the lights down low so that only the faintest glow remained in the kitchen and our shadows grew long in the corridors. Every few minutes she would lift the heavy drapes of the rear parlor window slightly to look out at the back garden for the new arrival.

Finally, around two o'clock in the morning, we settled in the kitchen with mugs of strong coffee. I hesitated for several minutes before speaking. There was so much I wanted to ask Krysia that I didn't know where to begin. "How did you…?" I began at last.

"Become involved with the resistance?" She stirred her coffee once more, then placed the spoon in the cradle of the saucer. "I always knew about Jacob's causes. He spoke to me about it because his mother was not that interested, and his father worried too much for his safety. I was concerned, too, of course," she added, taking a sip from her cup. "But I knew he was unstoppable." So did I, I thought. "He came here late one night shortly after the occupation," she continued. I realized she must have been talking about the night before his disappearance, when Jacob had not returned home for many hours. "He didn't exactly tell me what was going on, but he asked me to keep an eye on you, in case anything should happen to him. I asked what else I could do, and we realized together that my home and my position might be useful somehow. He put me in contact with people…the specifics did not come until after he was gone."

"But this is terribly dangerous for you! Aren't you at all afraid?"

"Of course I am, darling." The corners of her mouth pressed wryly upward. "Even an old widow with no children wishes to live. But this war…" Her expression turned serious. "This war is the shame of my people. Having you and the child live here with me is the least I can do."

"The Poles didn't start this war," I protested.

"No, but…" Her thought was interrupted by a light scratching sound at the back door. "Wait here."

Krysia tiptoed downstairs. I heard whispers, some movement, then a tiny click as the door shut. Krysia came back up the stairs, her footsteps slower and heavier now. When she reached the landing, her arms overflowed with a large cloth bundle. I stood to help her and together we carried the sleeping child to the third floor.

We set the child on the crib and Krysia unwrapped the blankets in which he had been swaddled. At the sight of the child's face, I gasped loudly. It was the blond child whose mother had been shot in the alleyway.

"What is it?" But before I could answer, the child, awakened by my gasp and Krysia's voice, began to whimper. "Shh," she soothed, rubbing the child's back. He settled into sleep once more.

Silently, we backed out of the room. "That child," I whispered. "That's…"

"The descendant of Rabbi Izakowicz, the great rabbi of Lublin. His mother was shot…"

"I know! I saw it happen from our apartment."

"Oh, you poor dear," Krysia said, patting my shoulder.

"You said he has no parents. What about his father?"

"We don't know. He was either shot in the woods near Chernichow or taken to a camp. Either way, it doesn't look good."

I squeezed my eyes tight then, remembering the scene in the alleyway. Surely they wouldn't kill the rabbi, I had said to my parents that night. "She was with child when she was killed," I added, my eyes beginning to burn. "His mother, I mean."

Krysia nodded. "I had heard that. It makes what we are doing that much more important. The child is the last of a great rabbinic dynasty. He must be kept alive."

Krysia and I took turns sleeping that night in case the child should awaken and be confused or upset by the strange surroundings, but he slept through the night and did not stir. The next morning, I went to his crib and lifted him, still in his street clothes. He was damp with sweat, his blond curls darkened and pressed against his forehead. He blinked but did not make a sound as I placed him on my hip. Instead, he wrapped his hands around my neck and rested his head on my shoulder as though he had done this every day of his young life. Together we headed down the stairs to the kitchen, where Krysia was once again preparing breakfast. At the sight of us in the doorway, her eyes warmed and her face broke into a wide smile.

A week later, Lukasz and I would walk into town for our debut appearance as gentiles at market. His eyes would light up at the sight of an ice-cream cart and I, unable to resist, would take a few pennies from our food money to buy him a vanilla cone. And this is how Lukasz, the son of the great rabbi of Lublin, and Emma, the daughter of a poor Kazimierz baker, came to live with the elegant Krysia Smok in a cottage that seemed like a palace in Chelmska.

CHAPTER 6

"We will be having a dinner party on Saturday," Krysia announces as routinely as though she is discussing the weather. The damp white towel I am holding falls from my hands to the dirt.

We are working in the garden, Krysia pulling weeds from around the spry green plants that are just beginning to bud, me hanging the linens we washed in a large basin an hour earlier. A few feet away, Lukasz digs silently in the dirt with a stick. It has been more than a month since Lukasz and I came to live with Krysia. I can tell that she is overwhelmed at times. Since arriving here, I have tried to take on as much of the housework as I can, but the labor has still taken its toll on her. Her delicate hands seem to grow more callused by the day, and her work dresses have become soiled and tattered. Yet despite her sacrifices, Krysia seems to like having us around. We are the first real companions she's had since Marcin died. She and I make easy company for each other, sometimes chatting as we work around the house, other times falling into deep silence. There is, after all, much to think about for both of us. I know she worries, as I do, about Jacob, and about us, how we must never be discovered, what would happen if we were.

The child's presence, however, keeps us from wallowing too deeply. Lukasz is a beautiful boy, calm and undemanding. In the weeks he has been with us, though, he has not spoken a word. We try desperately to make him laugh. Sometimes I invent childish games, and often in the evenings, Krysia plays lively tunes on the piano as I whirl him around in my arms to the music. But so far it has not helped. Lukasz watches patiently, as though the revelry is for our benefit, not his, and he is only humoring us. When the music and games stop, he picks up the tattered blue blanket in which he arrived and retreats to a corner.

"A dinner party?" I repeat, picking up the towel from the dirt.

"Yes, I used to throw them quite often before the war. I still do, from time to time. I don't enjoy it so much anymore. The guest list—" her mouth twists "—is a little different these days. But it is important to keep up appearances." I nod, understanding. Before the war, Krysia's guests would have been artists, intellectuals and socialites. Most of the artists and intellectuals were gone now—they had either fled abroad or been imprisoned, because of their religion or political views, or both. They had been replaced at Krysia's dinner table, I suspect, by guests of a far different sort.

Wiping her hands on her apron, she ticks off the guest list

on her fingers. "Deputy Mayor Baran," she pronounces the word mayor with irony. Wladislaw Baran was a known collaborator who, along with much of the present city administration, had been installed in office by the Nazis as a puppet of their regime. "The new vice director and his wife…"

"Nazis." I turn away, fighting the urge to spit.

"The party in power," she replies evenly. "We must keep them on our good side."

"I suppose." My stomach twists at the thought of being under the same roof as those people.

"You arrived several weeks ago. It would not do to have my niece living with me and not be properly introduced about town."

"B-but…" I stammer. I had not realized Krysia expected me to be at the dinner. I had envisioned hiding upstairs for the duration of the party, or at most helping in the kitchen.

"Your presence is essential." And I know from her tone that there will be no further discussion on the subject.

No sooner has Krysia spoken of the dinner party than the preparations begin, and they continue nonstop all week. For the occasion, Krysia brings back Elzbieta, the ruddy-cheeked housekeeper she had dismissed before my arrival. She returns without hard feelings, all energy and smiles, and immediately sets about scrubbing the house from top to bottom, putting my and Krysia's housekeeping efforts to shame.

Krysia is glad to have Elzbieta back again, I can tell, and not just for her cooking and cleaning skills: Elzbieta's boyfriend, Miroslaw, has a particular gift for procuring items that can no longer be found in the shops, delicacies we will need for the party. Within two days, he magically produces smoked salmon, fine cheeses and dark chocolate. "I haven't seen such items since before the war!" Krysia exclaims upon receiving the bounty. I can only nod; I have seldom seen such things in my life. To round out the meal, we pillage the garden, pulling up the few heads of lettuce that have already sprouted, bring up the remaining winter potatoes and cabbage from the root cellar, and buy from our neighbors what other vegetables we lack.

The morning of the party, Krysia helps Elzbieta to steam the fine table linen and polish the silver while I make dinner rolls and pastries. Kneading the dough, I am reminded of baking with my father. As a child, I used to grow frustrated with the resilience of the dough. No matter how hard I tried to make it take shape, long or round or flat, it always resisted, snapping stubbornly back to a nondescript mound. Only a few of my ill-shaped pastries even made it to the shelves, and those were always the last ones remaining late in the day. But now the challenge is a welcome one. I imagine my father working beside me, kneading the bread with his light, almost magical touch. His thick, gentle fingers could cajole the most stubborn dough into intricate shapes: braided challah, or hamantaschen for Purim, or obwarzanki, the crusty pretzels enjoyed by Jewish and non-Jewish Poles alike.

"Here," Krysia says, handing me a package wrapped in brown paper later that afternoon. We are in the kitchen, having just completed a final walk-though of the house to make sure everything is in order. I look at her puzzled, then set the package down on the table and open it. It is a new dress, light blue with a delicate flowered pattern.

"It's beautiful," I gasp, lifting it from the paper. Until now, I have made do with old dresses of Krysia's, pinning up the sleeves and hems to fit me. Growing up, all of my dresses were handed down or homemade. This is the first store-bought dress I have ever owned. "Thank you."

"You're welcome," she says, waving her hand as though it were nothing. "Now, go get ready."

A few hours later, I walk down the stairs once more. The house has been transformed. Scented candles flicker everywhere. Pots simmer on the stove burners under Elzbieta's watchful gaze, giving off a delicious aroma. Soft classical music plays on the gramophone; I think I recognize it as one of Marcin's recordings.

At fifteen minutes to seven, Krysia descends the steps from the third floor, wearing an ankle-length burgundy satin skirt and white silk blouse, her hair drawn neatly to a knot at the nape of her long neck, which is accentuated by a single strand of pearls. She looks restored and almost untouched by the war, as if all the care and hard work of recent months have been erased from her face. "You look lovely," Krysia says before I have the chance to compliment her. She brushes a speck of dust from my collar and then steps back to admire my dress.

"Thank you." I blush again. I have used a hot iron to curl my hair into ringlets, which cascade down onto my shoulders. The dress is the grandest thing I have ever worn. "I wish…" I begin, then stop. I had started to say I wished Jacob were here to see me, but I hesitate, not wanting to sadden Krysia.

She smiles, understanding. "He would think you are even more beautiful than he already does." I cannot help but beam. We walk into the dining room together. "Dinner parties are always so hectic," she explains, reaching across the table to adjust the orchid centerpiece. "No matter how many I plan and how well I prepare, there are things that cannot be done well in advance, which makes the last few hours chaotic."

I nod, as though I have thrown dinner parties all my life and understand. In truth, the few I had attended had been with Jacob, and they had in no way prepared me for this. Tonight is my debut as Anna Lipowski, the gentile orphan girl from Gdańsk. Since leaving the ghetto, I have scarcely spoken with anyone outside of the household, and I am terrified about my first full-fledged interaction in my new role. In my head, I have rehearsed my life story over and over again. Krysia has worked with me over the past several weeks, refining my behavior and mannerisms to fit the part, helping me to adjust the last few inflections and pronunciations to ensure that I speak with the generic accent of northwestern Poland. She has also schooled me intensely in Catholicism and I now know as much about saints and rosaries as any Polish girl outside of a convent. Still, I worry that some flash across my face or look in my eye, some gesture or intangible thing will scream out that I am a Jew.

But there is little time to be nervous. A few minutes after we enter the dining room, the doorbell rings. "Ready?" Krysia asks me. I gulp once, nod. The guests begin to arrive with a promptness characteristic of both Poles and Germans. Elzbieta meets them at the door and takes their wraps and coats. I wait at the first-floor landing with Krysia, who introduces me, and then I lead the guests into the sitting room and offer them a cocktail. Lukasz is trotted out briefly and admired for his blond hair and good behavior before being shuttled off to bed.

At ten past seven, five of our six guests are present: Deputy Mayor Baran and his wife, and three Germans: General Dietrich, an elderly widower who was highly decorated in the

Great War, and whose role in the present administration is largely ceremonial; Brigadier General Ludwig, a fat, bald, squinty-eyed man; and his wife, Hilda.

Ten minutes pass, then twenty, and still we are one guest short. No one comments on his lateness, and I know we will not be sitting down to eat without him. As Krysia told me earlier, Georg Richwalder, second in charge of the General Government, is the most important guest of all.

"How are you finding Kraków, Anna?" Mrs. Baran asks as we sit sipping our glasses of sherry.

"Lovely, though I haven't had as much time to see the city as I would like," I reply, amused at the notion of being a tourist in the city of my birth.

"Well, you and Lukasz must come into town one day soon and I will show you around. I'm surprised we haven't met at church," Mrs. Baran continues. I hesitate, uncertain how to respond.

Krysia steps up behind me, intervening. "That's because we haven't been yet. It's been so hectic with the children arriving, I haven't gone myself. And last week Lukasz had a cold." I look up at her, trying to mask my surprise. Since coming to live with us, the child has not had so much as a sniffle. It is the first time I have heard Krysia lie.

"Perhaps we can have tea one Sunday after mass," Mrs. Baran suggests.

I smile politely. It is not difficult to keep up appearances with such small talk. "That would be delight..." I start to reply, then stop midsentence, staring at the doorway.

"Kommandant Richwalder," Mrs. Baran whispers under her breath. I nod, speechless, unable to take my eyes off the imposing man who has entered the room. He is well over six feet tall, with perfectly erect posture and a thick, muscular chest and shoulders that seem ready to burst out of his military dress uniform. His large, square jaw and angular nose appear to be chiseled from granite. I cannot help but stare. I have never seen a man like the Kommandant before. He looks as though he has stepped off the movie screen or out of the pages of a novel, the epic hero. No, not a hero, I remind myself. The man is a Nazi.

Krysia crosses the room to greet him. "Kommandant," she says, accepting his kisses on her cheek and the bouquet of gardenias he offers. "It is an honor to meet you." Her voice sounds sincere, as though she is speaking to a friend.

"I'm sorry to keep you waiting, Pani Smok." His voice is deep and resonant. His head turns and he seems to swallow the entire room in his steely blue-gray eyes. His gaze locks on me. "You have a beautiful home." I look away, feeling the heat rise in my cheeks.

"Thank you," Krysia replies. "You aren't late, dinner is just ready. And please call me Krysia." She takes the Kommandant by the arm and, deftly sidestepping the other guests who have risen to greet him, leads him to me. "Kommandant, allow me to present my niece, Anna Lipowski."

I leap to my feet, far more light-headed than I should be from two small sips of alcohol. Up close, Kommandant Richwalder is even taller than he first appeared; my head barely comes to his shoulder. He takes my extended hand in his much larger one, sending a jolt of electricity through me, making me shiver. I hope that he has not noticed. He raises my hand smoothly, barely grazing it with his thick, full lips. Though his head is bowed, his eyes do not leave mine. *"Milo mi poznac."* His Polish, though stiff and heavily accented, is not altogether poor.

I feel my cheeks burn. "The pleasure is mine," I respond in German, unable to look away.

The Kommandant's eyebrows lift in surprise. You speak…?" He does not finish the sentence.

"Yes." My father, who had been raised in a town by the German border, had taught me the language as a girl, and given its close linguistic relation to Yiddish, it had come easily to me. When I arrived at Krysia's house, she suggested that I refresh my knowledge of the language. It only made sense that a girl from Gdańsk, which had once been the German city of Danzig, would be bilingual.

"Herr Kommandant," Krysia interrupts. With seemingly reluctance, the Kommandant turns to her so that she can introduce him to the other guests. Grateful that the introduction is over, I leave the room and step into the kitchen to recompose myself. What is wrong with me? I pour a glass of water and take a small sip, my hands shaking. You are probably just nervous, I tell myself, though in truth I know it is more than that—none of the other guests had such an effect on me. Of course, none of the other guests looked like Kommandant Richwalder. Picturing his steely gaze as he kissed my hand, I jump, sending water splashing over the edge of the glass.

"Careful." Elzbieta, who had been pouring the soup into bowls, comes to me with a dry towel. Enough, I think, as she helps to blot the water that has splashed onto my dress. Compose yourself. He's a Nazi, I remind myself sternly. And regardless, you are a married woman. You have no business having such reactions to other men. I smooth my hair and return to the parlor.

A moment later, Elzbieta rings a small bell and the guests

rise. As we make our way to the dining room, I try frantically to recall the seating cards Krysia had set out. Put me next to the elderly general, I pray, or even the endlessly carping Mrs. Ludwig—just not the Kommandant. There is no way that I can maintain my composure next to him for an entire meal. But no sooner have I made my silent wish than I find myself standing on one side of the table with General Ludwig to my left and the Kommandant to my right. I try to catch Krysia's eye at the head of the table, hoping she might somehow intervene, but she is speaking with Mayor Baran and does not notice. "Allow me," the Kommandant says, pulling out my chair. His pine-scented aftershave is strong as he hovers over me.

Elzbieta serves the first course, a rich mushroom soup. My hand shakes as I lift the spoon, causing it to clink against the side of the bowl. Krysia discreetly raises an eyebrow in my direction, and I hope that no one else has noticed.

"So," General Ludwig says over my head to the Kommandant. "What is the news from Berlin these days?" I am grateful that he has chosen to leave me out of the conversation, relieving me of the need to speak for a time.

"We are having success on all fronts," the Kommandant replies between spoonfuls of soup. Inwardly, I cringe at the news that the Germans are faring well.

"Yes, I heard the same from General Hochberg," Ludwig replies. I can tell from the way Ludwig emphasizes the name that he hopes it will impress the Kommandant. "I have heard talk of an official visit from Berlin?" He ends the sentence on an up note, then looks at the Kommandant expectantly, waiting for him to confirm or deny the rumor.

The Kommandant hesitates, stirs his soup. "Perhaps," he

says at last, his face impassive. Looking at him more closely now, I notice two scars on his otherwise flawless face. There is a deep, pale line running from his hairline to his temple on the right side of his forehead, and another, longer but less severe, traveling the length of his left jawbone. I find myself wondering how he got them, an accident perhaps, or a brawl of some sort. Neither explanation seems plausible.

"So, Miss Anna," the Kommandant says, turning to me.

I realize that I have been staring at him. "Y-yes, Herr Kommandant?" I stammer, feeling my cheeks go warm again.

"Tell me of your life back in Gdańsk." As Elzbieta clears the soup bowls, I recount the details I have been taught: I was a schoolteacher who was forced to quit my job and move here with my little brother when our parents were killed in a fire. I recount the story with so much feeling that it almost sounds real to me. The Kommandant listens intently, seemingly focused on my every word. Perhaps he is just an attentive listener, I think, though I have not noticed him so engaged in conversation with anyone else at the party. "How tragic," he remarks when I have finished my story. His eyes remain locked with mine. I nod, unable to speak. For a moment, it seems as though the rest of the guests have vanished and it is just the two of us, alone. At last, when I can stand it no longer, I look away.

"And you, Kommandant, where are you from?" I ask quickly, eager to take the focus off myself.

"The north of Germany, near Hamburg. My family is in the shipping business," he replies, still staring intently at me. I can barely hear him over the buzzing in my ears. "I was orphaned at a young age, too," he adds, as though our purportedly mutual lack of parents gave us a special bond. "Though mine died of natural causes."

"And what is it you are doing here?" I ask, amazed at the audacity of my own question. The Kommandant hesitates, caught off guard; clearly, he is accustomed to people knowing his role.

Ludwig interjects, "The Kommandant is Governor Frank's deputy, second in charge of the General Government. What the governor decrees, the Kommandant ensures that the rest of us implement."

The Kommandant shifts uneasily in his chair. "Really, General, you are overstating it a bit. I am just the owner of a shipping company doing his service to the Reich." He looks away, and I notice that his dark hair is flecked with gray at the temples.

"Not at all," Ludwig persists, his fat face red from too much wine. "You are far too modest, sir." He looks down at me. "Kommandant Richwalder was decorated for his valor at sea as a young man in the Great War." I nod, doing the math in my head. If the Kommandant served in the Great War, he must be at least forty-five years old, I think, surprised. I had taken him for younger. "He was gravely injured, and he served Germany with great distinction."

Looking at the Kommandant's face once more, I realize then that his scars likely came from battle. He touches his fingertips to his temple then, his eyes locked with mine, as though reading my thoughts. "Please pass the salt," I say abruptly, forcing him at last to turn away.

But Ludwig is not through with his praise of the Kommandant. "Most recently, he served the Reich overseeing Sachsenhausen with remarkable efficiency," he adds. I have not heard of Sachsenhausen, but Ludwig says the name as though its nature is self-evident, and I do not dare to ask what it is.

As the meal progresses, I try to keep focused, but my head grows heavy from the wine, and the Kommandant seems to refill my glass each time I take a sip. "Your German is flawless," he remarks as we finish the main course of pheasant with roast potatoes and carrots.

I hesitate. German, like Yiddish, came so naturally to me I had almost forgotten we were not speaking Polish. "We learned German in school," I manage at last. "There is a large German population in Gdańsk."

"You mean Danzig!" Ludwig interjects loudly, offended by my use of the Polish name for the city. Hearing his outburst, the other guests stop their conversations midsentence and turn to us.

"I'm sorry," I apologize quickly, feeling my face turn red. "It's just that Gdańsk is the name I grew up knowing."

Ludwig is not placated. "Well, fräulein," he continues haughtily. "It is time to adjust to the new reality."

"Really, General, this lovely dinner party is no place for politics." The Kommandant's voice is quiet but stern. Chastised, Ludwig turns his boorish attention to Mrs. Baran, who is seated to his left. I smile gratefully at the Kommandant. "It's a beautiful city no matter what one calls it," he offers, more gently than I have heard him speak before.

"I agree." Relieved, I reach across my plate with my right hand to lift my water glass. The Kommandant does the same with his left and our knuckles brush. I pull back, feeling my face grow red. His hand remains suspended in midair as though frozen. Neither of us speaks for what seems like several minutes.

"I am a great fan of German authors," I say at last, resorting to literature, the one subject about which I can always speak.

He replaces his water glass and retracts his hand. "Really?"

Elzbieta appears on my left then, and as I shift slightly to the right to allow her to take my plate, I am forced within inches of the Kommandant. I smell his aftershave once more, underlain by a heavier, more masculine scent. "Yes," I continue, when Elzbieta has moved on and I am able to straighten in my seat. "Goethe must be read in the mother tongue." I lift my napkin from my lap and blot my lips. "To read in the translation simply doesn't do it justice."

The Kommandant nods slightly and smiles for the first time that evening. "I agree." Reaching carefully this time, he lifts his wineglass and I follow, raising my own. "To German literature," he proposes, touching his glass gently to mine. I hesitate before drinking. My head is already cloudy. But the Kommandant downs his glass of wine in a single gulp, and under his watchful gaze, I have no choice but to take a healthy sip.

"Why don't we adjourn to the parlor?" Krysia suggests when Elzbieta has cleared the dessert plates. In the parlor, Elzbieta serves small glasses of cognac to the men and Krysia, and cups of steaming tea to the rest of us. I lean against the doorway to the parlor, the warm cup clasped in both hands. Too weary from the wine and rich food to carry on conversation, I escape to the kitchen. "May I help?" I ask, but Elzbieta, who now stands before the sink rinsing the dishes, only shakes her head.

I am drunk, I realize, as I stare numbly at the soap bubbles that overflow from the sink. I have never felt this way before. The only alcohol I tasted growing up was the kosher wine of Shabbes and the holidays, too sweet to manage more than a few sips. Once or twice with Jacob I had tasted some whiskey or a glass of wine with dinner and felt warm. But this is different. My tongue is thick and dry. There is a cool sweat on my forehead and the floor seems to move under me. "Elzbieta," I say uncertainly.

She turns, sees the paleness of my face. "Here." She brings me a glass of water. I drink it gratefully and hand the glass back to her. She returns to the sink, placing the glass in the warm water with the rest of the dirty dishes. I lower myself into one of the kitchen chairs, breathing deeply. Of all the nights of my life, I had to pick this one to drink too much.

Elzbieta touches my shoulder. I look up, and she nods her head toward the parlor. "Anna," I hear Krysia beckon, and I can tell by her tone it is not the first time she has called my name. I lift myself from the chair, make my way back to the parlor.

"*Tak?*" My head is clearer now from the water and brief rest.

"Come here." Krysia waves me over to where she and the Kommandant are sitting on the large sofa and pats the cushion between them. "Sit down." I perch uneasily on the edge of the sofa, just inches from the Kommandant. I do not look at him. "Anna," Krysia pronounces my alias with ease once more. "The Kommandant has a proposition for you." The room quiets as she turns to him expectantly. My breath catches. Though I cannot fathom what she is talking about, I am certain I will not like it.

"Anna, I am looking for a secretary, an assistant, really, to manage some of the daily administrative tasks of my office," the Kommandant says. "Your aunt thinks you might be interested." My stomach jumps into my throat.

"It is a flattering offer," Krysia adds. There is a message behind her words I cannot decipher.

"Me?" I ask, trying to buy time to formulate a response.

"Yes," the Kommandant replies. I can feel everyone staring at me.

"But I can't!" I say, my voice rising sharply. Noting the surprised looks on the faces around me, I modulate my voice. "I mean, I'm a schoolteacher. I'm hardly qualified for such a position." I am unsure which notion is more inconceivable: working in the Nazi headquarters or spending every day in close proximity to this terrifying man.

The Kommandant is undeterred by my response. "Your German is excellent. Krysia says that you can type. Other than that, only good judgment and a pleasant demeanor are required."

"But I couldn't possibly. I have Lukasz to care for and Krysia to help…." I protest. I look to Krysia for support, but she flashes me a pointed look.

"We will manage just fine," she says firmly.

"Well…" I hesitate, searching for further arguments.

"This is ridiculous!" Ludwig blusters, though no one has asked him. "One does not turn down such an honor."

The Kommandant turns to the fat man, glowering. "I would not force the girl." He faces me again. "It is up to you," he says, speaking softly now. "You can let me know later."

I swallow. Krysia obviously wants me to accept this bizarre offer, although I have no idea why. "No, there's no need for that." I force myself to smile. "I would be honored to work for you."

Krysia stands. "Well, that's settled. Now, I believe I promised Mrs. Baran I would play for her before the evening was over." She strides over to the grand piano, and ever diplomatic, she plays first Wagner, then Chopin. I am amazed at her talent, how her hands fly over the keys with the dexterity and grace of one decades younger, playing full classical pieces from memory.

"I thought that might happen," Krysia says a few hours later when the guests have gone. We are standing by the sink, drying the last of the teacups, aprons protecting our party clothes. She speaks in a low voice so that Elzbieta, who is sweeping in the next room, will not overhear. "I had heard the Kommandant was looking for an assistant, and I could tell from the moment he walked in that he had taken a liking to you."

I pause to brush back a lock of hair that has fallen across my eyes. "Krysia, if that was your concern, why did you seat me next to him?"

Krysia looks up, the bowl she is drying suspended in midair. "But I didn't! Now that you mention it, I specifically remember asking Elzbieta to put him next to me. I was hoping he might say something useful after a few glasses of wine." She sets down the bowl and walks to the kitchen door. " Elzbieta…?" she calls. The young woman appears from the dining room, broom in hand.

"*Tak,* Pani Smok?"

"Did you somehow switch the seating cards around?"

Elzbieta shakes her head. "*Nie,* Pani Smok. You said you were to be seated in between the Kommandant and General Ludwig. I was surprised to notice the order had changed."

"Thank you, Elzbieta." The young woman disappears into the parlor once more. Krysia turns to me, her brow wrinkled. "I don't know what happened."

"Perhaps it was an accident," I suggest, scrubbing harder at the stained pot and not looking up. The Kommandant must have switched the place cards in order to sit next to me. My stomach twists.

"Perhaps…anyway, I'm not sure that you working for the Kommandant would be entirely a bad thing."

"How can you say that?" I ask in a loud whisper. "This will jeopardize everything. My identity, our situation…"

"Anna," she interrupts. We had agreed that she should call me by this name all of the time, even when we were alone, to reinforce the habit. "This is the perfect cover. A hiding Jew would never walk into Nazi headquarters. And the Kommandant is one of the most important men in Poland right now." She pauses. "You may in time be able to get close enough to him to help with our work."

"Help? Krysia, I cannot work for the Nazis!" My voice rises, and Krysia quickly raises a finger to her lips, gesturing with her head in the direction of the dining room. "I'm sorry," I mouth, embarrassed at my outburst. In that moment, I am reminded of the precariousness of our situation. How much worse can this charade get, now that I am expected to bear up under the close scrutiny of Kommandant Richwalder day in and day out? A wave of nausea sweeps over me.

Later that night, I lay awake, staring up at the oak beams that run across the bedroom ceiling, listening to dogs howling in the distance. My life has changed again, I think, and for the third time since the war started, I am ending the day nowhere near where I started it. One day I woke up in Jacob's house and went to bed that night a prisoner in the ghetto. I had gone from being a Jew in the ghetto to a gentile in Krysia's home just as quickly. And now I am going to work for the Nazis. A chill races through me and I draw the blanket closer, oblivious to the fact that it is May and not at all cold.

My mind rewinds to a few hours earlier, when the party had broken up. Kommandant Richwalder had been the last guest to leave, lingering in the doorway in his long gray military coat. He had taken my hand in his own, now clad in smooth leather gloves, and raised it to his lips once more. "I will be in touch in a few days, once all of the paperwork is complete."

My hand shook as I retracted it. "Th-thank you, Herr Kommandant."

"No, Miss Anna, thank you." And with that he turned and departed. Lying in bed now, I shiver. The way he stared at me had reminded me of a spider eyeing a fly. Now I would be forced to go to work in the spider's web every day. I shiver again, listening to the dogs' howling echoing in the breeze.

We do not hear from Kommandant Richwalder for several days. "It probably takes time to complete the background check," Krysia explains when I comment about the delay.

"Background check?" I panic, certain that an investigation by the Nazis will reveal my true identity. But Krysia tells me not to worry, and a few days later, I learn that she is right. The resistance organization apparently extends throughout Poland, and there are people in Gdańsk who are willing to verify that they had known Anna Lipowski, lived beside her, worked and gone to school with her, and wasn't it too bad about the death of her parents? On Friday morning, nearly one week after the dinner party, I receive word via messenger that my clearance has come through and that I am to report to the Kommandant's office the following Monday.

"We need to go to town tomorrow," Krysia says that Saturday night after we have put Lukasz to bed.

"Tomorrow?" I turn to her in the hallway, puzzled. The stores are not open on Sundays.

"We have to go to church." Seeing the stunned expression on my face, Krysia continues. "The mayor's wife commented at the dinner party on the fact that I have not been there with you and Lukasz."

"Oh," I manage to say at last. I cannot argue with her logic. Krysia is a devout Catholic, and it only made sense that Lukasz and I would be, too. The fact that she normally went to mass every week but had not gone since our arrival might raise suspicions. Still, the idea of going to church sticks in my throat like a half-swallowed pill.

"I'm sorry," she says. "We don't have a choice. We have to keep up appearances."

I do not answer but walk to my bedroom and open the wardrobe. I study my few dresses, trying to figure out which one most looks like the ones I have seen young women my age wearing on their way to and from church. "The pink dress," Krysia says, coming up behind me.

"This one?" I hold up a cotton frock with three-quarter sleeves.

"Yes. I am going to have coffee. Care to join me?" she asks. I nod and follow her downstairs to the kitchen. A few minutes later, we carry our steaming mugs to the parlor. I notice her knitting needles and some bright blue yarn on the low table. "I am making a sweater for Lukasz," she explains as we sit. "I think he will need it for the winter."

Winter. Krysia expects us still to be with her then. I do not know why this surprises me. The Nazis' stronghold on Poland shows no signs of weakening, and we certainly have nowhere else to go. Still, winter is six months away. My heart drops as I think of Jacob, of being without him for that long.

Trying to hide my sadness, I lift the needles to examine Krysia's handiwork. She has only knitted a few rows so far, but I can tell from the small, even stitches that she is working with great care, and that the sweater will be lovely. The ball of yarn is kinked, and I realize that she must have unraveled a garment of her own to get it. "The color will match his eyes perfectly," I say, touched once again by how much she is doing for us.

"I thought so, too. Do you know how to knit?" I shake my head. "Here, let me show you." Before I can reply, Krysia moves closer to me on the sofa, placing her arms around me from behind and covering her much larger hands with my own. "Like this." She begins to move my hands in the two-step knitting pattern. The touch of her hands, thin and delicate like Jacob's, brings back a flood of emotions. My head swims, and I can barely feel the knitting needles. "That's all there is to it," she says a few minutes later, sitting back. She looks at the needles expectantly, as though I will continue on my own, but my hands fall helplessly to my lap.

"I'm sorry," I say, placing the needles and yarn back on the table. "I'm not very good at such things." It is the truth. My mother had given up on teaching me to sew when I was twelve, declaring my large, uneven stitches an abomination. Even now, looking down at the knitting needles, I know that Krysia will have to unravel and redo my few clumsy stitches.

"Nonsense, you just need practice." Krysia picks up the needles and yarn. "If you learn how to knit well, you can make something for Jacob."

"Jacob," I repeat, seeing his face in my mind. I could knit

him a sweater, perhaps in brown to bring out the color in his eyes. I see him pulling it over his thin shoulders and torso. Sometimes he seems fragile, almost childlike in my memory. It is hard to imagine him as a resistance fighter. I wonder suddenly if he took enough warm clothes with him when he left.

"You miss him, don't you?" Krysia asks gently.

"Yes, a great deal," I reply, forcing the vision of Jacob from my mind. I cannot afford to get caught up in memories right now; I have to stay focused on starting work Monday, on being Anna. "Krysia…" I pause before asking the question I have wondered about since the night of the dinner party. "What is Sachsenhausen?"

She hesitates, knitting needles suspended in midair. "Why do you ask?"

"Ludwig said that the Kommandant used to oversee Sachenhausen?"

Krysia frowns, biting the inside of her cheek. "Sachsenhausen is a Nazi prison, darling. It is a labor camp in Germany, near Munich."

My stomach drops. "For Jews?"

She shakes her head. "No, no! It is for political prisoners and criminals." Though I want to feel relieved, something in her emphatic response tells me she is not being altogether truthful. She sets down her knitting again and pats my hand. "Don't worry. Richwalder likes you. He will not be unkind."

"All right," I say, though her words are far from reassuring.

"Goodness!" She looks at the grandfather clock. It is nearly ten-thirty. "I had not realized the time. You should get some sleep. We need to get an early start tomorrow, and you'll need your strength."

For tomorrow, and everything that lies beyond, I add silently. I take another sip of my still-too-hot coffee and stand. I pause in the doorway. Krysia has picked up the knitting again, her hands making the small, quick circles over and over. "Good night," she says, without looking up. I do not ask if she is coming to bed. Even on a normal night, Krysia stays up late and sleeps little. She reminds me of Jacob in that way—he would stay up until all hours of the night and I would often find him asleep over a book or article he was working on in the study the next morning. But at least Jacob would sleep well into the next day when he could to compensate for his late hours. Krysia, I know, will be up before dawn, doing chores and preparing us for the day that lies ahead. I worry that caring for Lukasz and me may be too much for her. And now, with our foray into church the next morning and my starting work for Richwalder the day after, she has more on her mind than ever.

That night I sleep restlessly, dreaming that I am on a street I do not recognize in the darkness. In the distance, I hear voices and laughter and I rub my eyes, trying to find the source. Fifteen meters down the road, I see a group of young people wearing some sort of uniform, joking and talking as they go. One voice, a familiar baritone, stands out above the others. "Jacob!" I cry. I start to run, trying to catch him, but my feet slide out from under me on the slick, wet pavement. I stand quickly and begin running again. At last I reach the group. "Jacob," I repeat breathlessly. He does not hear me but continues talking to a woman I do not recognize. I cannot understand what he is saying. Desperately, I try to reach out and touch him, but I am brushed aside by the crowd as it moves forward and I fall once more. When I look up again, they are gone, and I am alone on my knees in the cold, wet street.

I awake with a start. "Jacob?" I call aloud. I blink several times. I am still in my bedroom, of course. It was only a dream. Nevertheless, I peer into the darkness for several seconds as though Jacob might have actually been there. Jacob, I think, the dream playing over and over in my head. I miss him so. And I am always chasing, but never reaching him in my dreams. What if he really is so preoccupied with his work that he has forgotten me? What if he's found another girl? What if…I cannot finish the most horrible thought of all, that something may happen to him and I may not see him again. I press my face into my pillow, soaking it with the wetness of my tears.

The next morning, Krysia knocks on my door at seven. I rise and dress quickly. Downstairs, Krysia already has Lukasz washed and fed. Seeing the child, I hesitate. I had hoped that he would somehow not have to go to church with us, but of course there is no one else to watch him. Without speaking, we make our way from the house to the bus stop at the corner. The bus, which comes along shortly, is almost full of mostly farmers and peasants. They are going to church, too, I can tell, from the way they have tried to press their worn clothes and clean the dirt from their nails.

I stare out the window as we bounce along the curving road, trying to pretend we are just out running errands. But the thought keeps repeating in my mind: I am going to church, actually walking inside for the first time. Often growing up, I would pass by the crowds that gathered at the various church doors around the city for mass. I would watch as they stood, heads bowed, swaying slightly to the chanting melody that escaped through the open doorways. Above their heads, I saw only darkness. I could not imagine the mysteries that existed on the other side of those enormous wooden doors. Today I will find out. In my mind, I see my father's face, staring at me with sad eyes, my mother shaking her head in disbelief.

At the edge of the Planty, we climb from the bus. Lukasz walks between us, each of his hands in one of ours. As we cross the square, the towers of the Mariacki Cathedral loom before us. Though there are hundreds of churches in Kraków, it is not surprising that Krysia attends the largest and most imposing. At the doorway of the church, I hesitate. "Come," Krysia says, stepping in between me and Lukasz and taking our hands. Inside, I blink several times to adjust my eyes to the dim light. The air is different here, a cool dampness emanating from the stone walls. Krysia pauses, lifting her hand from mine to cross herself. I see her look at me out of the corner of my eye, lips pursed. Did she expect me to follow her lead? I shake my head inwardly. I cannot manage it, at least not yet.

I allow Krysia to lead me down the center aisle, trying not to stare at the gold crucifix, many meters high, which dominates the front wall of the church. People seated on either side of the aisle stare at us as we pass, murmuring. Can they tell that I am not one of them? I wonder. In truth I know that they are just curious because we are newcomers. Gossip travels quickly in Kraków and many likely have heard of the orphaned niece and nephew who have come to reside with Krysia Smok. If Krysia sees their reactions, she pretends not to notice, nodding to people on either side of the aisle and touching a few hands as we walk. Then she guides us into an empty pew halfway up the aisle and we sit on the hard wooden bench. Organ music begins to play. I look around, surprised at how many people are there. The Nazis are against religion, and they have arrested many priests. In a country where the population was almost entirely Catholic, they have not dared to outlaw the church entirely, but I marveled that more people do not stay away out of fear of persecution.

A priest appears at the front of the church then and begins to chant in Latin. A few minutes later, as if on cue, Krysia and the others around us shift forward to kneel. I hesitate. Jews do not kneel, it is forbidden. But Krysia tugs on my sleeve at the elbow. I have no choice. I slide forward, putting my arm around Lukasz to bring him with me. I look at him. He is staring upward, eyes wide. We remain kneeling for several minutes. My knees, unaccustomed, ache as they press into the hard stone floor. I notice that Krysia's head is bowed and I quickly follow her lead. The priest continues chanting and the parishioners echo his words at certain parts. It is one of the many secret rituals I do not know. At one point, Krysia and the others cross themselves. Hesitating, I wave my hand in front of my face in a nondescript manner, hoping that it will suffice. Something catches the corner of my eye and I look down at Lukasz. The rabbi's child is waving his hand in front of his face, earnestly attempting to cross himself, to imitate Krysia and the others. Crossing himself. The hair on the back of my neck stands on end at the sight of this.

Stealing another glance at Krysia out of the corner of my eye, I see that her lips are moving slightly, as though memorizing something. She is praying, I realize, really praying. I look around, trying not to lift my head, and wonder if my prayers will work here, too. It has been so long since I have prayed anywhere. I don't know where to begin. I consider saying the Shema, the most basic of Jewish prayers. *Hear O Israel, the Lord our God, the Lord is one.* Then I stop. It does not feel right here. I try again. Please, I pray, uncertain what to say after that. Please, God. Suddenly, the words pour forth inside me like a fountain turned on. I pray for the safety of my parents and Jacob. I pray for Krysia, and Lukasz and myself, for the strength to keep up our charade as I work for the Kommandant. I ask forgiveness for being in this place, for kneeling. I pray that Lukasz will never remember being here.

Then the kneeling part is over. We sit up again, and I lift Lukasz to my lap, pressing his cool cheek against mine as the priest keeps chanting. The priest steps in front of the altar then, a silver chalice and plate in hand. People in the front of the church begin to rise and go forward. "Communion," Krysia whispers, so softly I can barely hear. I nod. I have heard of this before. A few minutes later, Krysia stands and touches my shoulder. She means for me to go with her. I rise, my legs stone at the prospect of going up. We make our way to the center aisle and join the line as it shuffles forward, Lukasz coming with us, although, I suspect, he is too young for Communion. When we reach the front, Krysia goes first. I watch as she kneels and opens her mouth, allowing the priest to place a wafer there. Then she rises and turns, taking Lukasz's hand from me. It is my turn. I step forward and kneel. "Body of Christ," the priest says as he places the wafer on my tongue. I close my mouth against the dryness, wait for lightning to strike me dead.

A few minutes later we are back in our seats. The collection plate is passed. It is almost empty when it reaches us. Krysia places a few coins in it, much less, I am sure, than she would have before the war. I wonder if she can afford it now. Then it is over, and we make our way from the church. I fight the urge to rush ahead as Krysia makes obligatory introductions and small talk with other parishioners by the front door. Finally, we step out into the light.

"That wasn't so bad, was it?" Krysia asks when we are far from the church. I shake my head, not answering. There are some things that, despite her best intentions, she will never understand. I feel violated by the experience, nauseous at the knowledge that we will have to go again.

When we arrive back at Krysia's house, my mind turns to the next day. Less than twenty-four hours from now, I will go to work for the Kommandant. I deliberately keep busy with household chores, preparing a rich beet soup for Lukasz's lunch, laying out the clothes he will wear the next day. "I can do that for him tomorrow," Krysia protests.

I shake my head and do not stop moving. "I need to keep moving," I reply, refolding one of the child's freshly washed shirts for the fourth time. "It's not like I'm going to be able to sleep tonight, anyway."

I do not go to bed until almost midnight, and even then I toss and turn. The thoughts I usually fight so hard to keep from my mind, of my family and the ghetto and all of the awful unknowns, are welcome diversions now, as I try to ignore the reality that awaits me the next morning. How had my life changed so much in a week, a month, a year? Jacob would not even recognize me anymore. I imagine writing a letter to him—where would I begin? Oh, yes, my beloved, I write in my head. Your wife is a gentile now. And did I mention I have a child? And that I start working for the Nazis tomorrow? I laugh aloud in the dark.

But in truth I know that the situation is deadly serious. By walking into the Nazi headquarters every day, I will be entering the lion's den. It is not just my own safety I will be risking: if my true identity is discovered, it will put everyone around me, my parents, Lukasz, even Krysia, in grave danger. Krysia. I can see the look on her face as she urged me to take the Kommandant's offer, the worried way she has watched me ever since. She, too, knows the stakes. She must have very good reasons for wanting me to do this. At last my eyes grow heavy and I finally doze off.

After what seems like only minutes, I am awakened by the predawn sounds of the neighbors' rooster crowing. I can tell by the way the early morning light falls through the maple tree outside my window that it is approximately five o'clock. I lie still for a moment, listening to the horses' hoofs pound against the dirt road as they pull the farmers' wagons down from the hills, carrying produce to the markets. Staring at the ceiling, I hesitate. Once I set that first foot on the floor, it will all begin. If I do not get out of bed, I think, perhaps I can stop time. It is a familiar game, one I played as a child when there was something I did not want to do. It did not work then, I remind myself, and it will not work now. And it will not do to be late my first day on the job. I take a deep breath and stand.

I rise and wash quietly. Hoping not to wake Krysia or Lukasz, I tiptoe downstairs, trying not to let the soles of my shoes squeak on the hardwood steps. Krysia is already seated at the kitchen table, reading the newspaper over a cup of tea. I wonder if she slept at all last night. *"Dzien dobry,"* she greets me, her voice fresh. She rises and looks me up and down, appraising my outfit. I have chosen from among her castoffs a white shirtwaist and a gray skirt, belting the oversize shirt at the waist. The skirt, which was supposed to be knee-length, falls nearly to my ankles. "Very professional," she remarks, gesturing for me to sit. She pushes a plate of steaming scrambled eggs across the table toward me. "Now eat."

I shake my head, nauseous at the smell. "I'm too nervous." Even as I speak, my stomach jumps and a wave of queasiness washes over me. "And I should be going, I don't want to be late."

Krysia hands me a small lunch pail and a light wool cloak. "Try to relax. You'll be more likely to make mistakes if you're nervous. Just stay quiet, observe as much as you can…and trust no one." She pats my shoulder. "You'll do fine. Lukasz and I will be here when you come home."

It is not quite seven o'clock when I set out. The residents of Chelmska are early risers; as I walk down the road, past the houses and farms, there seems to be someone out in every yard, gardening or tending livestock or sweeping their front porch. They look up as I pass, my presence at Krysia's still a curiosity to them. I nod my head and try to smile as I go, as though it is perfectly normal for me to be heading into the city at this early hour. At the end of the road where it meets the roundabout, I pause and inhale deeply. I have grown to love early mornings since coming to Krysia's house. There is a thin layer of fog hovering over the fields that I know will lift like a flock of birds by midmorning as the sun rises. The air smells of wet grass. As I take in the scene, my heart grows lighter, and for a second, I almost forget to be nervous.

At the bus stop I wait without speaking beside an elderly

woman carrying an assortment of garden herbs in her tattered basket. The bus arrives and I follow the woman aboard, passing one of the tokens Krysia has given me to the driver. The bus rumbles along the unevenly paved road, pulling over every half kilometer or so. The trees, bent toward the road with their heavy loads of leaves, brush the roof of the bus as it passes. When all of the seats are filled and still more passengers continue to board, I stand to give my place to an old man, who smiles toothlessly at me.

Twenty minutes later, I step off the bus and, after a short walk, find myself standing at the foot of Wawel Castle. Looking up at the enormous stone fortress, I inhale sharply. I have not seen Wawel since I went to the ghetto last autumn. Now as I approach, its domes and spires seem even grander than I remembered. For the centuries that Kraków had been the capital of Poland, Wawel was the seat of kings, and many royal figures were buried in its cathedral. The actual capital had long since moved to Warsaw, and Wawel had become a museum— until eight months ago when it became the seat of the Nazi General Government. Compose yourself, I think, but my legs tremble and threaten to give out from under me as I walk up the long stone entranceway to the castle.

"Anna Lipowski," I manage to say to the guard at the top of the ramp. He does not look at me, but checks my name off a list and summons a second guard, who escorts me into the castle through a stone archway. We proceed through a dizzying array of high-ceilinged hallways and marble staircases. The musty odor reminds me of the time when I visited the castle on a school trip as a child. But this is not the Wawel Castle of my childhood. The corridors are sterile now, the pictures of Polish kings removed. They are lined instead with endless red flags, each bearing a white circle with a large black swastika inside. Almost everyone we pass wears a Nazi military uniform and greets with a crisp, firm, "Heil Hitler!" I nod, unable to return the greeting. My escort, perhaps taking my silence as nervousness, answers loudly enough for both of us.

When at last it seems that we can walk no farther or higher, the guard stops before an enormous oak door bearing a plaque with Kommandant Richwalder's name on it. He raps sharply on the door twice, then, without waiting for a response, opens it and gestures for me to enter. The room is a reception area of some sort, windowless and too warm. A large-boned woman with a wide nose and bad skin sits at a small desk in the center of the room. Her head is bowed and her enormous brown coil of hair bobs as she works, filling in spaces on a lined graph with intensity. If she's here, I wonder, then what am I to do? Hope rises within me. Perhaps some mistake has been made and there is no position available for me. Maybe I can just go home. But even as I think this, I know that it is impossible; Kommandant Richwalder is not the type of man to make that sort of mistake.

I stand awkwardly by the door for several minutes. The woman does not look up. Helplessly, I turn around, but the guard who escorted me has disappeared into the hallway, leaving me alone. The woman behind the desk does not speak. *"Przepraszam…"* I finally say, excusing myself.

"Ja?" she replies, and I can tell from her pronunciation that she does not speak German.

"I am Anna Lipowski." There is no reaction or response. "Kommandant Richwalder instructed me to report here…."

"Oh, yes." At last she stands, inspecting me from head to toe with a sweeping glance. "You are the Kommandant's new personal assistant." There is an inscrutable hint of disdain in the way that she pronounces my job title that makes me uneasy. She gestures for me to follow her through a second door behind her desk. "This is the anteroom." I look around. The room is smaller than the reception area, but has nicer furnishings and a cool breeze coming from two large open windows on either side. "You will work here. The Kommandant's office is through that door." She waves her head in the direction of another door at the back of the room. "The Kommandant had a meeting this morning and apologizes for being unable to welcome you personally." It is hard to imagine the imposing Kommandant apologizing for anything.

The woman continues on as though giving a speech. "We are privileged to be working in the governor's executive offices. Only the most senior officials and their staffs are located in Wawel. The rest of the General Government is located in the administrative building across town on Pomorskie Street." I nod, trying to reconcile myself to the idea that working for the Nazis could somehow be construed as a privilege. "The Kommandant is the governor's first deputy. All of the various directorates in southern Poland report to him. He will explain your duties to you in greater detail when he returns. For a start, you will keep his calendar and answer his correspondence." She pronounces the word *correspondence* as though it were a matter of national security. "I am Malgorzata Turnau," she concludes. "If I can help you at all, please let me know."

"Thank you." I realize then that this woman's position is subordinate to mine, and the strange look I saw cross her face when she said my job title was one of jealousy. She probably hoped to move up to the very position I am to fill. But any sympathy I might have had for her is dampened by the reverence with which she described our work and the fervent look in her eyes. She is obviously one of those Poles whose loyalties have been swayed to the Nazis, and I can tell right away she will do anything to curry favor with the Kommandant. When Krysia had said to trust no one, she clearly had the Malgorzatas of the world in mind. I knew she would be watching me.

Malgorzata walks over to the desk that sits to the left side of the room under one of the windows. "This is the Kommandant's mail." She picks up a clipboard and hands it to me. "Open each piece and log it on this chart by sender, date and subject." She shows me then how to separate the mail into piles: one for those pieces of correspondence that require the Kommandant's personal attention, another for those that can be answered with a form response, and a final stack for those that need to be routed to other offices. "And don't open anything marked *confidential*," she instructs before leaving the room, slamming the door behind her.

Alone, I exhale, sitting down behind the desk. In addition to the letters, there is a small stack of office supplies that has been left on the desk for me, which I organize and place in the drawers. I pause to look around my new quarters. The anteroom is about three by five meters, with a small sofa located across from the desk. The windows, one each over the desk and sofa, are almost too high to see out of, but if I raise myself on my toes, I can just catch a glimpse of the river.

I reach for the stack of mail and begin opening the envelopes. Remembering what Krysia had said, I try to read as much of it as possible, but it is remarkably mundane, mostly invitations to social functions and dry-looking, official reports comprised of German military terminology that I cannot comprehend. About a third of the way down the stack, there is one envelope emblazoned with the word *Confidential* in red ink across the seal. I pull it out and hold it up to the light, but it is impossible to see through the thick paper. I examine the seal of the envelope. Perhaps I can open it and then close it again, I think, working at the edge of the seal with my fingernail.

The door swings open. I look up. The Kommandant strides into the anteroom, cloak flung over one shoulder. My breath catches. He is even more striking than I remembered. A smaller man, also in uniform, follows him, carrying two black leather briefcases. I rise to my feet. "Anna," the Kommandant says, smiling and walking toward me. He takes my right hand and I half expect him to kiss it as he did the night we met at Krysia's, but instead he simply shakes it in a businesslike manner. "Welcome." He gestures to the other man. "This is Colonel Diedrichson, my military attaché."

Colonel Diedrichson sets down the briefcases. He is not smiling. "What are you doing with that?" he demands, pointing to my left hand.

I freeze. I had forgotten that I am still holding the confidential envelope, the seal half open. "M-Malgorzata told me I was to open the mail," I manage to say.

"She didn't tell you that confidential mail is not to be opened?" he demands. I shrug and shake my head slightly, praying that he will not ask her.

"I'm sure it was just a mistake," the Kommandant interjects.

"This—" Colonel Diedrichson snatches the envelope

from my hand "—is why I wanted to import the clerical staff from Berlin."

"Thank you, Colonel, that will be all," the Kommandant says.

Diedrichson raises his right hand. "Heil Hitler." He picks up the briefcases before turning on one heel and leaving. When he has gone, the Kommandant turns back to me. He does not speak but opens the door at the rear of the anteroom and gestures for me to enter. My hands shaking, I pick up a notepad from my desk and follow him inside.

The Kommandant's office is like nothing I have ever seen. It is enormous, bigger than an entire floor of Krysia's house. The office is like three rooms in one. Immediately by the door are a sofa and a half-dozen chairs arranged around a low table in the manner of a living room. At the far end of the room stands a conference table surrounded by at least fourteen chairs. In the center, between these two areas, is an enormous mahogany desk. A lone framed photograph sits on the corner of the desk. Across from the Kommandant's desk, there is a towering grandfather clock. The thick red velvet curtains that cover the wall of windows behind the desk have been pulled back with gold ropes, revealing a stunning panoramic view of the river.

The Kommandant gestures to the sofa by the door. "Please, sit down," he says, walking toward the desk. I perch in the location he indicated and wait expectantly as he shuffles through a stack of papers. A moment later he looks up. "I'm sure Malgorzata informed you of your basic duties, correspondence and scheduling." I nod. "If that was all I needed, I could have anyone do it, including Malgorzata. Anna," he says, crossing the room to where I am seated. As he approaches, I shiver involuntarily.

"Are you cold?" he asks.

"N-no, Herr Kommandant," I stammer, cursing inwardly at my nervousness. I must do a better job of concealing it.

"Oh, good." He sits down in the chair beside me. As he draws closer, I suddenly notice a swastika pin fastened to his collar. Had he been wearing it last time? I had not noticed. Then again, last time I had not known what Sachsenhausen was. He continues, "Anna, I am the Governor's first deputy. That fool Ludwig was not entirely mistaken in what he said the night of the dinner party—I am charged with carrying out all of the governor's orders. All of them." His eyebrows rise, as if to emphasize his words. "A great many others would like to have my position." He stands up again, pacing the floor in front of me. "The General Government is full of vipers who, for all of their lip service to the ideals of the Reich, would gladly stab me in the back while shaking my hand." His voice is lower now. "As such, I need a personal assistant who is discreet, versatile and, above all, loyal. You are not just my assistant, but my eyes and ears." He stops, standing squarely before me once more. His eyes lock squarely with mine. "Do you understand?"

"Y-yes, Herr Kommandant," I stammer, marveling over the fact that he thinks I am loyal.

"Good. I chose you not only because you are exceptionally smart and speak German, but because I sense that you can be trusted."

"Thank you, Herr Kommandant." Trust. My stomach twists.

He continues pacing again. "Every morning you and I will meet to go over my schedule and any tasks I would like you to complete that day. For now, you can simply catch up on the backlog of correspondence. I have not had a personal assistant for more than a month, and I did not want anyone else to handle it." I wonder then what became of my predecessor. "And as you discerned from Colonel Diedrichson, you are not to open any correspondence marked 'confidential.' Understood?" I nod. "Good. You have been given the highest clearance for a Pole, but there are still some things that are off-limits." My heart sinks. Confidential correspondence would undoubtedly contain the information most valuable to the resistance.

"I will ask Colonel Diedrichson to stop by to see you later this morning. He can provide you with whatever you need, including guidance in my absence." The Kommandant turns and walks toward his desk then, and I realize that I have been dismissed. I stand and turn to leave. "Anna," he calls when I am at the door. I face him again. He is looking at me intensely, his expression deadly serious. "My door is always open to you."

"Thank you, Herr Kommandant." I retreat to the anteroom and collapse into my chair, shaking.

My first day of work at headquarters passes quickly after my meeting with the Kommandant. I spend the remainder of the morning opening the mail until Colonel Diedrichson returns to take me around the executive offices and introduce me to the staff. I can tell by the way that the secretaries and aides seem to be sizing me up that my arrival as the Kommandant's personal assistant has aroused great interest. Finally, Diedrichson takes me to the security office, where I am given a building pass. On our way back to the Kommandant's office we pass another set of large oak doors marked with a brass seal.

"The governor's office," Diedrichson says solemnly without stopping. His voice sounds almost reverent.

I spend the afternoon reorganizing file drawers in the anteroom. The files are in such complete disarray that it seems hard to believe that my predecessor left only a month ago. The librarian in me takes over, dividing the files first geographically, one section for Kraków and another for each of the outlying regions. Two hours later, I am finished, but I still have not seen any documents that seem significant. I wonder if the Kommandant receives materials through other channels.

I do not see the Kommandant for the remainder of that day. At five o'clock, I gather my belongings and walk to the bus stop. Once on the bus, I slump in my seat, my throbbing head pressed against the window. I am exhausted, more so from nerves than anything else. But I have made it through my first day.

I barely walk through the front door of Krysia's and set down my things when Lukasz wraps himself around my knees. "He missed you all day today," Krysia says as I pick him up and carry him upstairs. "I took him to the park and tried to play with him, but he just kept looking for you."

We walk into the parlor. Sitting down, I hold the child back from me a few inches and brush his blond curls from his face. His eyes dart back and forth frantically and his grip on my arms tightens, as though afraid I am leaving again. The poor child has seen so many people he trusted walk through the front door and never come back. "Shh," I coo, drawing him close again and rocking him back and forth. "I have to go away during the day sometimes, *kochana,* but I will always come back at night. Always." His grip unrelenting, he buries his head in my shoulder, still not uttering a sound.

"How was it?" Krysia asks a few hours later, when we have finished supper and carried our mugs of coffee to the study. I had eaten with Lukasz still wrapped around my neck and had only been able to put him to bed once he had fallen soundly asleep in my arms.

"Not so very bad," I answer carefully. How could I tell her the truth, that it was both horrible and yet strangely exciting at the same time? I hated being among the Nazis, but it was somehow thrilling to work in such a grand office in Wawel Castle. And then there was Kommandant Richwalder. The air felt electrified when he was present. But he is a Nazi, and to feel anything other than hatred and disgust…a wave of shame washes over me. After an awkward pause, I fetch my bag and show Krysia the pass Colonel Diedrichson had obtained for me from the security office.

"Yes." Krysia holds the pass up to the light and appraises it with a knowing eye. "This is the highest Nazi clearance a Pole can get. Our friends in Gdańsk must have really done their job at verifying your background. With this pass, you can go anywhere."

"There are still things I cannot see," I reply. "Confidential documents are off-limits. And most of what I saw was routine correspondence."

"Give it time, darling. You must be patient. When the Kommandant grows to know you more, you will gain his trust. Then he will take you into his confidence, share things with you." She hands the pass back to me. "I will let Alek know right away."

"Alek?" Tucking the pass back in my bag, I look at Krysia quizzically. Was he still in the ghetto, I wonder? How does

Krysia make contact with him? Does she have contact with Jacob, too? I hesitate, not wanting to ask too much or appear demanding. I am certain that if she had news about Jacob she would tell me.

"Yes, I sent word to him about your most fortunate position at Wawel. He thinks you may be able to be of use to us there." She pauses, sipping her coffee and looking out the front window to where the sun is setting behind the trees of Las Wolski. "Not right away, of course. The Nazis will be watching you closely for the first several weeks. They and their Polish spies." At this last sentence, her lips curl with distaste.

"I know, I think I have already met one of them." As I tell her about Malgorzata, the woman's hawkish features appear in my mind.

Krysia pats my hand. "Don't worry. You just do a good job for now. Gain the Kommandant's trust and confidence," she stresses once more. "Meanwhile, I will make contact with Alek and find out exactly what he has in mind."

CHAPTER 8

As the grandfather clock in the Kommandant's office chimes five times, I pick up my lunch pail and walk from the anteroom into the reception area. "I'm leaving," I tell Malgorzata, who is engaged in making another one of her administrative charts.

"Good night." She does not look up. I leave the office, shaking my head and marveling that she can put so much energy and concentration into projects that matter to no one but herself.

The sun is still high over the spires of Wawel Cathedral as I walk down the castle ramp. Instead of heading directly for the bus stop for the trip back to Krysia's as I normally would, I turn down Grodzka Street toward the city center. I have been paid today, and it is the first time since leaving my job at the library that I have had any money of my own to spend. I want to buy some treats for Lukasz, and perhaps something for Krysia as well.

It is Monday, the beginning of my third week working for the Kommandant. I can hardly believe time has flown so quickly. The first few days of work were terrifying. My every nerve stood on end. I jumped each time the door to the anteroom opened, and my hands shook so hard I could hardly type. At the end of the day, I would return to Chelmska gray and shaken. "You must learn to calm yourself," Krysia had admonished gently. "You are going to make yourself ill." Not to mention give myself away, I thought. Malgorzata had remarked more than once during my first week of work that I looked pale.

Finally, I had forced myself to calm down, breathing deeply and visualizing happier times with Jacob and my family. Now my nerves are better, and I do not shake as I walk up the ramp into Wawel each morning. But there are some things I know I will never get used to. I still avert my eyes from the endless parade of swastika flags that line the castle corridors. I avoid walking the hallways unnecessarily, only leaving my office once or twice each day to go to the water closet or to lunch. I dread running into the other staff members, who invariably greet me with an enthusiastic "Heil Hitler!" When someone says this, I am forced to raise my hand in return and mumble something that passes for the same syllables. In fact, under my breath I am actually mumbling, "Kill Hitler!" or some other obscenity that would never have crossed my lips a year earlier.

Each day at lunchtime, I take my pail and sit on a bench by the river, passing the hour by reading a newspaper borrowed from the office, or just looking at the water as it flows under the railway bridge. It has been so very long since I have been able to just sit by the Wisla. I had once taken it utterly for granted, playing by the water's edge as a child, walking along the banks with Jacob as we courted. Now I am here again on its grass-covered banks, only this time I am acutely aware that I do not belong. I should be in the ghetto, I often think, looking across to the far bank of the river, imprisoned there with my family and neighbors. Instead, I am able to spend each day at lunch sitting out by the water, enjoying a thick turkey sandwich and an apple packed by Krysia that morning. Often, I stare across the water in the direction of Podgorze, fantasizing about sneaking away and taking some food to my parents in the ghetto.

Though I prefer to eat lunch alone, I am often joined by a group of secretaries from the other offices at Wawel. These are young Polish women, indifferent to the fact that they were working for the Nazis, happy to hold a position of relative security and prestige, and to have a steady source of income in these dire times. "Don't blame them," I can hear my father say, as he had about those Jews who policed and ran the ghetto. "These are desperate times, and people are only doing what they need to do to survive." Still, I cannot help but resent these young women, who gossip as schoolgirls might, about clothes and movies and men, all the while profiting from the Nazi occupation. They are fascinated by the senior Nazi officers, particularly my boss, Kommandant Richwalder, and they constantly attempt to pepper me with questions about him. They want to know if he has ever been married, if he has a girlfriend, how he got his facial scars. "I really don't know," I always respond, trying to sound apologetic instead of annoyed. "He is a very private man."

I know they do not believe, or even like me. They think that

I am an out-of-towner, not one of them. Like Malgorzata, they envy my status and resent the way I suddenly appeared to begin working as the confidential assistant to one of the highest Nazi officials in Poland while they, who had toiled in lesser offices for months, had been passed over. Some of them think that the Kommandant and I are romantically involved, and that I was given the position for that reason. "The Kommandant's girl," I had overheard one of them call me in the corridor during my first week of work, when she did not know I was around the corner. I often wonder if Malgorzata is the source of such gossip. But there is no point in making enemies, so I continue to speak with them at lunch each day, pretending I have heard nothing.

Sometimes as I sit with these girls at lunch, listening to their inane conversations, I want to jump up and shout, "Don't you know? There is a horrible ghetto down the road, and there are people, neighbors you knew your whole life, who are suffering and dying there!" Of course, I bite the inside of my cheek and say nothing that might lead them to question who I really am. In their company, I can think of little else but my true identity, though, and the fact that I might be discovered at any moment. My rational mind knows that it is unlikely: my papers are in order, and no one here knows me from my other life. Unless I accidentally blurt out a Yiddish word or run into someone I once knew, my cover is likely to remain intact.

At the end of Grodzka Street, close to the market square, I pause before a small toy shop. Something for Lukasz, I think, looking at the toy trains and dolls in the front window. As I step inside, I realize that I am unsure what he would like. He is such a passive child and accepts everything so gratefully.

When Krysia or I hand him a kitchen pot, he relishes it as though it is a great gift, and plays with it for hours. I scan the shelves. The selection is limited, and I will not buy him toy guns or soldiers. Not wanting to linger too long and get home late, I settle on some building blocks and a wooden horse.

As I step out of the shop with my purchases and start across the street, the skin on the back of my neck prickles: I am being watched. I peer furtively over my shoulder, but I can detect no one unusual or suspicious in the rush-hour crowds. I continue on my way, purchasing some licorice at the candy store and then heading toward the nearest bus stop. At the corner, there is a fruit kiosk. I finger the remaining coins in my pocket. I should save some of the money, but I would like to get something for Krysia to show my appreciation for all that she has done for us. Perhaps just an orange, I think. As I stand examining the produce at the fruit stand, a small woman sidles up to me. I can feel her breath warm on my neck. "The dark ones are the juiciest," she says loudly enough for the merchant to hear.

I hesitate for a moment. The voice is familiar, but I am unable to place it. She means for me to play along, I realize. "Yes, but the light ones are sweeter."

"Walk with me," the stranger whispers after I pay the seller. Only when we are several feet away do I look over. Marta! I might not recognize her but for the thick glasses and bright eyes. Her dark curly hair has been straightened and made lighter, and her blue skirt and kerchief are those of a Polish peasant girl. There is something more mature about her, too; gone is the chubby, girlish figure, and in its place stands a curvy and mature woman. She has changed much in the months since our last meeting.

"Marta, what are you…?"

"Shh…" Instead of answering, she grabs my hand playfully, as though we were just two girls meeting up while out for an afternoon stroll. "Walk with me," she says softly.

I follow her, my mind racing. I have not seen Marta since I escaped from the ghetto, and there are so many things I want to ask her. How did she get out? How did she find me? I bite my tongue, knowing that it is not safe to talk on the street. "How did you…?" I whisper at last when I can stand it no longer, the blood pounding in my cheeks.

"Keep your head up," she singsongs through her smile, and I realize that I have tilted my head toward her in a conspiratorial gesture that threatens to give us away. "I got out on my messenger's pass just before the ghetto was sealed," she replies in a voice just slightly lower than normal. "Many of us are living outside Kraków now in the forests and villages."

I desperately want to ask her about Jacob. Perhaps she has seen him or had word through the resistance. But we have never spoken of my husband. "Where are we going?" I ask instead.

"Alek wants to see you." Alek. My breath catches. Perhaps he has some news of Jacob. I follow Marta, expecting that she will lead me in the direction of the ghetto, toward an abandoned building or alleyway or out of town, but she continues striding confidently toward the market square. It is a balmy summer evening, and the outdoor cafés ringing the square are crowded with Nazis and Poles enjoying a coffee or beer after work.

"Here?" I ask incredulously, as she leads me to a sidewalk café overflowing with people.

"Where better?" she replies, and I realize that she is right.

Much like my working in Nazi headquarters, no one would suspect that a bunch of Jews would have the audacity to meet at an outdoor café on the market square in broad daylight.

I hesitate, but no one looks up as I follow Marta through a maze of tables. Toward the back of the café sit two men. As we near, I recognize Alek and Marek. Alek has cut his hair so short that patches of white scalp shine through. Marek, his beard shaved, looks like a schoolboy. They rise as we approach and kiss each of us on our cheeks three times, as though this is a social gathering.

"Hello, Anna," Alek addresses me as we sit down. I notice that he used my pseudonym. I try to contain my excitement at seeing him. My mind buzzes with a thousand questions: How had he arranged my escape? Has he heard from Jacob?

A waitress approaches our table and Marek orders four coffees. "How's work?" Alek asks when she has gone.

"O-okay," I stammer, caught off guard by the nonchalance of his question.

"I saw your uncle from Lwów last Tuesday," Alek says. Puzzled, I start to reply that I have no uncle from Lwów. Then I stop, realizing that he is referring to Jacob.

"He is well?" I ask, my stomach jumping.

"Quite well." I relax slightly. He continues, "Very busy with his work. And he is missing his niece terribly." I smile, knowing he means me.

After the waitress has returned with our coffees and left again, Marta and Marek begin talking then in a loud, joking, conversational voice about nothing in particular. Alek addresses me directly in a lower tone. "Down the hall from where you work is the office of Colonel Krich, the director of administration. He issues all of the security passes that give access throughout the city." I nod. Krich had signed the security pass I'd received on my first day of work. "Each Tuesday morning, Krich and the other senior officials travel over to Pomorskie Street for a long meeting. Krich's secretary often uses this time to get her hair done or run errands outside Wawel. If the way is clear, you can get into his office. The key to his office is taped under his secretary's desk." He grabs my hand under the table and presses something into it.

"This is the combination to the safe. Memorize and destroy it. Inside the safe are blank passes, consecutively numbered. Take no more than a half dozen each week. Make certain they are always individual sheets from the middle or near the bottom of the stack, so they will not be missed.

"Each Tuesday afternoon, you will come here after work. Marek or I or someone else who will recognize you will come to have tea with you. You will set your satchel down by the foot of the chair, and when you go to leave, you will be given a new one. If you have not been successful that week, or if you think you are being followed, you are not to come. If it is not safe, the person will not be here to meet you. Do you understand?" I gulp, nodding. Alek means for me to steal security passes for the resistance.

Marek breaks from his conversation with Marta to interject in a harsh whisper. "It is essential that you get the passes this week! We need—"

Alek raises his hand, cutting Marek off. "Only if it is safe. We cannot afford to take chances." Marek bites his lip and looks away, chastised. Alek turns back to me and lowers his hand onto mine, his brow furrowed. "Anna, I'm not going to lie to you. This is dangerous work, as risky as any in the entire movement. But you wanted to help, and fortune has put you in a unique position to do so."

"I understand," I reply quickly. In fact, I could barely begin to grasp the magnitude of what he was asking me to do.

"It should only be two, three times at the most," he adds. I nod again. "Well, then." Alek swallows his coffee in one mouthful and stands. Marek follows. "It was a pleasure seeing you ladies." Marek tips his hat and the two stride off jauntily across the market square.

"Is he crazy?" I whisper to Marta once Alek and Marek are out of earshot. "Me, do this?"

Marta blinks rapidly several times behind her glasses, and I realize that I have made a mistake. Clearly she is unused to hearing anyone question Alek. "You heard him. You are the only one in a position to do the job."

"But me? I'm only a…" I hesitate, looking for the right word to describe my own sense of inadequacy.

"What?" Marta shoots back, her eyes flashing. "A girl?" It is the first time I have ever heard anger in her voice. I start to speak then stop, humbled. How silly I must sound! Marta is a girl, too, younger than me, and her work as a messenger has put her in constant danger.

"I'm sorry." I bite my lip, twirling the sugar spoon between my thumb and forefinger. "I just feel that I lack some sort of experience."

"No one trains for this," she replies flatly, not looking at me.

"You're right, of course. Again, I'm sorry."

We are silent for several minutes. Yet despite the awkwardness, we linger over our coffees. Our reunion, this fleeting moment of camaraderie, feels like standing by a fire before heading off into the cold. Neither of us wants to abandon it. "So…" Marta says at last.

"So…" I repeat. There is so much I want to ask her, I don't know where to begin.

"You are looking well," she offers.

"Thank you. I am very fortunate to be at Krysia's. She is so kind to me." Suddenly, I feel self-conscious about my cheeks, which have grown fuller and more colorful since I arrived at Krysia's house. I notice that Marta herself looks pale and tired, and I wonder what they live off of in the forest.

"It is not so bad out there," she says defensively. Like Alek, she seems to be able to read my mind. I must keep better control of my expressions. Such transparency will not serve me well at Wawel. "At least we are free," she adds.

Marta stands to leave then and I follow. "How is your mother?" I ask as we walk away, wondering if, through the resistance, she might still have some news from inside the ghetto. Marta looks down, shaking her head. "Oh, no! What happened?"

"Typhus. Two weeks ago." She clenches her jaw. Her young face seems so much harder than just a few months earlier.

"Oh, Marta." Tears well in my eyes, and I fight the urge to turn and hug her for fear of attracting too much attention. "How…?" Pani Nederman had been so strong.

"Things are very bad inside now." She pauses as a look of panic for my own parents crosses my face. Then she shrugs; there is no point in sparing me the truth. "They have little food, dirty water, far too many people, many more than when we were there. Disease is rampant. Parents of small children keep dying, and the orphanage gets more and more crowded.

They try to quarantine the sick children, but it's no use. That's where she caught it."

"I'm so sorry." In my mind, I see Pani Nederman's kind face. Without her, Marta and I never would have met. I would not have come to know Alek or the others and might have never escaped from the ghetto. My thoughts turn to my own parents then. The war has already weakened them so; surely they cannot be faring much better.

We continue walking past St. Anna's Cathedral. My namesake, I think with irony. I remember crossing this street each morning on my way to work at the library. The old man washing down the cathedral steps always said hello. I can still smell the musty odor of damp pavement drying in the morning.

"Marta, may I ask you something?" She nods. "The resistance, what is it all about?"

"You mean, why are we doing this?" She looks puzzled and I hope I have not angered her again.

"Yes."

"Because we have to do something. We can't just sit here and let our people be destroyed."

That part I understood. I had heard it from Jacob before. "But what's the goal?"

She pauses, as though considering the matter for the first time. "Various resistance members have different goals." I remember the conversation I overheard when eavesdropping on the back room at Josefinska 13, the one in which Alek and Marek and the other man were disagreeing about what the resistance should do. "Some just want to work quietly to help our people. Others want to strike back and attack the Nazis."

"Oh." Such a strike would be suicide, I think, though I do

not dare to question the resistance leadership in front of Marta again. I wonder which group Jacob is in, what he wants from all of this. How can I not know my husband's reasons for doing the very thing that keeps us apart? "But, Marta, striking back…it's symbolic, isn't it? I mean, they don't really believe they can make a difference, do they?"

She stops walking, turns to face me. "We have to believe that. Otherwise there is no hope."

We continue walking in silence. At the corner, where Anna Street meets the Planty, Marta stops again and I sense this is where we will part ways. I lean forward to kiss her cheek. She pulls back, hesitating. "Anna, there is one thing…."

I stop, my face still inches from hers. "Yes?"

"It's about your uncle from Lwów…that is, I have met Jacob."

My breath catches and I look away. "I don't know what you're talking about." Even after all Marta and I have been through together, my instinct is still to deny my marriage.

"I know the truth," she persists. "He is your husband. He tried to keep it from me, but I guessed. I could tell from his description of you."

"Oh." I look down, scuffing my shoes against the pavement. I am unsure what to say. "I'm sorry I didn't tell you. We have had to keep it a secret, you see, for everyone's safety."

"I understand. He's a wonderful man, Anna," she replies quietly, "and he loves you very much." There is a twist in her voice that I cannot quite comprehend.

"Tell him the same from me," I say, my voice even. "If you see him again."

"I shall," she answers, and her certainty of a rendezvous with my husband tugs at my heart. I grab her hand, as though the possibility that it had touched Jacob's offers some magical connection. Her lips are cool as she kisses my cheek. "Godspeed, Anna." Then she is gone.

Marta knows Jacob, I think in disbelief, as I make my way quickly toward the bus stop on the far side of the Planty. I suppose I should not be surprised. Surely the resistance cannot be that big. And she knows of our marriage. Jacob must trust her very much to have shared our secret with her. Unless…I shake my head, not wanting to think it. There was something behind Marta's voice that sounded so strange when she spoke about Jacob. I recall a conversation we had in the ghetto. Marta had said that there was a boy in the resistance for whom she had feelings. A boy who did not seem to notice her. I wonder now if the boy is Jacob. Marta is so outgoing, perhaps she had confessed her feelings to him, maybe even tried to kiss him, and he had told her of his marriage to hold her off and keep her from being hurt. My mind sears white-hot as I picture the scene. Stop it, I scold myself. Don't let your imagination run away from you. But still the image lingers. And she will see him again, I think uneasily as I board the bus.

Though I do not plan to tell Krysia about my meeting that day, she looks at me in a way that tells me she already knows, staring at me intently as Lukasz delights over his new toys on the living room floor. At last I can be quiet no longer. "I saw Alek today."

"Oh?" Her voice is devoid of surprise.

"Yes, he has an…errand for me to run." I tell her then about the passes, and what I am to do.

"Emma…" she begins, forgetting to use my pseudonym. I can read the conflict in her eyes. Krysia, herself a staunch resistance fighter, knows that Alek does not take unnecessary risks. If he has asked me to do this, it must be absolutely essential to the movement. At the same time, she is worried. "Are you afraid?" she asks.

"Terribly," I confess, letting loose the torrent of emotion I'd been unable to share with Marta earlier that day. "Not only for myself but for you, Lukasz, Jacob, my family…everyone."

"You are afraid of failing," she observes. I nod, feeling naked and ashamed.

"Yes. Afraid of getting caught, and what it would mean for all of us." I wait for her to reassure me, as she usually does, to tell me that everything is fine and that I will do a good job. But she remains silent for several minutes, her brow furrowed and lips pursed. At last I am the one who speaks. "It will be okay, Krysia."

"It will be what it will be, darling. These are uncertain times, and there is no need to give an old woman false comfort. But I do know one thing." Suddenly, her face relaxes. She takes my hand in hers, and I can see a light growing in her eyes. "The courage of young people such as yourself is the one thing that still gives me hope." And with Krysia's words, the weight of my mission has suddenly grown a thousand times heavier.

CHAPTER 9

The next morning, I awake even earlier than usual to find Krysia asleep on the sofa where I left her. Gently so as not to wake her, I take the knitting needles from her hands and place a blanket around her before tiptoeing into the kitchen. I putter around the kitchen, making tea and organizing things, trying to fight the urge to leave for work early. I must not be overeager on account of my secret mission, not do anything out of the ordinary to attract attention to myself.

I arrive at Wawel promptly at eight o'clock. Our routine today is the same every morning. I sit at my desk, organizing the various papers that have been delivered overnight until the Kommandant arrives at exactly eight-fifteen. A few minutes later he calls me into his office and together we review his schedule for the day, and discuss any important upcoming meetings. I share with him any correspondence that requires his personal attention, letters from high-ranking officials, or matters unfamiliar to me, and he dictates responses. He, in turn, alerts me to any special tasks he wants me to complete, meetings he needs me to schedule, and reports that he is expecting. Depending on how much we have to discuss, our meetings last anywhere from fifteen minutes to nearly an hour. I have come to learn that our meetings are a priority to the Kommandant. He has Malgorzata hold all calls and visitors for as long as our meetings take, and they are only rescheduled in the most urgent of circumstances.

Today, however, our meeting is to be brief. "I have to be over at Pomorskie at nine," he says briskly from behind his desk. I nod and take my usual seat on the sofa by the door, pen poised. He clears his throat and stands. "Please type a memo to the governor that reads..." I take notes as the Kommandant dictates a few sentences about rescheduled meetings. As he speaks, he paces back and forth, running his hands through his close-cropped hair in a way that makes me wonder if it used to be longer.

Suddenly he stops speaking midsentence and turns, staring out the window. He seems distracted, even upset. For a second I wonder if I have done something. The passes, I think. He could not possibly know about my plan to steal them, but even so... Finally, I can stand it no longer. "Herr Kommandant, is something wrong?"

He turns back. His expression is one of confusion, as though he has forgotten I am there. He hesitates. "I apologize. I am just preoccupied with a telegram I received from Berlin this morning."

He is not upset with me, I realize, a wave of relief washing over me. But the telegram from Berlin… perhaps it contains something that could be useful to the resistance. "Bad news?" I ask, trying not to sound too interested.

"I don't know yet. They want me to…" He stops midsentence, as if realizing that he should not talk to me about the matter. "Anyway, it's nothing you need worry about." He returns to his chair behind the desk. "Let's get back to that memo."

A few minutes later, when he has finished dictating, I look up. "Will that be all?"

"Yes." He holds up a stack of papers. "If you could take these…" I walk toward him. Out of the corner of my eye, I see a framed photograph I had not noticed before that sits on the corner of his desk. It is of the Kommandant and a younger, dark-haired woman. Who is she? I wonder. As I draw close to him, I cannot help but notice his eyes, more blue than gray now. My knees tremble. I reach out for the papers and our knuckles brush, as they had the night of the dinner party.

I grab the papers, then jump back. As I step away from the desk, I can feel my ears burning. "Th-thank you, Herr Kommandant," I say, starting for the door.

"Anna, wait…"

I turn back to him. "Yes?"

I can see him fumbling, trying to regain his train of thought. "Are you settling in all right here?" he asks. I hesitate, caught off guard by his question. "I mean, you've gotten everything you need, from Malgorzata and the others, to be able to do your job?"

"Yes, Herr Kommandant. Everyone has been very helpful."

"Good. And the trip to work?" I cock my head, puzzled. "I mean, it's not too long or difficult, getting into the city from

Krysia's house? I wouldn't want, that is, I could have my driver…" He stares at me helplessly, his voice trailing off. He is nervous around me, too, I realize suddenly.

"The ride is fine, Herr Kommandant," I manage to say, my heart pounding. "The bus runs quite smoothly."

"Good," he repeats. Our eyes remain locked. The room is silent except for the ticking of the grandfather clock.

Suddenly, there is a scratching sound at the door. I jump and spin around. Colonel Diedrichson stands in the doorway, briefcase in hand. "Sir, the meeting…" he says.

"Of course," the Kommandant replies, clearing his throat. He stands and walks past me, following Colonel Diedrichson out of the office without addressing me further.

Alone now, I return to the anteroom. My hands still tremble slightly, as they always do after an encounter with the Kommandant. But his reaction…it is the first time since I have come to work for him that I have seen him thrown off guard. I wonder… There's no time for such thoughts, I scold myself. Compose yourself. I hear the sound of deep voices and heavy boots in the corridor, other officers leaving for the meeting. When the noise subsides and several minutes have passed, I stand up from my chair and cross the anteroom into the reception area, carrying my notebook and a small stack of papers.

"Malgorzata, I have some errands to run around the offices," I say, trying to sound normal.

"I can help…" she starts to offer, but I raise my hand.

"Thank you, but no." I use the authoritative tone I have learned works best with her. Seeing her face fall, I soften my voice. "It's just that I am cooped up in that anteroom so much. The walk will do me good." She shrugs, indifferent now, and turns back to her work.

Colonel Krich's office is on the same floor as ours, at the far opposite corner of the castle. I walk down the corridor, nodding at the other workers I pass. When I approach Krich's office, I freeze; his secretary is still sitting at her desk. Alek's information must have been wrong. Or perhaps the woman has decided not to have her hair styled this week. Trying not to panic, I keep walking past the office and down the corridor, trying to decide what to do. I slowly circle the floor, walking past Colonel Krich's office a second time, but the secretary is still seated at the desk, showing no signs of leaving. I do not dare linger in the corridor longer for fear someone will notice me. Instead, I decide to run my other errand first—I had thought it best to have a real stop in case my whereabouts were ever questioned. I walk down one floor to the supply office and request that the clerk have some paper sent up to the Kommandant's office. If the clerk finds it strange that I have brought down my order personally, rather than phoning it in or having someone else do it, he gives no indication but simply accepts the completed requisition form. That's the thing about the Nazis, I muse as I walk away; Hitler himself could have come in asking for pencil erasers, and no one would bat an eye as long as the paperwork was in order.

I climb the staircase again, but instead of heading right toward the Kommandant's office, I turn left again toward Krich's. As I approach, I check over my shoulder in both directions to make sure no one is there to see me.

The secretary is gone, I observe through the glass window to Krich's outer office. Hopefully she's left for her hair appointment and not for some quicker errand. I turn the outer door handle and walk into the office. I run my hand along the underside of the desk. Held there by tape, as Alek promised, is a small skeleton key. Fearing that someone might see me from the hallway through the glass, I quickly take the key, turn it in the lock and slip through the door into Krich's office.

Inside, I scan the room quickly. Krich, far subordinate to the Kommandant, does not have an anteroom, and his office is about a third the size of the Kommandant's, with no view from its tiny windows. A large metal safe sits in full view, occupying the far right corner of the room. As I cross over to it, I repeat under my breath the numbers I have memorized: 74-39-19. I kneel by the safe and turn the knob carefully, hands shaking, moving the dial right, then left, then right again. Holding my breath, I pull. Nothing. A cold sweat breaks out on my brow. The combination's been changed, I think. I cannot do it. Try again, a calm voice, seemingly not my own, orders from deep inside me. I try the numbers again slowly, meticulously stopping on each. Please, I pray, pulling again. The door creaks and opens.

Inside there are three stacks of identical blank passes. Take from the middle of each pile, Alek had said. I remove the first stack and quickly slide two sheets from separate locations in the middle of it. As I start to return the stack to its original position, I hear a noise in the corridor outside. I jump, and my arm bumps the edge of the safe. The stack of passes falls from my hand. I gasp. The passes have scattered everywhere. Hurriedly, I gather them back together, and with shaking hands try to put them back in numbered order. This is taking too long, I think; the secretary will be back any minute now. I grab the last few scattered passes and put them on the bottom of the stack, hoping no one will notice. I look at the other two piles of passes. I should take from the middle of those but there is no time. I grab the top pass of one of the stacks and the bottom one off the other. It will have to do.

I close the safe door gently and spin the knob back to its original position. Grabbing the papers and placing them among the others I am carrying, I stand and start for the office door. Halfway across the room, I stop. In my hurry, I almost forgot my building pass, which is sitting on the edge of the file cabinet. It is as good as leaving a calling card.

I race back across the room, almost tripping in my rush. I pick up my building pass and quickly survey the room for any other telltale signs of my presence. Seeing none, I slip out of the inner office, replace the key under the desk and return to the hallway. I have encountered no one.

Malgorzata only half looks up as I reenter the Kommandant's office suite. "Did you get your errands done?"

"Yes, thank you." I walk past her, trying not to betray my nervousness. Once inside the anteroom, I tuck the passes inside a newspaper in my bag. At times, the staff members at Wawel are subject to inspection when leaving work. I have never been stopped, presumably because of my position, but I do not want to take any chances. For the rest of the day, I find it impossible to concentrate on my work. The hands on the clock over my desk seem to stand still. Finally, it is five o'clock and I gratefully escape, trying to act normal as I walk down the ramp to the bus stop.

I had planned to deliver the passes the following Tuesday, but the next day, it begins to rain. The summer to that point had been dry, almost drought-like. The grass on the Blonia, the large flat field just outside of town, had become parched and dead to the point that the farmers could no longer graze their horses on it. The Wisla River had dropped so low that boats could not pass for fear of becoming grounded. The Nazi government imposed water restrictions, but the residents of Kraków, perhaps more terrified of hunger than imprisonment, watered their gardens in the dead of night so that the desperately needed fruits and vegetables would not die.

But the day after I steal the passes, it seems that the eyes of the heavens, looking down on the sorrow of war-ravaged Poland, can no longer hold their tears. The rains burst forth. That night, a heavy sheeting storm begins, pounding fiercely down on our flat roof and against the windows. It rains the next day and the day after that, until the streets run with thick mud and the ditches back up, spilling filthy sewage into the streets and making the roads almost impassable. My journey to and from work becomes truly grim. No parasol or coat can keep the moisture out, and I arrive both at work and at home soaked to the skin, my shoes caked with inches of mud. Such conditions make a rendezvous with Alek or anyone else from the movement to exchange satchels at an outdoor market café impossible. I do not dare carry the papers with me each day, so I place them underneath my mattress. Each night I lay awake, acutely aware of their presence, recalling the children's story about the princess and the pea.

One day while wringing out my soaked stockings in the water closet down the hall from our office and cursing the weather for the hundredth time, I stop, shamefaced. I spent my days in a comfortable office, my nights in a warm bed. Where is Jacob? I wonder. I imagine him sleeping in the woods through these storms, without roof or floor.

Finally, after nearly two weeks, the rains subside and the sun begins to shine through. "The weather has broken," Krysia says on Tuesday morning, not looking up from the pitcher into which she is squeezing oranges. "It will be lovely weather at the café this afternoon."

I swallow the mouthful of cereal I had been chewing. "Yes." I have not spoken of my secret mission with her since the day I saw Alek.

She sets down an orange and walks out of the kitchen without speaking, her apron still tied around her waist. A few minutes later she returns. "Can you run an errand for me after work?" she asks.

"Of course," I reply quickly, without asking what it is. Krysia asks so little from me in exchange for all that she has done, it is the least I can do.

"Good. Here." She reaches into her apron pocket and pulls out a small bundle wrapped in cloth. I take it from her and my hand drops under the weight. It is filled with coins, I can tell from the hard, round shapes that protrude through the cloth. The weight suggests that they are real silver, the only currency that is worth anything these days. "Give this to Alek," she says. "Tell him to buy something useful." I nod, amazed. I knew that Krysia was connected to the resistance through Jacob. I did not know she was helping to finance it. I should not have been surprised.

The day at work seems interminably slow as I wait for my meeting with Alek. At last, the clock strikes five and I make my way to the market square, the papers and satchel of coins in my bag. I try to walk naturally, but I might as well be carrying a bomb—if I am caught, I am as good as dead.

When I cross the square and approach the designated café, only Alek and Marek await. Marta is not with them, and I wonder if she is avoiding me since our awkward conversation about Jacob. Perhaps, I think with a twinge of jealousy, she is on an assignment with him somewhere. "We needed these days ago," Marek snaps, taking the bag directly from my hands before I can even sit down. I catch Alek glancing over my shoulder, concerned that Marek's rough gesture might have drawn attention to us.

I am taken aback by his rudeness. "The rains were hardly my fault," I manage as I sit.

"Of course not. You did wonderfully." Alek's deep voice is soothing. "It's just that there was an *akcja,* and we were hoping to get some people out before it happened with these papers."

"An *akcja,*" I repeat in a hushed whisper. While still in the ghetto, I had heard rumors of *akcjas* in other cities. The Nazis would storm into the ghetto, ordering the residents out of their apartments to assemble in the street. Hundreds of Jews, seemingly chosen at random, would be cleared out in a single day and deported to labor camps. Those who resisted such deportations were shot on sight. "I didn't see or hear anything about it in the Kommandant's office."

"You wouldn't," Alek replies. "Most of the work involving the Jews is undertaken at the Directorate of Operations, over on Pomorskie Street. And the few papers the Kommandant likely received would have been classified."

"Oh."

"Next time you go into Krich's office…" Marek begins, but Alek, noticing my furrowed brow, interrupts him.

"What's troubling you?" he asks.

I pause, swallowing. "Alek, please, my parents are still in the ghetto." It occurs to me that after the *akcja* they may not be there anymore. "Isn't there something that can be done?"

Alek takes a deep breath, holds it. "You must understand…" he begins.

"We all had parents," Marek interjects coldly. I remember then hearing that his father had been shot in Nowy Sacz early in the war.

Alek places his hand on mine. "Emma," he begins gently. Emma. My real name sounds so foreign now. "The situation in the ghetto has changed much since you were there. The walls are sealed and heavily guarded. The only way to get people out is with a transit pass or with a work card or messenger's pass. That's why your getting these blank passes was so very important."

"Can't my parents have two of the passes?" I demand, surprised at my own boldness.

"The thing is this." Alek hesitates. "After you were taken from the ghetto, Jacob asked me to look in on your parents from time to time. And I have…Emma, your mother is sick."

"Sick?" I panic, my voice rising. "What's wrong with her?"

"Shh," Alek soothes. "She has one of the many things that spread through the ghetto like wildfire. I don't know if it is typhus." I think of Marta's mother then. "Or dysentery, or even a bad flu. But she has a high fever that she can't seem to shake, and she is bedridden. So you see why we cannot issue her a work card. Even if she could walk, she does not look strong enough to be a worker. The Nazis would see through the scheme right away, and her fate would be far worse, then."

I do not answer. I consider asking for help for my father,

but I know he would never leave without her. "Then I should go back to them," I say aloud.

"Back?" Marek splutters so loudly the couple behind us stares. When they have turned back to their coffees, he continues, his voice soft but full of anger. "Do you have any idea how bad things are there? How hard we worked to get you out in the first place?"

"It is impossible," Alek agrees. I slump in my chair, defeated.

"And if she gets better?" I persist.

"If she gets better, we will do all we can. That is the only promise I can make to you. Things in the ghetto are horrible right now, and they are growing worse by the day. We have to help as many people as we can as quickly as possible. That is why our work is so very important, and you must keep doing what you are doing for us. It is the only way to help all of our families. Do you understand?" Pulling my hand from his, I do not answer. "Same time next week, then?"

I nod and stand up. He has not mentioned Jacob and I want to ask if he is safe, if there has been any word from him. But I can tell from their faces they will say nothing further; I have been dismissed. "Yes," I say finally.

"Good." Alek rises and remains standing until I have walked away.

When I reach the far corner of the square, I stop, unable to hold my tears. Mama, I think, picturing her and my father sleeping the night I escaped from the ghetto. I never should have left them. Now my mother is very sick and my parents could be deported at any moment. There is nothing I can do and the resistance is unwilling to help them. What is the good of these spy games we are playing if we cannot even help our own families? For the first time, I am plagued with doubt toward those I had trusted most: Alek, Krysia, even my beloved Jacob.

I think for a second of the Kommandant, picturing his eyes and the kindly way he looks at me. Perhaps he can help.... No, don't be ridiculous, I remind myself. He is, first and foremost, a Nazi. If he thinks you have Jewish relatives, even the tiniest drop of Jewish blood, his affection will turn to revulsion and you will be dead, along with your family, the resistance and everyone who has helped you. Everyone you love. I wipe the back of my hand across my eyes, ashamed to have thought of him in such a way, even fleetingly. No, the Kommandant is no friend.

An hour later, I burst through the front gate of Krysia's house. She is in the garden weeding with Lukasz. Taking one look at my red eyes, she sets down the trowel, picks up Lukasz and leads me into the house. "What is it?" she asks when the door is closed behind her. As we walk upstairs, I tell her about my conversation with Alek and my mother's illness. "Oh, you poor dear," she says, drawing me in her embrace, rocking back and forth while Lukasz, sandwiched between us, looks on quizzically.

"Alek says there is nothing they can do," I add.

"I'm sure he would help if he could," she replies calmly. Krysia, like Marta, is completely trusting of the resistance leadership and their decisions. She leads me to the sofa. "You have to see it from his perspective. Things are very difficult for the resistance right now and they have thousands of Jews to consider. He can't risk everything to save any individual person."

I think of Pani Nederman, Marta's mother. Marta has been

fighting for the resistance much longer than I. They did nothing to help her mother when she was sick, and she died. "I never should have left them," I cry.

"Is that what you think?" Krysia lifts my chin. "Emma, listen to me. This is not your fault. There is nothing you could have done to keep your mother from getting sick. If you were there you might have caught the illness as well." I do not reply. Krysia continues, "Let me see what I can do." I look back at Krysia, surprised. Do? If Alek and his contacts, with access to inside the ghetto, could not help my parents, how could Krysia possibly help?

A few days later, when I am giving Lukasz his evening bath, Krysia comes and stands in the bathroom doorway. "Pankiewicz is an old friend of mine," she begins. I pause, washcloth suspended midair. I had almost forgotten about the kindly, brave pharmacist, a non-Jew who had chosen to remain behind at his pharmacy in Podgorze to care for the Jews as the ghetto walls went up around him. "He checked on your mother this morning. She is very sick, and his medicine supplies are quite low. But he promised to look in on her and give her the best care he can."

"Oh, thank you!" I leap up and throw my arms around Krysia's neck. "Thank you, thank you!" Pankiewicz might not be able to do much, but at least someone has said they would try to help.

"*Dank!*" Lukasz mimics, trying to repeat my words and splashing around in delight at the commotion. Krysia and I break from our embrace and turn to the child, stunned. It is the first time since he came to live with us that Lukasz has spoken.

Twenty minutes later, as I dry Lukasz, he is still babbling, a nonsensical torrent that has been bottled up inside him for months. I put him into his pajamas, thinking of my mother once more. My hope begins to fade and a nagging sensation returns to my stomach. Krysia's inquiries and Pankiewicz's attention are well-intentioned, but they are nothing in the face of the starvation, disease and despair that my parents face, not to mention that another *akcja* could come at any time to sweep them away. I brush these doubts from my mind. When one is trying to stay afloat in deep water, one grabs at any stick that is offered—and tries not to notice that the stick is in fact nothing more than a wisp of a reed, practically useless in the strong current.

CHAPTER 10

A few days after Krysia tells me about Pankiewicz, I am standing in the corner of the anteroom, putting the papers into the file cabinet. The new filing system I created has worked well, but I have to be sure to file the papers at least once a week so that I do not get behind. I pause to wipe my brow. It is mid-July and quite warm, despite the fact that it is not yet ten o'clock and both windows are open.

Suddenly, the Kommandant comes through the front door of the anteroom. Malgorzata is at his heels. "In my office, please," he says as he passes, without looking at me. I hesitate, surprised. We had our daily meeting nearly two hours ago and he has never called me in a second time so quickly, much less invited Malgorzata to join us. Something is wrong. A chill passes through me. The passes, I remember suddenly, my stomach dropping. Someone has noticed that the security passes I took are missing. Perhaps Malgorzata has told him that I was acting strangely the day they went missing, or that I was seen lingering outside Colonel Krich's office by one of the other secretaries. Feeling faint, I grab the edge of the file cabinet for support.

"Anna...?" I jump and spin around. Colonel Diedrichson has entered the anteroom and is looking from me to the door of the Kommandant's office expectantly.

"Yes, I'm coming," I reply. Willing my hands not to shake, I take my notebook from the top of the file cabinet. Colonel Diedrichson follows me through the door of the Kommandant's office.

"Sit down," the Kommandant says. Out of the corner of my eye, I study his face, looking for some sign of anger or accusation, but he is looking away from me, his expression imperceptible. Colonel Diedrichson places himself stiffly in the chair, leaving me the spot on the sofa beside Malgorzata, who has placed herself at the end closest to the Kommandant. As I sit, my mind races, trying to come up with a response if I am confronted about the passes, a reason why I was near Krich's office that morning. The Kommandant clears his throat. "We are to have an official visit from Berlin," he announces.

So this is not about the passes after all. A wave of relief washes over me.

"Sir?" Colonel Diedrichson sounds startled. It is the first time I have heard any emotion in his voice. "A delegation?" I, too, am surprised. Though I recall Ludwig mentioning a delegation visit at the dinner party, I have not heard or seen anything about it since my arrival.

"Yes, it was decided only yesterday. Three very senior members of the SS leadership. They arrive Thursday." The Kommandant takes a stack of papers from his desk and distributes a portion of it to each of us. "That is only three days away and there is much to be done. The governor will meet with the delegation, of course, but all of the arrangements are to be overseen by this office. Colonel Diedrichson will take care of the itinerary and logistics. Anna, you are to assist him, and to make sure everything here in the office goes smoothly." Though still not entirely sure what he needs from me, I nod. "Malgorzata, please see that the office is immaculate."

"Yes, Herr Kommandant!" Malgorzata replies, lifting her chin as though she has been asked to guard state secrets.

"Good. That is all for now." Colonel Diedrichson stands and starts for the door and Malgorzata and I follow close behind. "Anna, wait a moment, please." The Kommandant gestures me over to the side of the desk, but does not speak until the others have gone.

"Yes, Herr Kommandant?" Closer now, I can see that his face is pale, his eyes bloodshot.

"I don't have to tell you how important this visit is to me, to all of us in the General Government." I nod, wondering why he is telling me this. "Everything must go perfectly. I am counting on you to help make this happen."

"Me?" I cannot help but sound surprised.

"Yes. You are very capable and have an eye for detail. Make sure Colonel Diedrichson and the others forget nothing. If you think something is being missed or wrong, let me know immediately. Do you understand?"

"Yes, Herr Kommandant."

"Good." He lowers his head, placing his hands on his temples.

"Are you all right?"

"Just a headache," he replies, not looking up. "I've always gotten them, though they've been more severe of late with all of the stress."

"Perhaps an aspirin?" I offer, but he shakes his head.

"These headaches require something stronger. I have medicine that my doctor prescribed."

"Very well. Is there anything else that you need?"

"Not right now," he replies. He lifts his head slightly to look at me. "Thank you, Anna. I feel much better knowing that you are here." I do not answer, but turn and walk hurriedly from the office.

The next several days are a blur of activity. Word of the visit spreads quickly around the castle, and soon every office is abuzz with preparation. The cleaning staff of Wawel work around the clock to make the marble sparkle and the endless windows shine. The Nazi flags are taken down from the hallway, pressed and rehung. Malgorzata, seeming not to trust anyone else to clean our offices sufficiently, does most of the work herself. I watched as she spends a day and a half on her knees, scrubbing the floor.

My own role is limited. The day after our meeting, I help Colonel Diedrichson type the final version of the itinerary which, he tells me, is classified for security reasons. The delegation, a party of three high-ranking Nazis and their military attachés, will be here for one night, and will visit the labor camps Plaszow and Auschwitz and the ghetto. I shudder as I read the last part. In truth, I know that the ghetto is large, that there is only the slightest chance the delegation will see my parents, but still… I force the thought from my mind, keep working. On Friday, the Kommandant invites me to sit in on a review of the itinerary with himself and the colonel. When every last detail has been reviewed, the Kommandant declares that we are ready.

That night, my stomach twists as I think of the visit. "I wish there was some way I could be ill tomorrow," I confide to Krysia that night after dinner as I clear the table. "I haven't been this nervous since my first day of work."

"You'll be fine," Krysia reassures, still seated at the table. She is trying to spoon peas into Lukasz's mouth. "You work around the Nazis every day."

I shake my head. "These are different." They are SS from Berlin, I think. Surely something will give me away.

Handing me a plate, she continues, "Anyway, if they are like other self-important men, chances are they won't even notice you." Looking over at Krysia, I find that she is smirking.

"Krysia!" I exclaim, surprised. I cannot help but giggle. Her observation is both funny and true at the same time. With the possible exception of the Kommandant, men of stature, whether they are Nazis or professors, seem to look right through young women such as me. Suddenly, we are both laughing full and hard. It is not just her comment, but the ludicrousness of the entire situation and months of pent-up anxiety. Lukasz stares at us in amazement. He has never seen either, much less both of us, in hysterics. Soon he joins in, cackling wildly and banging his spoon against the table. Peas fly everywhere. The sight of him makes us laugh even harder. Later that night in bed, I find that my throat is scratchy from laughing. It is no longer accustomed to making such a sound.

The next day I arrive at work half an hour early. The Kommandant, Colonel Diedrichson and Malgorzata are already there, scurrying around with last-minute preparations as though the delegation was scheduled to arrive momentarily, instead of in the early afternoon. We do not take lunch that day. Even the Kommandant, usually so composed, paces from his office, through the anteroom, to the reception area and back again. For once, he barely seems to notice me. At exactly twelve-forty-five, the telephone in the reception area rings and Malgorzata throws herself across the desk to get it. "Herr Kommandant, they're here!" she exclaims.

"Early…" I hear him mutter under his breath, as though this was a bad sign. "To your desks, please, ladies." He straightens his jacket. "Colonel, come with me." As the men leave the office, I look at Malgorzata. She is sitting perfectly straight in her chair, smoothing her hair, her face flushed with excitement. I have never despised her more.

I return to the anteroom and close the door. I sit behind my own desk and assume what I perceive to be a professional position, tablet and pen in hand. A few minutes later, I hear heavy footsteps and deep voices in the hallway, followed by the sound of the front office door opening. The voices are louder now. Breathe, I think. Act naturally. The door to the anteroom swings open, and the Kommandant enters. He is followed by seven men. Though I keep my head low, I can tell that the three men immediately behind them in heavily decorated brown uniforms are the official delegation. The other three younger men who follow are clearly the attachés. None of the men are as tall or imposing as the Kommandant. Krysia was right, I think, as they pass me without looking in my direction. Perhaps if I do not have to interact with them, I can manage this after all.

The last of the party is Colonel Diedrichson. As he reaches the door of the Kommandant's inner office, he turns to me. "Anna, bring eight coffees. Quickly."

Inwardly, I cringe. I had not anticipated having to serve refreshments. For a moment, I consider asking Malgorzata to do it, but I know the Kommandant would prefer to have me. "Yes, Colonel," I reply, rising and heading for the small kitchen just down the hallway. A few minutes later, I return through the reception area, balancing a serving tray laden with a pitcher of hot coffee and saucers. Malgorzata opens the door to the anteroom without my having to ask her, and I can tell from the way she follows me that she is hoping to come into the office, too. "Thank you, Malgorzata," I whisper firmly when she has opened the door to the Kommandant's inner office for me. She turns away, defeated.

I had hoped that I could place the tray on the low coffee table and leave, but it is clear from the way the delegation is spread out across the room that I will have to serve. I walk first to the far end of the office where the Kommandant and two senior officers are clustered around the conference table, poring over a large map. Keeping my eyes low, I set down the tray and begin to pour the coffees. As I begin to pour the last cup, my hands tremble involuntarily. Hot coffee splashes over the edge of the cup, burning my hand and I jump, setting the cup back on the tray with a loud, clattering sound. One of the officers looks up at me, glaring.

"Anna," the Kommandant says softly. I expect him to sound angry, but he does not. Our eyes meet. He is staring at me intensely, his expression one of concern and, I think, something else I cannot describe. My breath catches. "Thank you." I nod, my eyes still locked with his.

"Kommandant Richwalder..." a male voice says. My head snaps to the right. For a moment I have almost forgotten where we are, that there are others in the room. The men at the table have stopped working and are staring at us. The officer who glared at me has turned slightly toward the Kommandant, bewildered. I can tell he is unaccustomed to hearing someone of the Kommandant's stature address his subordinates with kindness, and that he is even more taken aback by the way the Kommandant looks at me.

"Thank you, Anna," the Kommandant repeats. "That will be all." He clears his throat and rearranges the papers on the table in front of him before addressing the men. "Now, if you will turn to the chart on page three..."

Taking care not to spill again, I carry the tray to the Kommandant's desk, where the third delegation member sits, talking on the telephone. He does not look up. The photograph of the Kommandant and the dark-haired woman has been removed from the corner of his desk, I notice as I pour. I quickly pass out the remaining cups to Diedrichson and the other attachés who are sitting around the coffee table by the door. These are younger men, and as I bend over the low table I can feel their eyes on me, taking me in. My face burning, I straighten quickly and escape back to the anteroom.

I return to my desk, shaking. My head pounds. It will be over soon, I tell myself. The delegation is only scheduled to be in the office for a brief time, and they will not be coming back. Twenty minutes later, the voices inside the Kommandant's office grow louder and the door opens. The Kommandant, leading the group once more, does not look at or speak as he passes me, and for a moment I wonder if he is angry at me for spilling the coffee. But as he reaches the door, he turns back toward me. "I'll call you," he says. I nod. He told me yesterday that I am not to leave at the normal time tonight, but that I should stay in case the delegation needs anything. He has promised to let me know once they have retired for the night so I can go home.

When I hear the front door of the reception area close, I exhale. They are gone. A few minutes later, I pick up the serving tray and reenter the Kommandant's office to clean up the coffee cups. I could have left it for the Wawel cleaning staff, or even Malgorzata, to do, but I want to see if the delegation left any papers behind. The Kommandant's desk and coffee table are as clean as before they arrived, except for the empty cups. As I near the conference room table, I stop. There, spread out as it had been when I served, is the map the men had been poring over. Easy, I tell myself, as I approach the table. It's just a map. Surely they wouldn't have left it behind if it was important.

I look over my shoulder to make sure Malgorzata has not followed me. The door to the office is closed. Slowly, I edge my way toward the map, keeping the serving tray in one hand and an empty cup in the other, so that I can appear to be cleaning if anyone walks in. I look down. It is a map of Kraków, labeled in German. There are several buildings outlined in red: Wawel Castle, the administrative offices on Pomorskie Street,

Kazimierz, the ghetto. There are red arrows pointing from Kazimierz to the ghetto. Probably just all of the places they are
going to visit, I think, as I start to clean up once more. Then,
as I reach to pick up the last coffee cup, I stop again. The arrows, I realize, aren't pointing to the ghetto, they are going
through the ghetto toward Plaszow, the labor camp. And
drawn through the ghetto, in pencil, is a large *X*. I freeze, the
hair on the back of my neck standing on end. The ghetto has
been crossed out. What can it mean? Another *akcja?* Are all of
the ghetto inhabitants to be deported to Plaszow? Stop it, I
think, as my stomach starts to twist. Don't go imagining things
you know nothing about. I make a note to tell Alek when I
see him again on Tuesday.

I return the tray and cups to the kitchen, then return to my
desk. The rest of the day passes uneventfully. Except for a single trip to the water closet, I remain glued to my seat in case
the Kommandant should call. At five o'clock, Malgorzata
sticks her head in. "I can stay if you want," she offers.

I shake my head. I know she would like to linger in the hope
that I might share some details about the delegation. In truth,
I am not looking forward to staying in the empty office by
myself, but the thought of her prying company is more than
I can bear. "No, thank you. There's really nothing to be done."
As she departs, I can hear the other secretaries in the hallway,
leaving for the day. I spend an hour or so finishing the filing
I had begun earlier in the week and updating the Kommandant's address list. The office is completely silent, except for
the faint ticking of the clock above my desk. When my work
is complete, I look up. It is only six-forty-five. The delegation
is probably just beginning their first course at Wierzynek, the

elegant Polish restaurant I had recommended to Diedrichson. I could be here for several more hours. I reach into my bag and pull out my own supper, a cold stew left over from the night before and a thick wedge of bread. Looking around the silent, empty room, I sigh, imagining Krysia and Lukasz sitting down to supper without me. I wonder if the child will fuss because I am not there.

Another hour passes. Still the Kommandant has not called. I wonder if he has forgotten about me. Finally, when I can stand it no longer, I leave my desk and race to the washroom. As I reenter the reception area, I can hear the phone in the anteroom ringing. It may be the Kommandant, I think, running for it. *"Tak?"* I say breathlessly, forgetting to answer in German.

It is not the Kommandant, but Colonel Diedrichson. "Is he there?" he asks impatiently.

"Who?"

"The Kommandant, of course." He sounds annoyed. "He said he needed to stop back at the office and asked me to escort the delegation back to the hotel."

"I don't think…" I start to say, then look toward the Kommandant's office. Yellow light shines from under the closed door. "Oh, yes, he is here. He must have come in when I stepped away for a minute. Do you want to speak with him?"

"No, I just wanted to make sure he got back all right," he replies, his voice strange. "His car will be waiting downstairs when he's ready."

"I will tell him when I see him." I hang up the phone and look at the door to the Kommandant's office. Should I knock to see if he needs anything? I start across the anteroom, then hesitate. I will wait a few minutes, I think, turning around.

On the way back to my desk, I catch a glimpse of my reflection in the window and smooth my disheveled hair. I return to my seat behind the desk, staring uneasily at the door. It is not like the Kommandant to be in the office at night. Why has he come back? Ten minutes pass, then twenty. No sound comes from the Kommandant's office. I wonder if he has fallen asleep.

At last, I walk to the office door and knock lightly. There is no answer. I open the door a few inches. The Kommandant stands over the map with his back to me, looking down, head tilted toward his right shoulder.

"Herr Kommandant?" He does not seem to hear me. "Do you need anything?" I ask after several seconds of silence. He spins unsteadily from the conference table to the enormous glass window behind his desk. He has been drinking, I realize. My suspicion is confirmed as I cross the room and am assaulted by the thick odor of brandy and sweat. I am surprised; until now, the Kommandant has always appeared thoroughly composed. I have never seen him so much as touch the glass bottle of brown liquid that sits on the edge of his desk.

"Herr Kommandant," I repeat tentatively. He does not answer. I gesture toward the unfamiliar folder clutched in his right hand. "Is that for me?" He shakes his head unevenly, dropping the folder into the open top drawer of his desk. I make a mental note to try to look there the next time he is out. "Do you have some work you would like me to do in the morning when you are with the delegation?" As I walk closer, I notice a gray shadow of stubble on his jaw. He is unkempt and there is a distressed look in his eyes that I have never seen before.

He stares out the window once more at the dusky sky over

the river. "I saw Auschwitz today," he says suddenly. Auschwitz. The word sends a chill through me. We had heard rumors about the camp since before the ghetto, almost since the beginning of the war. Many of the stories had come from the rural Jews who were forced to migrate to Kraków. A labor camp, some had said originally, for political prisoners. During my last months in the ghetto, though, the stories had become more gruesome. Rumor had it that the camp was filled with Jews, not so much working as dying in tremendous numbers. I had heard nothing more about it since coming to Krysia's. No one working at Wawel ever spoke of it until the delegation visit was announced. Auschwitz. I understand now why the Kommandant has been drinking.

I am uncertain what to say. "Oh?" I try to make my tone inviting, hoping that he might say more, perhaps something useful I could relay to Alek. But he does not speak for several minutes.

"Yes," he continues at last. "I never thought…" He does not have to finish the sentence. I understand. The Kommandant considers himself a gentleman, a man of music, art and culture. In his twisted way of thinking, service to the Reich is something noble and patriotic, and the Jewish question is an ugliness to be tolerated from afar. He has sequestered himself in Wawel, ruling his dominion from a great height, shielding himself from the killing. From where he sits, the ghetto is just a neighborhood where the Jews are forced to live. Plaszow is just a labor camp. I am sure that he justified his time at Sachsenhausen, too, seeing it as a prison, its inhabitants criminals who deserved their surroundings. He hadn't seen, hadn't wanted to see the starvation, disease and murder of innocent civilians. Until now. Today he has been forced to go to Auschwitz, and the reality of what he has seen is so terrible it has unraveled him, driven him to drink. This terrifies me more than anything else has since the beginning of the war.

"Dreadful, I am sure." I wish that I could look inside his mind and learn what he has seen that day. Though I might have preferred it, I cannot bury my head in the sand like an ostrich as I once had done in the ghetto. I need to learn as much as possible, for the sake of my family and the resistance. But the Kommandant seems unwilling to say more.

"Herr Kommandant," I say again, when he has stared at the wall for several more minutes. He looks at me quizzically, as though he has forgotten, or is unsure why I am there. "You look tired," I offer. He half nods, leaning against the back of his desk chair with one arm. "Let me help you to your car." I go to the sofa where his military jacket lies in a heap and carry it to him. He holds his arms out and I help him into the sleeves as I would Lukasz. I can feel the warmth of his skin through the fabric. "Come," I say, guiding him by the arm out of the office. In the hallway, he straightens a bit and is able to make it down the stairs and outside.

At the end of the ramp, Stanislaw, the Kommandant's driver, stands by the awaiting sedan, emblazoned with a swastika on the side. *"Dobry wieczor,"* he greets us in his deep baritone as we approach the open rear car door. The Kommandant bends clumsily to enter the car, his head swinging within inches of the roof. Without thinking, I place my hand gently on the back of his neck and guide him into the car. He falls as he sits, his weight pulling on my outstretched arm. Caught off balance, I tumble into the car and land awkwardly, partially on top of the Kommandant. I quickly straighten to a sitting position, my face flushed.

"Well, I'd better be going," I begin, but before I can exit the car, Stanislaw shuts the door behind me. "Wait…" I protest. I look to the Kommandant for help but his eyes are closed, head back. "All right, I guess I will have to help get you home, too." He snores once in response.

As we make the short drive from Wawel to the Kommandant's apartment just off the Planty, I look around the interior of the car. I have been in precious few automobiles in my life, and certainly none as grand as this. Fingering the plush leather seat, I peer out the window. The streets are thronged with people running errands and heading home. They stop and stare as we pass in the large, dark sedan with a swastika on the side. I can see the fear in their eyes.

A few minutes later, the car pulls up before an elegant brownstone building. Stanislaw and I help the still-groggy Kommandant to his feet. The doorman unlocks the gate, then stands aside to let us pass. We guide the Kommandant up a flight of marble steps, and Stanislaw unlocks the apartment door. Once inside, the Kommandant is able to make it to the sofa on his own, where he sits, head slumped forward.

Stanislaw retreats from the room and closes the door quickly behind him, leaving me standing in the middle of the Kommandant's apartment. Taking up an entire floor of the brownstone, it is every bit a man's place: large and impersonal, with only a few pieces of heavy oak furniture and a single sofa covered in maroon velvet. The air smells thickly of stale cigar smoke and brandy, as though it has not been aired out for years. Heavy, dark curtains obscure what I imagine to be a spectacular view of the city skyline.

I shift my weight from one foot to the other, waiting for the Kommandant to speak, but he does not. "Herr Kommandant, it's late," I say at last. "If there's nothing else…"

"Anna, wait," the Kommandant mumbles, lifting his head slightly. "Don't go." He gestures for me to come closer.

Reluctantly, I walk toward the sofa. "Yes, what is it that you need?"

He hesitates. "Nothing. I mean that, I don't want…" he falters. "That is, if you could just stay awhile."

He doesn't want to be alone, I realize, surprised. I sit down at the far end of the sofa. "I can stay a few minutes," I say.

"Thank you." He reaches over and, before I can react, grabs my left hand. "Are you okay?" he asks, turning my hand over so the palm faces down. "Your hand…I mean, you burned it with the coffee didn't you?"

For a moment, I am too startled to respond. "It's the other one," I reply at last, pulling my left arm away.

"Let me see," he insists, his voice clearer now. I raise my right hand slowly and he takes it, cradling it in his two much larger ones, studying it. In the rush of the day, I had nearly forgotten about the burn, but the area just above my thumb is red and blisters are beginning to form. "Wait here," he instructs.

I start to protest but he disappears into the kitchen, leaving me alone in the enormous room. I've got to get out of here, I think uneasily, fighting the urge to flee while he is gone. Forcing myself to calm down, I look around once more. The room is devoid of any personal effects except for a framed photograph on the mantelpiece.

Despite my unease, I cannot help but be curious. I walk toward the photograph. It is a portrait of a woman, the same woman who is in the photograph that had been on the Kommandant's desk. She is beautiful, with flowing raven hair, high arched brows and flawless skin.

"Here," the Kommandant says as he reenters the room. I spin away from the photo toward him. He is carrying a damp cloth, a small jar and a bandage. "Sit down." Reluctantly, I allow him to lead me to the sofa, where he cleans and dresses my hand. "All done," he says a moment later. His hand lingers atop mine. Our eyes meet.

"Thank you," I manage to say, pulling my hand back.

"Of course." He straightens but does not look away. "I can't have an assistant with a bad hand, now can I?"

"I suppose not." I force myself to look away, then stand and walk to the photograph on the mantelpiece once more. "What a beautiful picture," I remark, lifting the frame gently.

"Margot," he replies from the couch, his voice now barely a whisper.

"Your wife, Herr Kommandant?" I venture.

"She was." Suddenly, he is beside me. He grabs the picture from my hands and looks at it intently, as though his gaze might bring the image to life. What became of her? I wonder. I look up at him, hoping he will say more, but he continues staring at the picture silently, as though he has forgotten I am there. Sensing that this is my opportunity to leave, I walk quickly to the door and open it. "It's late, so I'll be going now." Still staring at the picture, he does not respond. "Good night," I say as I slip out of the apartment and down the stairs.

At the entrance to the building, Stanislaw waits by the car.

I climb in, and without question or remark, he shuts the door behind me and starts out the long, winding road to Krysia's. He knows the way, I realize, from having driven the Kommandant to the dinner party. I lean my head against the cool glass of the car window, seeing the Kommandant's face in my mind. There was a desperation about him tonight that I had not seen before, especially when we were in his apartment alone together. He did not want me to leave, I realize, perhaps because he was drunk. Or maybe he just didn't want to be alone.

Suddenly, I remember waking that last morning in the Baus' apartment, finding Jacob, and then my parents gone. It was the one time in my life I had been completely alone and it terrified me. Some people manage to live perfectly well on their own, I know, like Krysia before Lukasz and I arrived. Still, it must be awful for the Kommandant to spend his nights in that empty, enormous apartment, haunted by the memory of his wife, Margot. I'd heard rumors around Wawel that the Kommandant had been married, but he had not spoken of her before. Tonight, though, it was as if he had seen a ghost. Maybe it was just the alcohol. Or perhaps there was something about what he had seen that day at Auschwitz that stirred his memories.

Auschwitz. A chill passes through me suddenly. I must tell Alek about the Kommandant's visit there, and about the map I saw on the table, at our next meeting. It could be important, I think, seeing the Kommandant's hollow, haunted eyes before me. I shiver as we speed past the trees and houses, leaving the last smoky traces of sunset behind us.

Krysia and Lukasz are asleep when I arrive home, so I tiptoe upstairs and undress quietly. Despite my confusion about the events of the evening, I am exhausted from all of the preparations for the official visit and my eyes grow heavy as I climb into bed. I immediately begin to dream that I am on a train that is speeding toward the mountains. Jacob, I am certain, is on the train, if only I could find him. I make my way through the crowded passenger cars, searching. Finally, I see the back of a man that looks familiar to me walking through the car several meters ahead. He has Jacob's slight build and the same-color hair. I walk faster, then begin running in an attempt to catch up. Finally, I am just a few feet behind him. I reach out, grab the man's shoulder. "Jacob!" I call as he spins around. I freeze. The face is not my husband's; it is the Kommandant's.

"Oh!" I cry aloud, sitting up in bed, breathing heavily. My mind races. For months, I have had dreams of chasing Jacob. That made sense; I miss my husband. But now this…? I cannot fathom it. Stop, I tell myself finally. It was only a dream. You are under a lot of stress at work, you are troubled because you had a bizarre conversation with the Kommandant. That is the only reason for the dream. I lay back down and pull the duvet up, not reassured. A disturbing thought creeps into my brain: perhaps the dream means something else. No. I shake my head in the darkness. It does not, cannot mean anything. I force myself to think pleas-ant thoughts of Jacob until I am able to fall asleep once more.

The Kommandant is not in the office when I arrive the next morning. The itinerary indicated that he would be meeting the delegation at their hotel, and escorting them to the ghetto and Plaszow before they depart for Berlin at noon. Not want-ing to be caught away from my desk again, I do not go out for lunch that day. At exactly twelve-fifteen, the door to the anteroom opens and the Kommandant strides in. "Anna, come in, please," he says crisply as he passes.

I follow the Kommandant into his office. He walks to his desk and picks up the stack of papers I left for him. I stand a few feet away and study his face, wondering if he will say anything about the previous night. But if he feels embarrassed about his drunkenness, he gives no sign of it. Perhaps he does not remember. Except for two faint, dark circles under his eyes, he looks completely normal. He looks up from the papers. "I will be leaving for Berlin tomorrow."

"Berlin tomorrow?" I repeat, unable to mask my surprise.

"Yes. There are some matters that arose from the delegation's visit that require me to follow up personally."

He hands me several pieces of paper. "My travel itinerary." He crosses the room, gesturing for me to follow. I sit on the sofa and look up, expecting him to pace the floor as he usually does. To my surprise, he sits down on the chair beside me. The cool pine scent of his aftershave wafts under my nose, making my stomach twitch. "As you can see, Colonel Diedrichson has made my travel arrangements," he continues. I can barely hear him over the buzzing in my ears. The Kommandant's unexpected departure and the masculine smell of aftershave combine to make my head feel light.

"I will be gone ten days," he concludes a few minutes later, looking up from the papers and meeting my gaze. I blink, realizing I have not heard most of what he has said. "Anna, are you all right? You look a bit pale."

"Is it safe to make such a trip these days?" I ask. The words from my mouth surprise me, as though they had been spoken by another.

"Relatively," he replies. "I have to go, regardless. I have been summoned to an important meeting, and it would not do for me to appear concerned for my personal safety." I nod, still unable to look away. "All right then. I think that's everything for now."

Taking my cue, I rise. My right leg has gone to sleep and I stumble slightly. The Kommandant reaches out and grabs my arm to steady me. "Careful," he says softly, still holding on to my arm. Our eyes lock.

"I—I'm sorry," I say, straightening. "It's just that…" I hesitate, uncertain how to finish. His hand feels warm though the sleeve of my dress.

"You've been working hard lately," he finishes for me. "You put in so many hours with the delegation visit."

"Yes, that must be it," I reply, grateful for the excuse.

"I will need your assistance with my travel preparations today. But you should take a day off while I am gone."

"Thank you, Herr Kommandant." I move quickly toward the door. I can feel the Kommandant's eyes on my back as I retreat to the anteroom. Seated at my desk once more, I sort through the pile of papers he has given me with trembling hands. For the past few weeks, I have a nagging sense of what Krysia had noticed the night of the dinner party: Kommandant Richwalder is attracted to me. But it is not only the Kommandant's behavior that concerns me. Why had I asked him if the trip would be safe? It is good for Anna to feign concern, I tell myself, though I knew the question had not been as calculated as I would like to imagine. My dream the night before had not been calculated, either. I sink back in my chair, shaken. Perhaps the Kommandant's absence might be a good thing.

The rest of the day passes quickly. Five o'clock comes and goes, and the Kommandant remains in his office with the door closed. Another forty-five minutes pass. A wave of exhaustion comes over me. The Kommandant was right; I have been working long hours. I feel as though I have not seen Lukasz and Krysia in a month. A few minutes later, the door to the Kommandant's office opens and he emerges carrying two briefcases. I rise to my feet.

He sets down the briefcases. "Well, I'm off."

Seeing the bags, the reality suddenly hits me: the Kommandant is leaving. "Have a good trip," I manage to say, swallowing over the lump that has formed in my throat.

"Thank you. Don't hesitate to send a telegram if there is anything urgent. Or if you need anything at all." I nod. He steps forward until he is just a foot or so away and I wonder if he is going to reach out and touch me. We stare at each other in silence, neither speaking. What is this? I wonder. What is happening between us? It is everything that has occurred these past few days, I tell myself. The strain of the delegation's visit. The fact that he is leaving. "Well…" he continues after several seconds of silence.

"Be safe," I say, meaning it. I am immediately ashamed to be wishing godspeed to a Nazi whom I should in fact want dead.

The Kommandant nods, picking up the briefcases once more. He clears his throat hard. "Goodbye, Anna." He lingers another moment and then he is gone.

CHAPTER 11

Five days after the Kommandant's departure for Berlin, I stand in his office, organizing the many papers that have arrived during his absence into piles on his desk. The Kommandant is scheduled to return three days from now, although I wonder if he will be delayed by the weather. I have learned from the incoming telegrams that they are still having heavy rains to the west, making the train tracks impassable and slowing German military supply lines. Munitions, food and medicine had all been delayed, stalling the German army's progress. Upon reading this, I found myself secretly cheering the rains I had cursed just a few weeks earlier.

The Kommandant's absence has enabled me to make an additional foray into Krich's office. But when I delivered the most recent shipment of passes to the market square café the previous Tuesday, Alek told me not to take any more and instructed me to await further guidance. I will obey him, of course; I am relieved to no longer have to make the secret, nerve-racking trips. I feel a bit lost, though—the mission gave me a sense of purpose and even a bit of excitement. Now, with my task for the resistance complete and the Kommandant still gone, the days seem lackluster. I struggle to keep up my energetic demeanor, lest anyone at work notices the difference.

As I straighten the piles of papers on the Kommandant's desk, my eyes linger on the framed picture of the Kommandant and his wife, which reappeared on his desk following the departure of the delegation from Berlin. In the photograph, they are wearing light, summery clothes and look as if they were on a seaside holiday. The Kommandant wears a playful expression unlike any I have seen. His wife's hair is pulled back beneath a handkerchief, and she is smiling up at him lovingly. Her eyes are dark and her skin surprisingly olive-toned for a German. I wonder once again what became of her. I pick up the picture to dust it, searching the woman's eyes for a clue that would tell me more about her, and about the Kommandant.

"*Dzien dobry,* Anna," a deep, familiar voice says behind me. I jump and spin around. The picture drops from my hands, hitting the carpet and bouncing softly to a rest.

"G-g-good day, Herr Kommandant," I stammer, scrambling to pick up the photograph and replace it on the desk. Straightening, I turn to him. "I was just organizing the papers for your return."

If he notices that I am flustered, he gives no indication. "Yes, well I am back now." He looks different somehow, I observe as I step aside to let him get to his desk. His hair seems grayer, the lines around his eyes more pronounced. It is as if he aged years during the few days he was gone. Perhaps it is just exhaustion from the travel, I think, noticing the fine coat of stubble that covers his jaw.

"We were not expecting you until Friday," I offer as he sits down.

"I decided to return early. There is much work to take care of as a result of my meetings. Many trains have been canceled due to the floods, so headquarters arranged a flight for me."

"An airplane?" I look at him in amazement. Though I know from the movies and newspapers that people do travel by airplane, commercial air travel is nonexistent in Poland. The only planes I have ever seen are the Nazi bombers that occasionally pass overhead.

"Yes," he replies. "It is quite a remarkable experience."

"I am sure," I reply. "Anyway, it is good to have you back." The words come out involuntarily. My breath catches.

The Kommandant's eyes meet my own. "It's good to be here," he says slowly. "I missed…that is, Berlin is a very stressful place, with all of the politics and such. Kraków is much quieter."

"Of course." We look at each other for several seconds, neither of us speaking. "Would you like to go over the schedule now?" I ask finally, desperate to break the awkward silence.

He looks up at the grandfather clock, which reads three-thirty. "I would like some time to get situated first." I can tell from the way he bites his lower lip that he is preoccupied with something. "Would you mind staying a bit late? We could go over the papers at five."

"Certainly." I retreat quickly to the anteroom. Once seated at my desk, I find that my hands are shaking. The Kommandant's return, early and unannounced, has caught me off guard. I can hear my own voice: it's good to have you back. Why did I say that? Because it is what Anna would have said. But the line had not been rehearsed; the expression was genuine. I spend the next hour and a half trying to compose myself, but as I try to distract myself with work, I keep seeing the Kommandant's bluer-than-ever eyes.

When the bells in the tower of Wawel Cathedral have tolled five times and I hear Malgorzata depart the outer office, I gather another stack of mail and other papers that have accumulated during the Kommandant's absence that I have not yet had the opportunity to place on his desk. As I cross the anteroom, I can hear the scraping heels and chatter of the other secretaries walking down the castle ramp through the open windows.

The door to the Kommandant's office is ajar. I knock lightly, then push the door open wider. The phonograph is playing softly and strains of a Mozart sonata fill the room. I had expected the Kommandant to be sorting through the papers I left for him, but he is sitting with his chair turned away from the desk, staring out the window toward Podgorze. I have often wondered what he sees while looking out those windows: does he hear the cries of the Jews in the ghetto, just across the river? Or is he elsewhere, lost in visions of his wife and other faraway things?

After standing for several seconds without his acknowledgement, I clear my throat. The Kommandant turns. He stares at me blankly, as though he has forgotten who I am or why I am there. "You wanted to go over the schedule?" I offer.

His puzzled expression disappears. "Oh, yes, of course. Come in." I sit on the sofa and the Kommandant comes over and takes the chair beside me. I begin to summarize verbally all of the key correspondence that has arrived in his absence, invitations, newspaper clippings and reports. "The minutes from the meeting at Pomorskie last Tuesday note that..." I hesitate, and look up. The Kommandant is staring at me intently. "Is something wrong, Herr Kommandant?"

He shakes his head. "No, please continue."

I look down at the paper but have lost my place. Flustered, I can feel the heat creeping up my neck. I clear my throat. "You have been asked whether you will attend the directors' banquet next Friday evening," I say, jumping to the end of my notes. "But there is a conflict with a dinner invitation you have accepted from Mayor Baran and his wife." I look up, expecting him to say which he will attend, but he is still staring at me, as though he has not heard what I am saying. "Herr Kommandant...?"

He blinks rapidly. "What is it?"

"The conflict between the directors' banquet and Mayor Baran's invitation...I need to know which you will attend."

"Oh." He looks puzzled, as though the question is a difficult one. "What do you think I should do?"

I hesitate, surprised to be asked my opinion. "Well," I begin carefully. "I think the directors' banquet is more important politically. Even though you accepted Mayor Baran's invitation first. I would send my regrets, and perhaps flowers to Mrs. Baran."

"Excellent," he says, as though I have said something terribly bright. "That's what I'll do."

"I'll make the arrangements." He is still staring at me. Suddenly, the room seems to have grown impossibly warm. "Is there anything else?" I ask, eager to leave.

He shakes his head. "No, that's enough for tonight. Thank

you, Anna." The Kommandant turns in the direction of the window once more. I gather up the papers I had placed on the coffee table and stand to leave. Just then, the phonograph needle jumps with a click, and the music shifts. It is a long, mournful piece that I recognize as one of my father's favorites. He used to play it whenever he was sad. Once or twice I heard him humming it under his breath in the ghetto. Now, as I listen, the cello chords seem to stroke my soul. A lump forms in my throat. "Wagner," I say aloud, in spite of myself.

The Kommandant looks up. "You like German composers?" His voice sounds as surprised as the night of Krysia's dinner party when I quoted Goethe to him in German.

"Yes." I can feel the heat rising to my cheeks.

He stands up, just a few inches from me now. "Anna, wait." He places his hand on my forearm, and I shiver. "I…" The Kommandant pauses, adjusting his collar with his free hand. "Would you like to join me for the symphony Friday night? The orchestra is playing Wagner, and I have tickets."

I hesitate, stunned. The Kommandant just asked me out on a date. "Th-that is very kind of you," I manage to say, trying to buy time to figure out how to respond.

"Then say you'll join me," he presses. I falter. I cannot go out with him. I am a married woman. But Anna is not. Desperately, I search for an excuse, a reason why I cannot attend. "If Friday is not convenient, we can go another night," he adds, seeming to read my thoughts.

He is my boss, I realize. Refusing is out of the question. I swallow hard. "Thank you, Herr Kommandant. That would be lovely."

"Then it's settled. Friday night. I'll pick you up at your

aunt's at seven o'clock." I bow my head and flee to the outer office, feeling his eyes on my back as I go.

I manage to stay calm during the long trip home, but once through the front gate, I lose all composure. I climb the stairs to the parlor, breathing heavily, my face red. Krysia is seated on the balcony overlooking the garden. "This situation with the Kommandant is getting out of control!" I explode.

She sets her book down. "What is it?"

Realizing that Lukasz is already asleep, I lower my voice. "He has asked me out on a date."

Krysia points to the chair beside her. "Tell me what happened." She does not sound surprised.

Sinking down, I begin with the Kommandant's return from Berlin just a few hours earlier. "And then he said he had tickets for the Philharmonic."

"Which is highly unlikely, since he has been out of the country for the past week," Krysia observes.

"Exactly! And if the tickets had come in through the office while he was in Berlin, I would have seen them." She nods, understanding the significance: the Kommandant did not just "happen" to have tickets, he was getting them specifically for our date.

"Georg Richwalder is the governor's first deputy," Krysia reminds me. "A powerful man, not to mention an attractive one. Anna Lipowski should be flattered."

I falter at this. Krysia is right; I know from hearing the other secretaries chatter that, if I really was a single young Polish woman, I would welcome the Kommandant's attention. "But I'm married!" I exclaim, tears filling my eyes.

"I know." Krysia pats my hand. "You are in a difficult position."

"And I am a Jew." It was the first time in months I have uttered the word, and it sounds strange on my tongue.

"Perhaps this is a way to help the Jews." I look up at Krysia, puzzled. "You must try to think of the bigger picture. Getting closer to the Kommandant may be useful to the resistance. You may be able to help in even greater ways than you already have."

I breathe deeply. I had not thought of it that way. "But Jacob…"

"Jacob would understand," she replies firmly. She is right, of course. Jacob loves me, but he is dedicated to the resistance. If my going on a date with a Nazi official would help the movement, he would forgive me. I cannot not help but wonder, though, if the tables were turned, would I be so understanding?

"I know. It's just that…" I stop, embarrassed at the selfishness of my thoughts.

"You miss Jacob," Krysia finishes for me. I can tell from the emotion in her voice that she understands. Krysia misses Marcin the way I miss Jacob. The difference is that I will see Jacob again—I know I will, I cannot allow myself to think otherwise. We have the promise of a future together. Krysia and Marcin do not.

"I'm sorry," I say. "I know you miss Marcin, too."

"It's okay, really." A faraway look comes to her eyes. "It's the little things I miss. The way he would bring me water and aspirin after we had a late night out, and tea the next morning, without my ever asking. The way he said my name—Kreesha—as if it had a long e. Most of all I miss having someone there in the middle of the night to wake up and share my dreams with. He never minded at all. Sometimes I open my eyes in the darkness and think he's still there."

I am unsure what to say. Her eyes are wide and I wonder if she is going to cry. "You loved him very much," I offer at last.

She turns to me, smiles. "I still do. It doesn't go away. He's my best friend." She does not speak for several minutes and I can tell she is lost in her thoughts. "It's been a long day," Krysia says at last. "You need a bath."

I nod. "Thank you," I say. I climb the stairs wearily. As the hot water fills the tub, I wipe some of the steam away from the mirror. The girl I see looks tired and careworn—her eyes are ringed with gray and her lips pull downward. The face in the mirror suggests a worldliness I have never seen before. "Who are you?" I ask aloud. Surely not Emma Bau née Gershmann, daughter of the Orthodox baker and his wife. Emma was someone else. I remember her faintly, like a childhood friend nearly forgotten.

Why does the Kommandant like me, anyway, I wonder, as I climb into the bath? I grew up believing that I was perfectly ordinary-looking, not hideous but nothing particularly special. Jacob and my father called me beautiful, but I had always dismissed it as something nice that men who love you just say. I was less noticeable than the dozens of secretaries who came to work at Wawel each day dressed up in tight skirts and too much makeup, and certainly nowhere near as striking as the Kommandant's wife had been. Perhaps it is because I speak German and he is homesick, I think, though the explanation seems unlikely. There is an intensity to the way he looks at me, a certain fascination in the way he listens to me speak that tells me it is something more.

As I soak in the water, I think of Krysia. Though we speak often, she seldom talks about herself. Until tonight. It's as though for just a few minutes her flawless exterior cracked open a bit, and I could see the love and hurt inside. I reflect on what she said about Marcin. Best friends. I wonder if I can say that about Jacob and me. I love him deeply and, despite my fears, I know he feels the same. But when he left, we'd known each other only a year. It was still so unfamiliar and new, there was so much we hadn't yet learned about each other. It must take a lifetime to become like Krysia and Marcin, I decide with a sense of relief as I dry myself and climb into bed.

For the remainder of the week, I see little of the Kommandant. He is occupied with meetings following his return from Berlin, while I am inundated with the multitude of tasks he leaves for me to do. On Friday afternoon, I leave work a few hours earlier than usual and hurry back to Krysia's house to prepare for our date. With Lukasz looking on, Krysia sets and styles my hair and works it into a smooth knot, then helps me to apply face powder and lipstick. I slip into the pale pink, short-sleeved frock of Krysia's that she has had taken in to fit me for the occasion. "Lovely," she remarks as I stand before the full-length mirror in the dressing room just off her bedroom.

"Thank you so much." I shift angles slightly, taken in by my own transformation. The last time I dressed up had been for the dinner party, just weeks after leaving the ghetto. Then I had still been pale and gaunt. Now the months of eating well at Krysia's house have restored the fullness to my breasts and hips, and brought color back to my cheeks. If only I were dressing for a truly happy occasion, I think, and the sense of dread at my date, which I had momentarily forgotten, returns.

As the hallway clock chimes seven times, the doorbell rings. Krysia scoops up Lukasz and heads for the stairs. "You wait here." I pause for several more minutes before the mirror, studying myself. I have only worn short sleeves a handful of times in my life, and I am unaccustomed to seeing my pale arms and bony elbows exposed. I study my hands. An hour earlier, Krysia showed me how to buff and polish my nails. Now they are round and smooth, the refined hands of someone I do not recognize.

Below I hear Krysia's footsteps descending the stairs and the click of the front door. I cannot make out the pleasantries she exchanges with the Kommandant, only the tones of voices, his deep and courteous, hers smooth and welcoming. I lift the ornate glass bottle of rosewater perfume Krysia has loaned me and press softly once. A cool spray of liquid caresses my neck and the delicate, flowery scent wafts upward. I return the bottle to the dresser. Steeling myself with one last look in the mirror, I head down the stairs.

"Good evening, Herr Kommandant," I say, when he appears on the landing beneath me. He turns and I can see a light come into his eyes as he takes in my restyled appearance. You look lovely, I expect him to say in his smoothest voice. But he remains silent, a helpless expression on his face, and I realize that he has been struck speechless.

"Well, you'd best be going," Krysia interjects, after an awkward moment of silence. "Here, take this." She hands me a light, gray silk coat I've never seen before. "It may get chilly later."

"Thank you." I kiss her lightly on the cheek and follow the Kommandant down the lower stairs. Outside, Stanislaw waits by the open car door. He nods courteously as we approach and extends a hand to help me into the back seat, as though it was not out of the ordinary for the Kommandant to be escorting one of his staff to the symphony on a Friday night.

The Kommandant slides into the back seat from the other side of the car, leaving several inches of space between us. We sit stiffly, facing forward in silence as Stanislaw maneuvers the car onto the main road. "So your trip to Berlin went well?" I ask at last. I try to keep my tone light, though I hope he will mention something of significance.

"Things went very well." He pauses for a moment, then turns to me. "Anna, I wish to be candid with you. The reasons for my trip were not entirely professional."

"Oh?" I try to keep my voice even, devoid of curiosity or surprise.

"Yes, it had to do with my wife, Margot. The woman in the pictures." I lift my head to meet his gaze. "You see, she died two years ago this past month." I detect a slight crack in his voice as he speaks the last sentence.

I hesitate, wondering why he is telling me this, desperately wishing that he would say more. "I'm so sorry."

He looks down, brushing a piece of lint from his uniform. "I needed to finalize her affairs."

I nod. "That must have been very difficult."

"It was," he replies, his voice full of candor. "I had put it off for some time for that very reason. Because I didn't want to acknowledge…" He pauses, looking out the window at the rolling fields. Suddenly, the car hits a bump in the road, jostling us unexpectedly. I lurch forward toward the Kommandant and he raises his hands to steady me. Our faces are just inches apart, his breath warm on my cheek. Neither of us moves for several seconds. "Are you all right?" he asks softly.

"Yes, thank you." I grab the back of the front seat and straighten, red-faced. "You were saying…?"

"Just that it was time to finalize matters regarding my wife's estate. Time to move forward." He clears his throat. "I went for the meetings, too, of course. From an official perspective, the trip was a complete success."

"I'm so glad to hear it," I reply. I can tell from the tone of his voice that he will say no more about Margot.

I turn to face forward and neither of us speaks further for several minutes. As we approach the city center, the Kommandant pulls out a pocket watch. "We're a bit early," he remarks. "I didn't realize until I looked at the tickets just before picking you up that the concert doesn't start until eight. We could go to the market square for a cocktail at one of the cafés, or have a stroll around the Planty."

I hesitate. I had assumed that the concert started at seven-thirty and we would be able to go directly to our seats without more conversation. "A-a walk would be nice," I reply. The idea of sitting across from him in a café, having to meet his eyes, terrifies me. I know, too, that it will be easier to keep my composure if I do not have a drink.

"Very well." He leans forward and says something to Stanislaw, who pulls the car over along the side of the Planty. The Kommandant steps out and comes around to help me from the car. His hand feels large and warm against the small of my back as he guides me onto the pavement. "Which way?" he asks.

I gesture to the left with my head. In truth, the path to the right is much more pleasant, winding past the stone buildings of the university. But I dare not choose it, in part for fear of running into someone I know, in part because it is so closely tied to my memories of Jacob that I cannot bear the idea of being there with another man.

As we walk down the path, I inhale deeply. The evening air is warm and thick with the sweet smell of honeysuckle. I look up at the maple trees that line both sides of the path, forming a thick canopy of leaves above us. Soft beams of late-day sunlight make their way through the branches. Out of the corner of my eye, I see the Kommandant. He, too, is staring up at the trees, humming to himself. I have never seen him look so relaxed.

He looks down at me. "It's lovely here, isn't it?"

"Yes," I reply quickly, hoping he did not notice me looking at him. I face forward once more, feeling my cheeks blush.

"I so miss being outdoors," he continues, stretching his arms high above his head. "When Margot and I were first married, we would take long trips to Bavaria. We would hike for days, sleep under the stars. But that was before…" His voice trails off. I look back up at him. The relaxed expression is gone from his face, replaced by its familiar heaviness. An impulse rises in me to say something, anything, to make him happy again.

"I also love hiking," I offer.

He looks up at me, surprised. "You do?"

"Yes." In truth, I had seldom been outside the city growing up. "Our parents used to take us on holiday in the lake district," I lie. "And we would go for marvelous walks."

"Perhaps…" the Kommandant begins. Suddenly, he looks ahead on the path to where a middle-aged couple sits on one of the park benches, a large dog on the ground before them. Without speaking, he starts walking quickly toward the couple. Confused, I follow him. Noticing the Kommandant approaching, the man puts his arm around the woman and whispers something to her. An expression of horror crosses her face. They must be terrified, I realize, at the sight of this large man in a Nazi uniform approaching them.

"What a beautiful animal!" the Kommandant exclaims as he nears the couple. He gestures to the dog. "May I?" The man, looking puzzled, nods, and the Kommandant drops to his knees. The couple and I watch as the Kommandant pets the dog, which appears to be a shepherd with a black-and-brown mottled coat. "I had a dog just like this when I was a boy," he says, not looking up as he rubs the animal between its pointy ears. I have never heard such excitement in his voice before. "His name was Max. He was a wonderful animal."

Just then a bell chimes in the distance. "Herr Kommandant," I say gently. "It is a quarter to eight. We should be getting to the symphony."

"Yes, of course," he says quickly. He gives the dog a final pat, then stands, brushing the dirt from his knees. We bid the stunned couple good-night and make our way to the Philharmonic. Dozens of people are clustered on the sidewalk outside the large stone concert hall, smoking cigarettes and talking. There are many men wearing Nazi uniforms with younger Polish women by their sides, I note, cringing inwardly. The occupying army and their local women. I hate being part of such a cliché, even if it is only an act in my case. Still holding my hand under his arm, the Kommandant leads me up the steps. Several uniformed men salute the Kommandant as we pass.

Inside, I blink several times to adjust my eyes. Though I have passed the Philharmonic many times in my life, I have never set foot inside, and I am utterly unprepared for its grandeur. The lobby is enormous, with marble floors and columns and a crystal chandelier the size of a small car. Its beauty is marred only by the two red flags bearing swastikas that hang from the rafters. No sooner have we entered than a bell sounds, which I know from Krysia is intended to summon us to our seats. We proceed directly to a set of stairs off the right of the lobby and an usher leads us to a private box just above the side of the stage. Before retreating, he apologizes for the lack of printed programs, which he says is a result of the wartime paper shortage. He tells us that the orchestra will be playing Wagner and Mozart. Another high-ranking officer and a large woman I do not recognize are already seated in the box. They nod as we join them.

The orchestra begins tuning up. There are fewer musicians than I had thought would be the case, and the large stage looks strangely empty. As the conductor steps out and the music begins, I remember Krysia saying once that the orchestra had been devastated by the loss of its many Jewish members, who had either fled or been imprisoned. Her eyes had grown moist as she spoke of Viktor Lisznoff, a cellist she had known for decades, who is now in the work camp Plaszow just outside Kraków, forced to labor by day and play with the other imprisoned musicians for the pleasure of the camp officials by night.

As the orchestra begins to play and the music drifts upward, I find myself slipping into the kind of thoughtful, meditative trance that only classical music can provide. I think of my father, who had never had the chance to attend the symphony. He would have loved to be here, to hear the music that he played over and over on his beloved, scratchy phonograph brought to life. He should have been here, not me. Once upon a time, Jacob had spoken of taking my father to a concert. Jacob. I will not think of him here, not while I am with another man.

I find myself observing the Kommandant then, studying him out of the corner of my eye. You are supposed to hate him, I remind myself for what seems like the millionth time. He is a Nazi and the cause for all of our pain. But I don't hate him, I realize, I can't. If not hate, then what…? Gratitude, admiration, attraction? I cannot swallow any of the words that run through my head. I am indifferent, I tell myself finally, just doing a job I have been asked to do. The conclusion sticks uneasily in my throat.

At intermission we rise and join the crowds in the lobby. The Kommandant disappears momentarily and returns with two glasses of champagne. As we stand beneath the crystal chandelier, sipping the cool, bubbly liquid and admiring the endless parade of beautiful gowns and jewels, it seems inconceivable that we are in the middle of a war. I almost forget to be nervous.

"Are you enjoying the concert?" the Kommandant asks.

"Yes," I answer honestly. Though I had grown up listening to classical music, I had never heard a live symphony before and I was struck by the intricacy of the pieces we had heard.

"It's a good program," the Kommandant offers, finishing his champagne. "I do think, though, that the second movement was a little slow." I do not hear the Kommandant as he continues to speak. Across the foyer, I notice a young woman with striking, long dark curls looking over, brow furrowed as though trying to place me. She must have mistaken me for someone else. No one I knew, with the exception of Krysia or

Jacob's parents, would even attend the symphony. But the woman continues to stare, her puzzled expression deepening. She raises her hand to her cheek then, and with that gesture, a wave of recognition sweeps over me. She is Eliana Szef, a wealthy, gentile student I knew from the university. I can see her mind working as she stares at me: is it really Emma Gershmann, she is wondering, and if so, what is a Jewish girl doing at the opera? I know that her confusion will soon give way to recognition, that she is only seconds away from realizing my true identity.

"Herr Kommandant, I must freshen up," I say as Eliana starts across the floor toward me.

"I will wait." Just then the bell rings, recalling us to our seats.

"No, you go in." The Kommandant's eyebrows rise. In my nervousness, my voice had taken on a surprisingly authoritative tone. "I won't have you missing the first movement on my account." I pat his arm. "I'll be along presently."

I press him toward the theater door and duck away through the crowd, just feet ahead of Eliana. Skipping down the marble stairs as fast as my long skirt will allow, I enter the ladies' room and peer hastily in the mirror. My face has matured in the years since Eliana and I had last met, and my hair is lighter now, bleached from being outdoors at Krysia's in the summer sun. It is still possible that she might recognize me, though. I duck hurriedly into a stall as the outer door of the washroom starts to open. Through the crack in the door I can see a flash of dark curls. Eliana and I stand motionless on opposite sides of the door. Clearly, she saw me enter the washroom and followed me; she isn't going to leave anytime soon.

I wait several more minutes, hoping she will leave. Finally,

I realize I have no choice but to come out. The Kommandant will wonder if I am gone any longer. I take a deep breath and open the door. Eliana turns toward me with a warm smile. "Emma…" She is stopped short by my blank, unfamiliar expression. "Aren't you…? I'm sorry," she says. "I must have mistaken you for someone else." I nod, afraid my voice might give me away. Stepping around her with my head held high, I walk out of the washroom.

I hurry up the stairs. Before entering our box, I pause to wipe the cold sweat from my forehead with my handkerchief. I sit down once more beside the Kommandant in our box, trying not to shake.

Eliana Szef. Of all the people to see! For months I have successfully eluded everyone from my past. Hiding in the bathroom stall, I had to fight the urge to confront her. Did she know how I had been fired from the library, then forced to move to the ghetto? Would she even care? Suddenly, I am seized by anger at her and everyone she represented, all of the Poles who worked and lived and went to the symphony while the Jews they had known for years hid or lived like animals in the ghetto. I hate those people worse than the Nazis. Eliana. I dig my nails hard into my palms. I should have ripped her luscious dark curls from her scalp.

I try to calm myself. Breathe, I think, gripping the armrests of the chair. Suddenly, I feel something warm on my right hand. I freeze. The Kommandant, noticing my fidgeting, has placed his much larger hand over mine. I freeze, my heart pounding. Several minutes pass and he does not take his hand away. Both of us continue to look down at the orchestra. What is happening here? I wonder. Clearly the Kommandant is attracted to me. Perhaps it is something more. But, I remind myself, whatever he feels, he does not feel it for you. He has feelings for Anna, and she does not exist.

An hour later the performance is over and we follow the crowds through the lobby. "Would you like to go somewhere for a light supper?" the Kommandant asks as he helps me pull on the coat Krysia gave me.

I hesitate. I should accept, I know, in hopes that the Kommandant may say something useful to the resistance after some wine. But the evening's events have drained me and I do not think I can manage to keep up conversation through a meal. "You are very kind, Herr Kommandant, but I must decline. It is getting late and Lukasz will have me up at dawn."

His face falls. "I understand." We step outside where Stanislaw is waiting with the car. We both speak little on the way home. Sitting silently beside the Kommandant, I realize there is a part of me that has enjoyed the evening and is sorry to see it end.

As the car pulls up to the house, I see a single light still burning on the second floor. Krysia must be waiting up for me. "Thank you again," I say as I turn to get out of the car, hoping to escape quickly.

"Anna, wait." Reluctantly, I turn back to face him. "I almost forgot…" I watch, puzzled, as the Kommandant reaches into his jacket pocket. He pulls out a small, cloth bag and removes from it a rectangular box, which he places on the car seat between us. "I brought this for you from Berlin."

"Herr Kommandant…" I begin, surprised. He pushes the box across the car seat toward me. Slowly, I reach for the box and open it, gasping. Inside there is a delicate silver necklace with a light blue stone. I lift it gently from the box. It is the grandest piece of jewelry I have ever touched.

"A small gesture of appreciation for all of your hard work while I was away." He does not meet my eyes as he says this, and I cannot help but think that his explanation is a lie, that he surely has not brought such a present for Malgorzata or Colonel Diedrichson. "Here, let me." He takes the necklace from my hands. I turn away from him slightly and lift my hair. As he fumbles with the clasp, I feel the warmth of his breath, then the light brush of his fingers across the nape of my neck.

"Thank you," I say, turning back to him when the clasp is fastened. I touch the stone, which lies atop the cross I was already wearing. Together they feel like a heavy noose around my neck. "It's beautiful, far too grand."

"Nonsense, it is you who makes it beautiful…" He stops, seemingly embarrassed by the effusiveness of his own words. I nod, unable to thank him again over the lump in my throat. Quickly I turn and start to get out of the car. "Wait," he says, leaping from the car. He comes around to my side and opens the door. "Here, allow me." He extends his arm and, reluctantly, I take it and allow him to help me from the car. When I straighten, we are just inches apart, my nose practically brushing against the front of his wool coat.

I take a step back, embarrassed. "Thank you once again."

"My pleasure," he replies, his voice sincere. He reaches down toward me. I panic. What is he doing? Is he going to try to kiss me good-night? Before I can react, he lifts my arm and points to the cuff of my coat. The strap around the wrist cuff has come loose and is hanging from the sleeve. "Here." He slides the strap back through the loop and fastens the button. He hesitates, still holding my arm. I can feel his breath on my forehead. Neither of us speaks.

"Good night," I say a moment later, pulling back my arm. "See you Monday." I walk quickly toward the door before he can offer to escort me.

Inside, I close the door and lean against it, my heart still pounding. The sound of Chopin drifts downward from the second floor. Trying to compose myself, I make my way upstairs. Krysia sits in the parlor listening to the phonograph and reading, a large glass of red wine beside her. "How did it go?"

"Great."

Hearing the sarcasm in my voice, she looks up. "Are you okay? Your face is so flushed...." I do not answer. Her eyes drop, freezing on the necklace. "What on earth?"

"Exactly!" I exclaim.

"He gave you a gift?"

I nod. "From his trip to Berlin."

Her eyes widen. "This is getting serious."

"And that's not the worst of it." Dropping down beside her on the sofa, I tell her of my encounter with Eliana Szef.

"That must have been nerve-racking," she empathizes. "But I am really more concerned about this." She lifts the stone that hangs around my neck. "It's topaz, very expensive. What did he say when he gave it to you?"

"Just that it was in appreciation for my hard work."

She nods. "Did he say anything else important?"

"He told me that his wife died two years ago, and that he had taken care of her affairs while in Berlin." A strange look passes across Krysia's face. "What is it?"

"Nothing, nothing at all," she replies. I am unconvinced.

I can tell by her expression that there is something she does not want to say, but I do not press her. "And what about you?" Krysia asks.

I tilt my head, puzzled. "I don't understand."

"How do you feel about all of this attention from the Kommandant?"

"I hate it, of course," I answer, too quickly. "I mean, I am married to Jacob." Krysia does not speak and I shift uneasily in my seat. "I suppose there is some part of me that is flattered…."

"Naturally. The Kommandant is a handsome man, and a powerful one, too." She reaches over and takes my hand in hers. "I don't mean to pry. It's just that, well, you and the Kommandant have a certain chemistry. I could tell the night you met at the dinner party, the way you spoke to each other."

"But…" I start to protest. My mind whirls back to that night, how it seemed at times as though the Kommandant and I were the only two people in the room.

Krysia raises her hand. "It's all right, darling. I know that you love my nephew. I mention it only to tell you that it is okay. Sometimes people have chemistry they cannot help, or even feelings for more than one person. But better to recognize it and be careful." I nod, overwhelmed by what she has said, unable to speak. "Anyway," she continues, "I've had a message from Alek today."

"Oh?" I quickly forget about my night at the symphony and our disturbing conversation. "What is it?"

"He needs to see you again. Meet him at the usual time and place." I nod, my mind spinning. I am glad to hear from Alek. But it is unusual for him to summon me, especially now that I am not stealing passes for the resistance. What does he want? I wonder. I have a feeling that this time, it is something more difficult than papers. I finger the charm around my neck, exchanging uneasy glances with Krysia and wondering just how far this charade will go.

CHAPTER 12

The Tuesday after my date with the Kommandant, I leave work at the end of the day and head toward the market square. It is early August with the kind of stifling hot weather that comes to Kraków for just a few days each summer. The pavement seems to liquefy under the late afternoon sun. Flies swarm around bags of garbage left out for pickup. I wrinkle my nose at the stench and try not to breathe too deeply as I pass.

Checking to make sure I have not been followed, I cross the square to the café where we usually meet. Underneath one of the bright yellow umbrellas that shields the tables from the sun, sits Alek. I am surprised to find him alone. "Marek had some business to take care of," he says as I sit down. I nod, though his explanation seems strange; I have seldom seen one man without the other. I wonder if things are more dangerous for them now, and whether they feel it is safer not to be in the same place at the same time.

"So how are you?" Alek asks. I notice that his face is darker and the skin around his nose is peeling, as though he has spent time outdoors since our last meeting.

I hesitate. Though I do not doubt the sincerity of his question, I am uncertain how to answer. How am I as Emma, missing and worrying about my husband and parents? How am I as Anna, keeping up appearances while working at Nazi headquarters for the Kommandant, and trying to ignore the growing attraction between us? The answer in either case, I suppose, is "tired and sad and worried." But as a Jew, I am far better off than most, and I know I have no business complaining. "Fine," I reply at last.

Alek smiles gently, unfooled by my response. "I hear your mother is doing better." I nod. Krysia told me a few days earlier that my mother's fever has broken and she is now able to stand. *No thanks to you,* I cannot help thinking. "Perhaps in a few weeks or months we will be able to help her and your father," he adds.

"Perhaps," I reply without emotion. Once the promise of his words would have filled me with joy, but I am too afraid to get my hopes up anymore. In a few weeks, the situation in the ghetto could have changed completely. Who knew what would or would not be possible then?

"How has work been?"

"Okay. Actually I'm glad that you called me." I tell him then about the Kommandant's trip to Berlin and a few meetings I have seen on the schedule that might be significant.

"Anything else?" he asks when I finish. I shake my head. "Thank you for the information. We already knew most of that, but it's still helpful."

"Certainly," I reply, glad to have finally offered something that was marginally of use.

"Emma, I can't stay long, so let me get to the point. I called you here for a reason. There is something else we need to ask you to do." He has dared to use my real name in public, I realize. The request must be serious.

"Of course, anything." I am unsure what more I have to offer.

He raises his hand. "Don't say that until you've heard me out. Emma, for several months now, we have had reason to believe from other sources that there are major Nazi plans afoot related to the Jews in the Kraków ghetto. We have tried to get specific information about where, when, how. But all of our contacts, even our best sources, have come up empty. If we can find out what is going to happen, perhaps we can stop it or at least create delays. We need information urgently." I nod, swallowing hard. If their best sources could not get information, what is it Alek thinks I can do? He continues, "If there truly is something going on, some plans about to be set in motion, Richwalder will know about it."

"But he doesn't…" I start to say that the Kommandant does not involve himself in Jewish affairs, then stop. The map I saw during the delegation visit clearly indicates otherwise.

"I know the good Kommandant doesn't usually dirty his hands in Jewish matters," Alek replies bitterly. I nod. I can see the hypocrisy in the Kommandant's role, overseeing the enslavement of the Jews from a distance, not looking closely enough to acknowledge the everyday atrocities that are taking place. "But if something major is to occur, it cannot happen without passing across your boss's desk and getting his stamp of approval. You are our only hope for finding out what that is."

"What do you want me to do?"

"Have you noticed anything unusual in Richwalder's office?"

I shake my head. "Nothing." I have access to almost everything in the Kommandant's office. He does not even have a private safe. "The only things that come in that I have not seen are the classified cable traffic, but there hasn't been much of that lately."

Alek strokes his goatee. "Then it is as I thought. He must keep papers at home."

"He does have a home office," I offer. Alek looks at me strangely, as if wondering how I know that. "Sometimes the Kommandant has me pack a briefcase of work for him to take home at night," I explain quickly.

Alek pauses for several seconds. "Emma, there is something you can do."

Something else, I want to say; I am already helping. "Yes?"

"I can hardly bring myself to ask…"

"I'll do anything I can to help." But even as I say this, I am filled with dread.

"I know that. But this is different from anything you, or any of us, have done before." He looks me squarely in the eyes. "You have to find a way to get into the Kommandant's home study."

"I can do that," I reply quickly.

"Not so fast—you must listen to me carefully." I have never heard Alek sound so serious before. "This is not a case of merely going into an office at Wawel to snatch some passes and leaving again." Merely, I think, remembering my first terrifying foray into Krich's office. I wonder to myself if Alek has any idea how difficult that was. He continues, "You are going to have to get into Richwalder's study and look around. We're not sure exactly what it is you will be looking for. Correspondence, memos, directives, possibly. Anything having to do with future plans for the Jews. This will not be easy," he cautions again. "Richwalder is a notoriously private man, and these are not the type of documents he would leave lying about. We're talking drawers, file cabinets, that sort of thing. You must be extremely careful." I nod. We both know what will happen to me and many others if I get caught.

"I can do it," I repeat. There is a confidence in my voice that I do not recognize. "He…trusts me."

"Yes, we know," Alek says. "That is why we have asked you." It occurs to me then that I may not be the resistance movement's only spy at Wawel. There may be someone else there, perhaps even observing me. Of course, I laugh inwardly. This is war. No one is to be trusted.

Suddenly I am overwhelmed by everything that is happening. "I have to go," I say, standing to leave.

Alek reaches up and grabs my hand. "I know this will not be easy for you."

Easy, I think. Easy is a concept from another lifetime. "It's all right," I reply, though nothing could be further from the truth. I look down at him. "Just one question—does Jacob know about this?"

He shakes his head. "Only that you are working for the Kommandant. He's mad enough about that since he didn't want you getting involved in the first place. I haven't told him about this latest assignment."

"Good. Promise me that you won't tell him?"

"I swear it. Your husband will never know." Looking into his unblinking, solemn, eyes I know he can be trusted not to say anything. "He's worried enough as it is."

"Thank you." I pull my hand away and start to turn.

"Emma, one last thing." I turn back toward him. "Time is of the essence. If you find something, anything that you think might be important, don't wait for our Tuesday meetings. Send word through Krysia and we'll find a way to get the information from you."

"I understand." I turn again to leave, feeling Alek's eyes still on me as I walk away.

Several meters across the square, as I cross through the archway of the cloth hall, a voice explodes behind me. "Anna!" I freeze, terrified that someone has recognized me. Then I realize that the speaker has used my pseudonym; this is someone who knows Anna, not Emma. I turn to find that the shrill, nasal tone belongs to Malgorzata.

"Hello," I reply, trying to smile. Hoping to cut off any questions she might ask, I gesture to her bag. "Doing some after-work shopping?"

But Malgorzata is not easily distracted. "Who was that?" she asks, and I can tell by the direction in which she jerks her head that she has seen me with Alek.

"I don't know what you're—" I begin.

"You don't have to play coy with me, Anna," Malgorzata interrupts. " I saw you having coffee with that handsome young man."

"Oh, that." I wave my hand, trying to sound casual.

"Don't worry," she winks, dropping her voice conspiratorially. "I won't say a word to the Kommandant." Yet I know that was exactly what she would do, if he ever gave her half a chance.

"That's Stefan," I fib quickly. "He's an old friend of my aunt Krysia's."

"Oh." I can tell from the way her voice goes flat that she accepts my explanation, and is disappointed that there isn't more to the story.

"Well, it's a long trip home," I say. "I must get going. *Dobry wieczor,* Malgorzata."

"*Dobry wieczor,* Anna."

Knowing that Malgorzata will watch my retreat, I try to walk rather normally across the square. I turn the corner onto Anna Street and stop, feeling as though I might be ill. Malgorzata had seen me with Alek. Thank goodness she is stupid enough to believe my story. But it might not have been Malgorzata. It could have been one of the officers from Wawel who had spotted me, I think, leaning against the side of a building. Or worse, the Kommandant himself. We have gotten entirely too cavalier about these meetings. My identity, our plans, could all go up in smoke, just like that. And they mustn't, I tell myself. Not now, when we have so much to lose.

I intended to head directly home after my meeting with Alek, but instead I find myself instead cutting south from the city center toward the river. The towpath by the water is crowded with pleasure-seekers this warm August evening: young couples, strolling as Jacob and I once had, children running ahead of their mothers to chase the birds. I walk past them, barely seeing, my mind wrapped up in what Alek has asked me to do. Get into the Kommandant's personal study to find out what is going to happen to the Jews. This was not a simple matter of slipping into an office and grabbing some papers. I would have to go to the Kommandant's apartment repeatedly, become familiar with his desk and study, and learn what he keeps there. Unlike my forays into Krich's office for blank passes, Alek could give me no key or secret code to gain access when the Kommandant is not home, and breaking in was out of the question. No, I would have to go to the Kommandant's apartment deliberately, find some pretext for spending time there with him. It would not be difficult; I know that the Kommandant likes my company and would invite me over if given a hint that I would accept. Perhaps if we have dinner and some wine, and then when he is asleep…

I stop walking, freezing in the middle of the path. Stay at the Kommandant's apartment at night, perhaps even sleep with him…is that what Alek is really asking me to do? I picture his grave expression as he described how I would have to get the passes. No wonder he cautioned me against agreeing to the task too readily. He wants me to become intimate with another man and betray my husband. Suddenly I cannot breathe. There is no way I can be unfaithful to Jacob. It is impossible.

Jacob. His sweet face appears in my mind. He will never know, Alek promised. I had not known the full meaning of his words at the time, but now their impact hits me like a rock. Betray my husband, lie to him. If this were somehow to happen, it would be a secret forever between us. And if he did somehow find out… I shiver.

"No!" I say loudly. Passersby, who are making their way around where I stand motionless in the middle of the path, turn to look at me. "No," I repeat under my breath. I walk to a bench by the river's edge, still thinking about Jacob. What would he do if the situation was reversed? Jacob believes in this cause, I realize, perhaps even more than in us. Otherwise he would be here with me instead of underground with the resistance. And I would not be faced with this dilemma.

Enough, I think. There is no point despairing over what could have been. And this is not Jacob's decision. He did not even want you involved with the resistance, I remind myself. But it is too late for that now. Anyway, this is not about Jacob, I know, or even about me and Jacob. It is about me. I am here, alone, and the decision is mine. Or was. Suddenly I regret having accepted the assignment so readily. Alek had given me the choice and I could have said no. But there had been something in his expression and tone of voice that I had not seen or heard before, a kind of muted desperation that said I was the only one who could possibly get close enough to this man to do what needed to be done.

But this is not just any man, I remind myself. The Kommandant is a Nazi. I suddenly picture the Gestapo shooting the rabbi's wife, Lukasz's pregnant mother, in the doorway in the ghetto. I see Lukasz standing over her as she lay dying on the ground, her head wreathed in blood. The Nazis killed her and they have killed so many others. And the Kommandant is one of them. And now, to show him affection...? My stomach turns.

Even as these dreadful thoughts run through my mind, though, I think again that getting close to him would not be hard. Since the Kommandant's return from Berlin, it has been impossible to ignore the fact that he is attracted to me. I sometimes wonder if it goes beyond physical attraction and he has actual feelings for me, despite the fact that I am one of his subordinates and, in his eyes, a lowly Pole. Until now, I have deliberately kept him at arm's length. The Kommandant is polite, even if he is a Nazi, and I know that he would not take improprieties with me uninvited. It would take time, of course, to make him believe that the attraction is mutual and real. But with the right encouragement…

Stop! a voice inside my head shouts. This is madness. The magnitude of what I am contemplating crashes down upon me. I cannot do it. I lean over the water. Who are you? I demand of my reflection. The image does not answer, but asks back: what is it that matters most? My family, I think, without hesitation. My husband and my parents. The answer has not changed.

A siren erupts on the far side of the river then, breaking me from my thoughts. I look up; the place where I have stopped is exactly parallel to where the ghetto sits, several blocks back from the far bank. *My parents.* With every passing day they spend in the ghetto, their situation is becoming bleaker, their chances more remote. Every day they become sicker and weaker and at greater risk for deportation or worse. Every day people like them are dying, or being killed by the Nazis. That's why Alek has asked me to do this. He needs me to get this information so that the movement can try to save my parents and the other Jews in the ghetto. To get close to the killers so that we can try to stop the killing. I can do this; I can help.

Even as my resolve strengthens, my nagging doubts persist. How will I be able to convince the Kommandant that I really like him? Will I be able to go through with becoming intimate with a man such as him? Perhaps it will not even come to that, I tell myself. Maybe I will be able to find the information without letting things get that far. It is a lie that I desperately want to believe. But whether I do or not is of no consequence. My mind is made up: if there is any chance that my actions might help my family, I have to try. Jacob will never have to know.

Perhaps, I venture, something I discover might actually bring him back to me sooner. Lifting my chin, I turn and begin the long walk home.

CHAPTER 13

The next morning I walk up the ramp to Wawel Castle filled with newfound purpose. Time is of the essence, Alek said. In any event, there is no point in delaying getting close to the Kommandant. It is like pulling off a painful bandage, I analogize; best to do it quickly. The only question is how. Once at my desk, I review the Kommandant's schedule. He has meetings over at the offices on Pomorskie Street all day. Usually on days when the Kommandant has afternoon meetings out of the office, he returns to his residence rather than the office, and has work delivered to his home for the evening. As I pass through the reception area later that morning, I overhear Colonel Diedrichson telling Malgorzata to arrange for a messenger to deliver files to the Kommandant at the end of the day.

"Colonel, I can take the files on my way home," I interject.

Diedrichson looks in my direction, an eyebrow raised. "There are some matters the Kommandant wanted to go over this morning, but we did not have the chance because of his meetings," I continue smoothly. "Matters that require his personal attention."

"I don't know…" Diedrichson hesitates. He is a typical Nazi, thrown off by anything that is not strictly by-the-book.

"I have to go that way, anyway, to run an errand," I persist. The reluctant expression remains on his face.

Just then, the telephone on Malgorzata's desk rings. *"Jawohl,"* she says into the receiver, then looks up. "Colonel, it's for you."

Taking the receiver, Diedrichson looks over at me and shrugs. "Fine with me. The files are heavy, though. Arrange to have Stanislaw take you over." Inwardly, I breathe a sigh of relief. Then my stomach tenses again. I've just committed myself to going to the Kommandant's apartment, I realize. The most difficult task of my life has begun.

At five o'clock that evening, I leave work carrying the files for the Kommandant. Stanislaw drives me to the apartment building and lets me in the front door. I climb the steps carefully, not wanting to drop the files. Standing in front of the Kommandant's door, I hesitate. I cannot do this, I think, panicking. I will just leave them on the doorstep and go. I set the files down on the mat in front of the door, then turn to leave. As I step forward, a floorboard creaks loudly. "Hello?" the Kommandant calls from inside the apartment. My heart sinks as I hear his heavy footsteps shuffling toward the door. It is too late now to run. With a deep breath, I bend over and pick up the files again. As I straighten, the door to the Kommandant's apartment swings open. "Anna!" The Kommandant's stubbled jaw drops and his eyes widen.

"The messenger was gone for the day," I lie, knowing that he is too surprised to doubt my story. "Colonel Diedrichson said you needed these." I jog the files slightly as an indication.

"Come in, come in," he repeats, stepping back unsteadily. The Kommandant's jacket is off and his sleeves are rolled up. His shirt has several buttons undone at the collar, revealing a small patch of hair flecked with gray. I have never seen him dressed so informally. Setting the files down on the end table where he has indicated, I stand awkwardly in the middle of the dimly lit room. The Kommandant's steamer trunk lies on the far corner of the bare wood floor, open and still unpacked from his trip to Berlin. The temperature is too warm, and the mixed odor of brandy and perspiration hangs heavily in the air.

"Welcome." He swings his arm in a wide, sweeping gesture and the liquid in the glass he is holding sloshes precariously. He's been drinking, I realize. A wave of concern flashes through me; I have not seen him like this since before his trip to Berlin, and I wonder what has set him off again. "Come in, have a seat." Reluctantly, I walk to the sofa and perch on the edge. "Would you like a drink?" he asks.

My stomach twists, and I fight the urge to turn and run. "Please." Perhaps if he gets drunk enough to pass out, I can search the apartment without having to get close to him. "Thank you." I accept the glass of amber liquor he offers and take a small sip. The liquid burns my throat like fire. It is stronger than anything I have ever tasted.

The Kommandant finishes his drink in one gulp. He walks to the window and draws the heavy curtains aside. The glass is unwashed, coated with a film of gray. "Do you miss the ocean, Anna?"

I hesitate, caught off guard by his question. "I have never…" I stop midsentence. I had almost said that I had never seen the ocean. Anna is from the seaport town of Gdańsk. In that moment, I had nearly forgotten who I was supposed to be.

"Never what?" He looks back at me.

"N-never seen such dry weather in late summer," I improvise, trying not to panic.

"Mmm," the Kommandant murmurs, and nods in agreement, too inebriated to notice my slip. "The weather is much milder on the coast," he adds. Suddenly I feel as though my life is a balloon balancing on a needle; the slightest misstep could burst it.

I take another sip, welcoming the burn that now reaches to my stomach. The Kommandant is looking out the window again. I hesitate, unsure what I am meant to do. Get close to Richwalder, Alek said. But how? I know nothing about flirting with a man, much less seducing one. When I met Jacob, it was different, we courted like young people… Stop, I order myself, knowing that if I allow myself to think of my husband even for a moment, I will never be able to do this. But it is too late. Suddenly, Jacob's face burns in my mind and I know I must get out of there.

I stand up quickly. "Well, it's getting late. I should be going." I hesitate again, torn between wanting to escape back to the safety of Krysia's house, and hoping he will stop me from leaving so I can go through with my mission. "Thank you again for the drink." The Kommandant follows me as I leave.

"Anna." Suddenly, the Kommandant is in front of me, standing between me and the door. He reaches out and I freeze, watching his hand as if it is moving in slow motion, fighting the urge to jump backward. He touches my temple, brushing back a lock of hair that has fallen from behind my ear. His fingertips graze my cheek. "Good night," he whispers, not moving out of the doorway.

"Good night," I say, turning away from him, my face burning. My hand reaches around him and grasps the cool brass doorknob. I slide through the narrow opening, take a step.

"Anna," he calls again through the half-open door. I can barely hear him through the blood that pounds in my ears. I hesitate and, in a moment that I know I will wonder about for the rest of my life, turn around. The Kommandant's lips crash down upon me like a wave.

I do not know how we got back inside the apartment, nor can I remember taking my coat off. Suddenly my memory and most of my senses are gone—it is as if I can no longer see past the star-bursts in my mind, nor hear above the roaring in my ears. Only taste and smell and touch remain, the saltiness of his ear on my tongue, the grating of his stubbled cheek against my collarbone. I have forgotten my role: Anna should be a virgin, a faraway voice in my head reminds me, tentative and shy. Instead, the noises that come from within me, the way I clutch at his shoulders and back are those of a woman who has known desire. But surely I am not Emma, either, for by the time the Kommandant carries me to his bedroom, lips still glued to mine, I am half dressed and kissing him back with an urgency that gives no hint of the deception this is meant to be. Later, I will tell myself that my passion was part of the role, the mission, to get close to him. But in that moment, as he lays me across the bed, my skirt lifted and crushed under me, I am lost in his musky scent, and in the strong hands that claim me for their own.

I lay trembling on the sweat-soaked sheets some hours later. My limbs throb with an ache that tells me there will be bruises later, as much of my own making as his. The Kommandant snores, one arm thrown back over his head, the other draped heavily across my midsection. Earlier, when his breathing had subsided to a level where he could speak again, he had apologized. "I'm sorry," he said, stroking my face. I knew he meant for the roughness of it all, that what he thought was my first time should have been gentle and romantic. I pressed my lips together in what I hoped passed for a smile and nodded, afraid of what might have come out of my mouth if I tried to speak. Taking my silence for contentment, he soon drifted off to sleep.

Now, lying awake beside him, the reality of what has happened begins to sink in. I have slept with another man. A Nazi. I tried to leave, I tell myself, but even as I think it, I know that my walking away was part of the seduction, the chase. No, my betrayal was calculated. *Not here. Do not think of it here.* But it is too late; panic rises within me and I can stand lying there no longer. Carefully so as not to wake the Kommandant, I slide out from under his weighty limb, dress hurriedly and run from the apartment.

At the door to the building, I hesitate, worrying that Stanislaw has waited for me with the car. I cannot bear to face anyone. But of course he is gone. Hours have passed since my arrival, and I can tell from the position of the moon that it is nearly midnight. The streets are deserted, residents terrified of what will happen if they are found breaking curfew. Normally I would be, too, but I am too preoccupied with getting home and away from all that has happened. I begin to walk in the direction of the road that will lead me to Krysia's house.

My mind races. I never expected this to happen so soon. I thought there would be days, even weeks, of build-up. But in no more than an instant, we were upon each other... *Stop,* I command myself once more. *Do not think about it.* I begin walking faster, taking deeps breaths with each long stride. *You did it. The hardest part is over. You survived.* A strange sense of calmness overcomes me.

Suddenly an image flashes through my mind of the Kommandant's face above me in the darkness, his weight pressed down on mine. As though watching a film, I see myself reaching up to embrace him, meeting his movements with my own. I stop, sickened by the memory. A wave of nausea overwhelms me. Ducking behind a tall bush, I manage to muffle the involuntary retching sounds I make as I bring up the brandy and what little else was in my stomach. Even on the deserted road in the middle of the night, I know better than to attract attention. When my stomach has calmed, I stand up, wiping my mouth and breathing deeply. The street is empty, except for a single rat that pops up from the gutter and glares at me disdainfully. I had to do it, I explain silently. I had to make it look as though I really liked him and was enjoying the moment. The rat turns and runs away from me, not convinced. I smooth my hair and begin the long walk home.

When I have gone about a quarter of a mile, I stop again. The documents, I think. I left the Kommandant's apartment in such a hurry that I forgot to look for the documents and information Alek sent me to find in the first place. Never mind, a calm voice inside me says. It would not do to be rummaging about the Kommandant's apartment on your first visit. You must learn his sleep habits in order to make sure he doesn't wake. First visit. I shudder. That means there will have to be others. My stomach turns menacingly once more.

It takes me more than an hour to walk back to Krysia's. When I reach the front gate, the house is dark. Krysia and Lukasz are long asleep, I think. I wonder if Krysia had worried about me when I had not come home. Though I had mentioned to Krysia that morning that I might have to work late, I had not been able to bring myself to tell her about my new "mission." It is possible, I realize, that she may have known, anyway. She seemed to have a great deal of information about the resistance that did not come from me. In any event, I am grateful that she is not awake. I could not face her questions right now.

Upstairs, I fall to the bed, drained. My body aches from head to toe. More than anything, I want to soak in a hot bath to scrub away my filth and shame, but I do not dare to run one and wake the others. Instead, I slip under the covers. Though exhausted, I lie awake, imagining the dreaded moment when I will have to face the Kommandant at work, to meet his eyes, both of us knowing what has happened. To act like I want it to happen again. Perhaps…I try to picture the calendar that sits on my desk, the one that keeps all of his appointments. Tomorrow is August 12th. The Kommandant will be at Pomorskie all day for meetings, I realize. I will not have to face him. A wave of relief washes over me and I exhale.

Suddenly, I stop mid-breath. August 12th is the anniversary of my marriage to Jacob. How could I have forgotten? It was one year ago tomorrow that we stood together underneath the marriage canopy in his parents' parlor. After the ceremony and a small lunch, we had traveled by train to Zakopane, a small town sixty kilometers south of Kraków, nestled in the High Tatra mountains on the border between Poland and Czechoslovakia, for our honeymoon. For three days, we stayed in a tiny guesthouse nestled at the foot of the mountains, taking long walks outdoors and wandering through the town. I had bought Jacob a sweater, knitted by the mountain peasants and still smelling faintly of sheep, and he gave me a necklace of round amber stones.

I remember now how we lay together those first few nights. I had known little about sex, but the smoothness of Jacob's touch made me wonder if I was his first. He was gentle and patient with my inexperience, introducing me to this strange, newfound joy that brought a perpetual glow to my cheeks.

On the last day of our honeymoon, we took a cable car up the mountainside. Looking over the border into Czechoslovakia, I stared at the jagged, snowcapped peaks, gasping in wonder at enormous vistas I had seen before only in paintings. Jacob squeezed my hand. "We'll come back in the winter and I'll teach you to ski," he promised.

It is hard to believe that was only one year ago. It seems like another lifetime. I wonder what our anniversary would be like if he was still here: another trip to Zakopane, perhaps, or even just a picnic by the river. I sigh. He has been gone longer than we had been together. I still love him as much as I had on the day we were married, but sometimes I have trouble seeing his face clearly in my mind. And now I've betrayed our marriage and slept with another man, I think, tears rolling down my cheeks. It was for Jacob that you did it, I try to tell myself, for him and the cause he believes in. The thought is of no comfort. I roll over and cry myself to sleep.

The next morning, I awake and depart for work early, leaving a note for Krysia so she will not worry. I cannot face her yet. As I walk to the bus stop, my thoughts turn to the Kommandant. Walking home the previous night, my humiliation still fresh on my skin, I had not been able to imagine going to work and seeing him ever again. But in the calm light of morning, I know that I have no choice. I hope to be first in the office so as not to be forced to walk past Malgorzata—I am certain that to her, my shame would be apparent. Fortunately, my plan works, and the office is empty. I look at the Kommandant's schedule and am pleased to discover that he is out of the office all day for meetings. Though I am too exhausted to actually get much work done, I am able to sit at my desk in the anteroom uninterrupted until it is time to go home.

When I arrive at Krysia's that night, the garden is quiet and empty. I am surprised; usually on summer evenings, Krysia and Lukasz are playing there, waiting for me to come home. I wonder for a moment if their absence was some sort of rebuke for my returning home late the night before and leaving early that day.

I open the front door. "Hello?" There is no answer. Something has happened, I think, racing up the stairs. In the parlor, I find Krysia holding Lukasz, wrapped in a blanket, pacing the floor. "He's sick," she informs me, her eyes wide.

"Here, let me." I try to take him from her but she moves away.

"We don't need you getting sick and missing work," she replies coldly.

"Krysia, please," I insist, at last wresting the child from her. Lukasz's face is pale and his half-closed eyes are glassy. His forehead, plastered with damp blond curls, is burning. But the most alarming part are his sobs. Lukasz, usually so quiet and complacent, wails openly now, and I can tell from his swollen, red-rimmed eyes that he has been crying all day.

"He has been sick to his stomach several times, and he can't hold anything down," Krysia says, hovering over my shoulder. It is her lack of composure that frightens me most. Her hair, usually immaculate, is loose and wild, and her dress is soiled. I have never seen fear in her eyes before.

"Perhaps a cool bath?" I suggest, but Krysia shakes her head impatiently.

"He's had two already."

"Well, then, another." I begin to strip the blanket and clothes from the child, unsure of what else to do. Krysia walks wordlessly upstairs, and a moment later I can hear the water running.

As I carry Lukasz past the kitchen toward the stairs, a flash of something bright red catches my eye. I pause. A bouquet of red roses, still wrapped in paper, sits on the table. I know who they are from without asking.

"I tried all of my home remedies," Krysia says a few minutes later, as I cradle the child in the tub and trickle water on his head. He has stopped crying and is still now, but he does not feel any cooler.

"Children get ill. It is normal," I reply without conviction. In truth, Lukasz has not been sick at all in the time he's been with us. I cannot help but feel that his sudden illness immediately following my interlude with the Kommandant is not a coincidence. Surely I am being punished for my sins.

The problem, of course, is not just that Lukasz is sick—it is that we cannot take him to the doctor. Jewish boys are circumcised, Polish boys are not, and a doctor inspecting the undressed child would immediately know his true identity. There are no Jewish doctors to call and no Polish doctors who can be relied upon not to turn us in for hiding the child. It seems to me a great shame that, with all of Krysia's underground contacts and all of the people she knows, there is not a trustworthy physician among them. Even Pankiewicz, the ghetto pharmacist, can no longer help us—Krysia had mentioned a few weeks ago that he'd been deported from the ghetto to one of the camps as punishment for caring for Jews.

Finally, when the child's fingertips are wrinkled like raisins and the water is turning from cool to cold, I draw Lukasz from the bath and wrap him in fresh towels. As I dry him, he seems to drift off into a fitful sleep, his eyes dancing beneath their lids. What does a child his age dream about? I wonder. I cradle him to my breast. In another lifetime, he would have nothing but safe and warm experiences to fill his dreams. Instead, Lukasz has nightmarish visions of his mother being shot and his father taken away, of being hidden and taken through the woods at night to strangers. No matter how warm and safe a world Krysia and I might try to provide, nothing could take away the haunting experiences the child has suffered in his young life.

We redress Lukasz in fresh pajamas and put him to bed. "We should take turns staying with him," Krysia says, and I nod in agreement, although in fact neither of us can bring ourselves to leave the child to sleep first. So we both sit, Krysia in the small chair by his crib and I on a pillow on the ground, watching him and touching his head every few minutes.

"The flowers, they're from the Kommandant," Krysia whispers when at last Lukasz's eyes have stopped moving and his breath has evened.

"I know," I reply flatly.

"Are you all right?" I shrug, unable to speak. "It will be okay, darling. I promise."

Neither of us speak further. When I look over a few minutes later, Krysia is dozing lightly in her chair, head back against the wall, mouth slightly open. So the grande dame of Kraków snores, I cannot help but think. Once it might have surprised me, but these days I know that nothing is as it appears.

I sit on the pillow on the floor and watch them sleep, these two people I have come to call my family. I don't think either Krysia or I realized until tonight what Lukasz has come to mean to us. Once caring for him had been a task, a way to help with the resistance and defy the Nazis. Now he is our child, the son I someday hope to have with Jacob and the grandchild Krysia knows she will never see.

For the first time, I stop to think about what will happen after the war: will the rabbi, by some miracle, survive the camps and come to reclaim his child? If he doesn't, will Lukasz stay with Krysia or with me? To envision the answer means trying to picture what my life will be like after the war. In my dreams, I am always reunited with Jacob and my family. I cannot bear to imagine otherwise. But the backdrop is clouded and obscured. I have no idea where we will be. I doubt we will be able to stay in Kraków. The Jewish quarter has been shattered and will never be whole again. Indeed, judging from the comments I occasionally overhear on the street, and the way the Poles seem to carry on unperturbed with their daily lives, Kraków is more glad to be rid of its Jews than I would care to admit. It is unlikely that Jacob and I would return to a big apartment in the city center and to our jobs at the university. And would the rest of the world be so much better for us? I've heard of the magical kingdoms before: New York, London, even Jerusalem. I cannot imagine these fairy-tale places I have never seen. These thoughts overwhelm me then and I fall into a light sleep of my own.

I awaken, sore and stiff, on the floor at first light. Krysia still sleeps in the chair, and I stand to place a small blanket around her shoulders. I peer into the crib. Lukasz is awake, not crying but holding his feet and talking softly to himself. "Lukaszku," I coo softly. I reach for him and he extends his arms toward me as though it were any other morning. He wraps his arms around my neck. I place my lips to his forehead and it is cool.

"Thank you," I whisper, my eyes wet. God, it seems, has not chosen to punish me in this way. "Thank you."

Lukasz looks up at me and smiles, perhaps the first real smile I have seen since he has come to us. "Na," he says. "Na."

"Anna?" I ask, emphasizing the second syllable.

"Na," he repeats, reaching out to pat my nose. Now it is my turn to smile. He is trying to say my name. It hardly matters that the name isn't really mine. Lukasz is healthy, and happier than I have ever seen him. The scare last night made me aware of how precious he is and how, in this world, even the very little we had could be taken in an instant. Tiptoeing so as not to wake Krysia, I carry the child downstairs for breakfast.

CHAPTER 14

That morning, I am reluctant to go to work. "I should stay home," I say for what seems like the hundredth time. "My leaving will upset the child too much."

Krysia shakes her head. "You need to go to work." Her eyes drift to the bouquet of roses, now sitting in a white ceramic vase, and I realize then she is worried that my missing work now might set off some sort of alarm with the Kommandant.

"Okay," I concede at last. But I linger in the doorway carrying my coat and basket, not wanting to leave.

"He's okay," she reassures me, bending to ruffle Lukasz's hair. Looking at his bright eyes and pink cheeks, I know that she is right. He appears as though he was never sick. Still, I am haunted by the memory of his illness the night before, the prospect of losing him. I fight the urge to pick him up and kiss him good-bye, not wanting to draw attention to the fact that I am leaving.

At last I turn and head for the stairs. "I will be home on time," I say as I go.

"Don't worry," Krysia calls after me. "We will be fine."

Once out the door, I hurry to the bus stop. A bus appears momentarily and twenty minutes later, I am at the foot of Wawel. Still, my dawdling has made me late; Malgorzata is already in the office, wearing a smug expression as I arrive. I have barely set down my belongings behind my desk when Colonel Diedrichson steps out of the Kommandant's office into the anteroom. "The Kommandant has been calling for you," he says. Is he looking at me strangely? I wonder. Perhaps he knows something. But there is no time to worry about it. Grabbing my writing pad and smoothing my hair, I brace myself and step into the Kommandant's office for our first meeting since our night together.

The Kommandant is pacing behind his desk, reading a report. I wipe my hands on my skirt, take a deep breath. "G-good morning, Herr Kommandant," I say, trying unsuccessfully not to let my voice shake.

He freezes midstep, lifts his head. An expression flashes across his face that I do not recognize. Anger, or perhaps relief? "You're late," he replies, though his voice does not sound accusing.

I walk toward him. "I'm sorry," I offer. "I…"

He raises his hand. "There's no need to apologize. It's just that it's not like you. I was worried that…" He falters and looks away. I hesitate. Though he did not finish the sentence, I understand what he is trying to say. He is afraid that I did not want to come to work because of what happened between us. The Kommandant is nervous, too, I realize, astonished.

"It's not that, Herr Kommandant," I say quickly. I am

standing beside the desk now, his face inches above me. I can smell his aftershave and it takes all of my strength to block the memories of two nights earlier. "It's just that Lukasz was ill." I regret my words immediately. I have said too much. The Kommandant sets down his report, takes my hand.

"Is he okay? Is it serious?" The expression on his face is one of genuine concern.

I swallow; it is hard to speak with his warm fingers squeezing mine. "Yes, thank you, he's fine now. It was one of those fevers that children get."

"You should have called me. I would have had my personal physician look at him."

Which is exactly why I did not say anything. "That is very kind," I reply, praying that he will not insist that the doctor still look at the child. "But it isn't necessary. Everything is fine now." I pull my hand away and gesture toward the coffee table. "Shall we go over the day's agenda?" He nods, following me over to the sofa and sitting in the armchair beside it. I review the schedule and all of the correspondence that came in during his absence the prior day. When we have finished, I look up. He is staring at me intently. "If that is all...?" I ask, lowering my eyes.

"Yes, thank you," he says. I stand and start for the door. "No, Anna, wait a moment, please." I turn back toward him. He does not speak for several seconds and I can tell from the way his Adam's apple moves up and down that he is struggling to find the right words. I know then that he is trying to ask me out again. "There is one other thing..." He hesitates. "I was wondering if you are free tonight. I thought we might have dinner together."

I am never free. If I were free I would not be here. "I would love to, Herr Kommandant, but with Lukasz just recovering, I really should be at home this evening." This is not a lie, but I also decline knowing that it would not be proper to accept a last-minute invitation so readily.

He nods. His face is expressionless as though trying to mask disappointment or surprise. "I understand. Perhaps Saturday night instead."

I pause. There is part of me that wants to say no, to write off two nights ago as something that only happened once, a mistake, while I still can. But that will not help the resistance and my parents. "That should be fine, Herr Kommandant," I reply at last. "Assuming Lukasz continues to be healthy."

"Very well. I will send a messenger to Krysia's early Saturday afternoon to confirm." I turn and walk out the door into the anteroom, shaken and torn. Part of me had hoped that the Kommandant would regard the other night as just a one-time occurrence and not pursue me further. In reality, though, I had known that was not the case—the flowers, and the way he continued to look at me, said otherwise. And though I did not like to admit it, I was relieved that he wanted to see me again. It's not because you care what he thinks of you, I lie to myself as I sit down behind the desk. You simply have to get back into his apartment to look for papers.

The fact that I am to see the Kommandant again means I will have to say something to Krysia. I intend to speak with her as soon as I get home that night, but I find her and Lukasz playing in the garden, and the sight is such a happy one I cannot bring it up. Later, after we have eaten and put Lukasz to bed, I follow Krysia into the parlor. She sits down and

picks up the blue sweater she has been knitting for Lukasz. "It looks almost finished," I offer.

Krysia holds up the sweater, studies it. "I think I will add a hood," she says.

Still standing, I shift uneasily. "So, the Kommandant has asked me out again for tomorrow night."

Krysia looks at me evenly. "I see."

I look down, studying the top of my shoes. "I wanted to let you know, I mean, to explain…"

Krysia interrupts, "You don't owe me any explanations."

"Thank you," I reply awkwardly. "But it's important to me that you know. Alek has asked me to…that is, he thinks it is important for the movement."

"And what do you think?" she asks.

I hesitate. "I think I do not have a choice," I say, sinking to the sofa beside her.

"There's always a choice, Emma," Krysia replies. "We have to take responsibility for our actions. It is the only way we can avoid becoming victims and keep our dignity."

Dignity. How ironic. I forfeited mine two nights ago in the Kommandant's apartment. But Krysia is right about taking responsibility. I bite my lip. "Then I am choosing to see him again. For my parents and for the resistance."

Krysia places her hand on my shoulder. "I know it's not an easy decision."

"Do you think it's the right one?"

"That's a question only you can answer." I sigh, then reach over and kiss her on the cheek. "Good night, dear," she says. Upstairs, I check on Lukasz before going to the bathroom. As I wash my face, I think about what Krysia said. I am choosing to do this, to be with the Kommandant in order to help the resistance. Still, I do not feel brave, but filthy. It is not merely the act by which I have betrayed my marriage that fills me with disgust; it is the undeniable fact that some part of me actually enjoyed it. And even that would not have been so bad, I realize as I soak, if it had merely been a physical reaction. I could have attributed that to loneliness and the fact that I hadn't seen my husband in almost a year. No, the problem was this chemistry thing that Krysia had spoken of—part of me liked the Kommandant, liked talking to him and being close to him. That was what made the situation so unbearable.

The next day, the Kommandant's messenger arrives with a handwritten note inviting me to dine at Wierzynek at seven o'clock that evening. Reading the note, I hesitate. I would like to decline, to hold off on being with him for even one more day. But there is no excuse: Lukasz is better and I must try to get the information as soon as possible. I send back a message that I will attend.

At a quarter to seven, Stanislaw comes to pick me up in the car. He explains to me that the Kommandant has been delayed by business and will meet me at the restaurant. Alone in the backseat of the enormous car, I stare out the window. As we near town, I wonder how the evening will go. Since our first night together, I have only seen the Kommandant the one time in his office. I worry that now the conversation will be stilted and awkward.

A moment later the car stops in front of a grand building just off the market square. The Kommandant is waiting in the doorway of the restaurant. "I was sorry not to have been able to meet you," he apologizes as he escorts me inside. The maître d' takes my coat and leads us upstairs to a secluded table on a balcony overlooking the main dining room. "I have taken the liberty of ordering for us," he says as we sit.

I nod, grateful to not have to worry about choosing the proper items on top of everything else. "Lukasz is better?" he asks.

"Yes, thank you." A waiter appears to pour two glasses of red wine, then leaves again. The Kommandant raises his glass. "To health."

"To health," I repeat, raising my glass and taking a small sip. "The wine is delicious."

The Kommandant drains his glass. "Italian. Have you ever been?"

"To Italy?" I shake my head.

"Wonderful country." Two waiters appear with silver-covered plates, which they set before us and uncover in unison to reveal the first course, a smoked salmon terrine. When they have gone, the Kommandant launches into a story about a ski holiday he had taken in the Italian Alps with some friends in his younger years. He speaks very quickly, pausing only for quick bites of salmon and sips from his wineglass, which one of the waiters refilled before leaving.

A few minutes later, the waiters reappear, removing the plates and replacing them with two larger silver domes. The main course is some sort of roast bird, with a gamey taste that I do not enjoy. I pick at the dish, grateful that I ate at Krysia's before leaving. If the Kommandant notices my distaste, he gives no indication, but devours his own plate with relish.

"Have you been back since?" I ask when the waiters who have refilled our glasses have gone again.

"Not to the Italian Alps," he replies. "I've been to other

parts of Italy, of course, Rome, Florence, Venice." I marvel at the way these destinations, which seem so exotic to me, roll so easily off his tongue. He continues, "And to the French and Swiss Alps. But I haven't gone to Turin again since my university days."

I tilt my head. "I'm trying to picture you as a student."

"It was a long time ago," he admits, laughing.

"What did you study?"

"History," he replies, wiping his mouth with his napkin. "I wanted to be a professor. Of course that was before…" He looks away and takes a sip of wine.

"Before what? What happened?"

"Before I no longer had a choice." He pauses. "I was the middle of three children. My older brother, Peter, was supposed to take over the family shipping business. When the war started, he and I joined the navy together." I realize that he is speaking of the Great War. "He was killed at the Battle of Jutland."

"I'm sorry," I say, reaching over the table and touching his forearm.

He clears his throat. "Thank you. He was a brave man and I looked up to him immensely. Anyway, with Peter gone, it fell to me to learn the family business, so I could run it when my father was someday gone. I never had the chance to finish my studies."

I sit back in my seat, uncertain what to say. We eat in silence for several minutes. "How did you enjoy the pheasant?" he asks when the waiter returns to clear the table.

"Delicious," I lie, hoping he did not notice my almost untouched plate.

He turns to the waiter. "Two coffees, one black with brandy, one with cream and sugar," the Kommandant says. I am surprised that the Kommandant knows how I take my coffee, since I never drink it in front of him in the office. He must have remembered from Krysia's dinner party. That was May, I realize, nearly five months ago. It seems like a million years. A moment later, a waiter returns with our coffees and a dessert cart bearing a dazzling array of pastries. My mouth watering, I choose a slice of German chocolate cake and the Kommandant takes a piece of apple strudel.

"How is it?" I ask after he has taken a bite.

"Not bad," he replies, swallowing. "Not as good as my sister's, though. She is married to an Austrian. They live outside Salzburg."

"Are you and she close?"

He nods. "Quite, though I haven't seen her since before the war."

"Perhaps soon…" I begin, then stop, unsure of how to finish. I had started to say that perhaps soon the war would end and he would be able to see her again. But speaking of the end of the war seems strange somehow.

"I know what you were going to say," the Kommandant replies, stirring his coffee. A crumb of strudel is stuck to his face, right by the cleft in his chin. I have to fight the urge to reach out and brush it off. "You were thinking of the war ending. It's okay, Anna. It's not disloyal to wish for an end to the fighting. We all do. I'm just not sure what that means anymore, even if we do win." I am shocked. It is the first time I have heard anyone German speak of Nazi victory as anything other than a foregone conclusion. He continues, "The Führer's plan is quite good in the abstract, but what does it mean, really? Are we to keep occupying Poland and the rest of Europe indefinitely?"

I hesitate, wondering if he expects me to answer. Suddenly I am reminded of the days before the war when Jacob and I would debate political issues. Those conversations were different; there were no right or wrong answers. Here, everything I say is a potential land mine. "I—I don't know," I manage to say.

"You don't have to answer. I'm not a fool, Anna. I know what the Poles think of us. We are the occupying force." *Not occupiers,* I think. *Murderers.* He continues, "They hate us, think we're monsters. I understand it."

"I'm a Pole," I offer. "And I don't…"

"Hate me?" He smiles sheepishly. "I know. That's the part I don't understand." He pauses, taking another bite. "No, the problem with the war is that nothing is certain."

"What about the Jews?" I blurt. The question seems to fly from my mouth involuntarily, as though placed there by another.

The Kommandant stares at me, his fork hovering midair. "I don't understand. What do you mean?"

I hesitate, wishing the floor would open and swallow me up. I should never have asked the question, but it is too late now. "When you spoke of the Führer's plans long-term…" I look down at my coffee cup. "I—I was just wondering about the Jews in the ghetto, what will be done with them?"

"Do you know many Jews, Anna?" the Kommandant asks sharply.

I shake my head quickly. "Only the ones I saw around the city before the war. None personally."

He clears his throat. "The Jewish question will be resolved. You needn't worry about that." He looks up and signals to the waiter for the bill.

My heart pounds. Why did I ask him that? Does he now

suspect something? As he signs the bill, I study his face. But if he thinks anything is amiss, he gives no indication. A moment later, the maître d' reappears with my coat. We make our way downstairs and outside to the car. Inside, the Kommandant turns to me. "I suppose you need to be getting back to Lukasz," he says.

I hesitate. He is asking me if I want to come over, I realize. I do not have to go—he has given me the perfect excuse. But backing out now would defeat the purpose of everything I have already done. I shake my head. "It's okay," I reply. "Krysia is with Lukasz. I don't have to hurry home." The Kommandant smiles slightly and leans forward to speak with Stanislaw in a low voice.

Neither of us speak again until we are inside his apartment. "Would you like something to drink?" he asks, taking my coat and laying it across a chair.

"No, thank you." We stand awkwardly in the middle of the parlor, looking at each other. There is no unexpected moment to bring us together now. Taking a deep breath, I step forward.

"Anna," he says, opening his arms. I take another step toward him and he reaches for me. Wordlessly, we walk to his bedroom. His embrace is tentative at first, but then our lips meet and it is as if we have been together a thousand times. The sex (I refuse to think of it as lovemaking) is less animalistic now, a slower, more tender passion. At one point, I break from the hypnotic trance to a moment of consciousness. Suddenly, it is as though I am hovering above us by the ceiling, looking down on our bodies. I am pinned beneath the Kommandant, my face contorted. Go back inside, I think as I look down, hating myself.

Then it is over. A few minutes later, he is asleep. Watching him breathe evenly, eyes closed, I cannot help but think of Jacob. We would lie awake for hours after making love, holding each other and talking. You should be glad that the Kommandant is asleep, I remind myself. It is time to make this all worthwhile.

Slowly, carefully, I slip out of bed and tiptoe across the apartment in the darkness. Feeling my way along the wall, I find the door to his study. I turn the knob and open the door slowly, so that it does not creak. Inside the unlit room, I can make out nothing and I do not dare turn on a light. *This is pointless.* The only way to do this is to wait and look in the light of very early morning, before the Kommandant wakes up. But I cannot bring myself to stay, not tonight. I need to be home when Lukasz awakes in the morning. Returning to the bedroom, I dress quietly and tiptoe from the apartment. Downstairs, Stanislaw is still waiting by the car. I cannot bear to meet his eyes as I climb into the back seat. If he thinks something untoward has taken place, though, he gives no sign of it, but rather closes the car door behind me and drives me home.

The situation with the Kommandant falls into a pattern after that day. He asks me out several times each week. I think he would see me every day if he could, but the demands of his work keep him from trying. I accept most of his invitations, usually to dinner, or occasionally to the cinema or a play. The evening always ends at the Kommandant's apartment. A few times I stay until the earliest dawn, slipping into the study to look for papers, but I do not dare to shuffle more than a few papers at a time for fear of waking him. So far, I have found nothing of consequence. The situation remains the same for several weeks. Once or twice, Krysia asks in a roundabout way whether I need to see Alek and I always say no. I know that things are more dangerous for him and the other resistance members now, and that they cannot risk a meeting unless I have something significant to report.

One Friday morning in early November, I am seated at my desk in the anteroom opening the mail. Toward the bottom of the pile, there is a small, vanilla colored linen envelope containing a note card. I do not recognize the writing, but I can tell that it is female. *Georg,* the message begins, *I am looking forward to the gala on Saturday. Fondly, Agnieszka.* I freeze, dropping the note card to the desk. Who is Agnieszka? I wonder, and where is the Kommandant taking her? I open the Kommandant's appointment book, but there is nothing listed for Friday night. Maybe it is a mistake. But he has not asked me for a date for that night, as usually would have been the case....

Just then the anteroom door flies open and Malgorzata barrels in, carrying a stack of folders. "These are for…" she begins, setting the folders on the edge of my desk. Then, noticing my expression, she stops. "Is something wrong, Anna?" she asks. "You look rather pale."

"N-no, of course not," I reply, hastily trying to shove the note card under the stack of mail. The last thing I need is Malgorzata thinking I am concerned about the Kommandant's personal life.

But it is too late. She reaches down, picks up the note card. "Ah, the Baroness Kwiatkowska."

"Agnieszka Kwiatkowska?" I repeat. The Kwiatkowskas are a well-known Kraków family with an aristocratic bloodline.

"Yes, I have heard that the baroness has designs on our Kommandant," Malgorzata says, dropping the card back on my desk and winking. "Oh, don't be too sad, Anna. Of course the Kommandant would date a wealthy, cultured woman like Agnieszka Kwiatkowska. You didn't really think he would wind up with a lowly staff person, did you?"

"No, of course not," I start to say, but Malgorzata has walked away, laughing cruelly over her shoulder as she leaves the room. I sit for several moments, staring at the card. Finally, I place it back in the envelope and return it, along with the rest of the mail, on the Kommandant's desk. Still, the idea of it gnaws at me all morning: the Kommandant is going on a date with another woman. Well, why shouldn't he? I muse angrily as I work on the filing that afternoon. He is a very eligible man, single, handsome and powerful. The fact that he is sleeping with a member of his staff should hardly matter. I feel foolish for ever thinking that it might be something more to him.

Once I am seated on the bus heading toward Chelmska, my mind turns to the Kommandant once more. So he has a date with another woman. It should not matter at all. You are only with him because you have to be, I remind myself. It is a mission for the resistance. It is not as though it is Jacob who is betraying you. No, it is I who is betraying him, I think, pressing my head miserably against the cool glass window. I betray Jacob, the Kommandant betrays me. It is pathetic. As I get off the bus at Krysia's, it begins to rain—thick, cold drops that soak through my coat and stockings. The miserable weather suits my mood perfectly.

Opening the front gate to Krysia's, I pause. Something is not right. There are lights burning everywhere in the house, yet the second-floor curtains, usually flung wide open, are tightly shut. I hurry up the path, wondering if Lukasz is sick again. "Hello?" I call as I open the front door. I walk up the stairs to the second floor. "Hello?"

"Surprise!" a chorus of voices bursts out, startling me. Krysia, Lukasz and the Kommandant leap out of the kitchen. Elzbieta lingers behind slightly, holding a cake with lit candles. "Happy birthday!" they cry. I blink repeatedly, trying to process what is happening. Tomorrow is my birthday, I remember, my real birthday and Anna's, too. The resistance gave her the same birthday as me to minimize confusion. I had almost forgotten, though I know Krysia has not. But the Kommandant is here, too. A birthday celebration made up of the Jewish child we are hiding, my husband's aunt who is sheltering us, and the Nazi she is protecting us from, who happens to be my lover. The irony is really too much.

"Thank you," I manage to say at last. Suddenly I am mindful of my disheveled hair and mud-soaked stockings.

Elzbieta steps forward with the cake. "Are you surprised?" she asks.

"Yes," I reply, blowing out the candles. It is one of the great understatements of my life.

"Happy birthday, Anna," the Kommandant says, taking a half step toward me. I do not answer or meet his eyes. For a moment when I first saw him, I had felt a rush of warmth. Now I am reminded of his date with the baroness and his presence seems hypocritical. Of course he is here tonight, I think. Tomorrow, on my actual birthday, he will be with someone else.

Lukasz breaks the awkward silence. "Ca!" he says gleefully, stepping toward the cake with outstretched fingers.

"No, darling," Krysia admonishes gently, catching his hands. "We need to eat our meal first."

"Dinner is ready," Elzbieta says. "Why don't you go sit down?"

"Come, Lukasz." The Kommandant holds out his hand. The child hesitates, looking up at the giant man in uniform. Then he places his tiny hand in the Kommandant's. I shudder. It is all part of the plan, I know, having the Kommandant warm to Lukasz. It means that our disguises are working. Still, I cringe at the sight of the rabbi's child holding the hand of a Nazi.

"I'm sorry," Krysia whispers as we make our way to the dining room. "He found out that it was your birthday and contacted me. I had no choice but to invite him."

I nod. She could not know why I was really upset. Why make the effort, pretend that he cares about me enough to celebrate my birthday? I wondered. This time tomorrow night he would be on a date with the baroness.

"Happy birthday, Anna," the Kommandant says again once we are seated. I do not answer but turn slightly away. Out of the corner of my eye, I can see the puzzled expression on his face. He does not know that I know about the baroness. I am silent through the meal, leaving Krysia to keep up most of the conversation.

After dinner, Elzbieta serves coffee and the birthday cake, which is a yellow cake with lemon icing. "It's delicious," I say, knowing that white flour and sugar cost dearly these days, even for Krysia. Krysia stands and returns to the table with two boxes wrapped in paper. "Thank you," I say, touched. I had not expected anything. I unwrap the presents. One is a pale pink scarf that Krysia has secretly knitted for me. The other is something made from sticks that Lukasz has put together. "I love it!" I exclaim, circling the table to hug and kiss him. He giggles, squirming to get away.

"It's late. I'd better get this youngster to bed," Krysia says, standing up and picking up Lukasz. "Say good-night, darling."

Lukasz raises his hand. *"Salom,"* he says.

"What's that?" the Kommandant asks.

"Sabat salom," Lukasz repeats. I freeze. Lukasz is trying to say *shabbat shalom,* the Hebrew greeting on the Sabbath.

The Kommandant turns to me. "What is he trying to say?"

"Nothing," I reply quickly, shooting Krysia a warning look. "He is just babbling because he's tired." Krysia carries the child hurriedly from the room, leaving the Kommandant and I alone. Where did Lukasz learn that? I wonder frantically. I have never spoken Hebrew around him. It must have been something he recalled hearing from his parents as a young child. Surely the Kommandant would not have recognized the words…. I study his face, but he does not appear to have noticed anything suspicious. "I need some air," I say, standing up. I step out onto the balcony off the parlor. The Kommandant follows me. The rain has cleared, leaving a gorgeous, crisp autumn evening sky freckled with a thousand stars.

"Anna." The Kommandant comes to stand beside me. "This is for you." He draws from his pocket a small wrapped box, the same size as the one he gave me the evening we went to the orchestra.

"I can't accept it." My voice is cold. The hurt expression returns to his face once more. "There is no need to give presents to a lowly member of your staff."

"I don't understand," he says. "Are you angry that I am here?"

"It's just that perhaps your time would be better spent with someone else. Someone more your equal."

"Someone else?" he asks, puzzled. "What on earth are you talking about?"

I take a deep breath. "You should give that to Baroness Kwiatkowska," I say, gesturing toward the box. "I am sure she would like it very much." He stares at me, still not comprehending. I continue, "I know about your date tomorrow night."

"The baroness!" he exclaims. "Is that what's bothering you?" I wait for him to deny it but he does not. "Anna, listen to me. The baroness is a cousin of Governor Frank's wife. He asked me to escort her to the gala as a personal favor to him. I would have told you about it, but I didn't think it was important. I knew that I was seeing you tonight, and you never agree to see me more than once in a weekend, anyway." I do not answer. The Kommandant's explanation makes sense, but I still feel hurt. A date is a date.

"Thank you for coming," I say firmly, signaling that it is time for him to go.

He places the box back in his pocket, defeated. "Good night, Anna. Happy birthday." I do not look up as he reenters the house. I can hear his heavy footsteps on the stairs, the door closing below. As I hear Stanislaw starting the car engine, I shudder. I wonder if I have just allowed my ego to ruin my mission by ending things with the Kommandant.

CHAPTER 15

"I heard the Kommandant leave," Krysia says, stepping out onto the balcony a few minutes later. "What happened?"

I take a deep breath. "I sent him away."

"I don't understand…"

"I refused to accept his present and he left." Briefly I explain to Krysia how I found the baroness's note at work that day, finishing with the Kommandant's explanation when I confronted him just a few minutes earlier. "I know that I shouldn't care if he is seeing someone else," I finish in a low voice. "I mean, this isn't real."

"But you do care."

I look away, staring out into the darkness. "Yes."

"You feel that you are being disrespected somehow," she offers.

"Exactly!" I reply quickly. It is much easier to accept her explanation than the only other one: that I am hurt because I have feelings for the Kommandant. "But now I may have made him so angry that he won't want to see me again. I won't be able to get into his apartment again to get the information for Alek."

Krysia shakes her head, taking a step closer to me. "I doubt it." She draws her shawl closer around her shoulders. "For whatever it is worth, darling, I believe Richwalder's feelings for you are legitimate. I can tell from the way he watches you. I don't think he will give up so easily."

I shift uncomfortably. "I suppose that does help the mission, his legitimately having feelings for me."

"I suppose," Krysia replies evenly. "Well, I'm exhausted. I am going to turn in. I hope you had a nice evening."

Suddenly I remember the dinner party. She had tried, really tried, to make my birthday special, despite the circumstances. "It was lovely," I say, hugging her. "Thank you so much for everything."

When Krysia has gone back inside the house, I look up at the black, star-filled sky. On our honeymoon, Jacob had taught me to locate some of the more basic constellations. Orion, I think now, searching the darkness above. Jacob used to say that when he felt lost, he would find the three contiguous stars that formed Orion's belt to center himself. But I cannot find it. Perhaps it is the wrong time of year. Giving up, I remember how as a child I used to wish on the evening star. Staring up at the sky, I pray that Jacob is all right and that he is thinking of me, too.

I sleep dreamlessly that night, and the next morning I awake early. Memories crash down upon me quickly of the night before and the Kommandant's hurried departure. What have I done? I wonder. I roll over, pulling the blanket high over my ears. At least it is Saturday and I do not have to face him at work. I will sleep awhile longer, I decide. But a few seconds after I have closed my eyes again, I hear my door opening and low voices in the hallway. "Say happy birthday," Krysia whispers.

"Birday!" Lukasz cries, running in and trying unsuccessfully to climb into my bed. I sit up and lift him into my lap.

"Thank you, sweetie." I kiss his cheek, looking up at Krysia.

"Sorry to barge in, but he has been waiting to do that for an hour," she says.

"I should get up, anyway. We need to get the laundry done and…"

Krysia holds up her hand. "This is your birthday. No work." I know better than to argue with Krysia when she uses that tone of voice. Instead, after we've washed and dressed, the three of us pack a picnic basket and walk to the park. The ground is thick with freshly fallen leaves, and after we finish eating, I show Lukasz how to make a pile of leaves and then jump in it. By the time we return home, it is late afternoon and nearly dark. As I bathe Lukasz, my mood sinks again. The gala starts at seven o'clock. I imagine the baroness getting ready for her evening with the Kommandant, him picking her up. It should have been me on his arm tonight. I cannot help it, I realize. Right or wrong, I am jealous.

"Would you like to play a game of cards?" Krysia asks when I have put Lukasz to bed and come downstairs. She has set out two plates of reheated food left over from my birthday party.

I shake my head. "No, I'm sorry. And I'm not hungry, either. I'm going to go read upstairs." I can see the concern register on Krysia's face.

"Darling, I know you are upset. These are confusing times, and sometimes it's hard to make sense of things…."

"I don't want to talk about it," I interject. "I'm sorry."

She smiles gently. "Good night. Sleep well." I retreat upstairs. It is too early to sleep, so I take a bath and wash my hair, then climb into bed with a book. It is *Pride and Prejudice,* one of the first books Jacob gave me, though of course that copy is still back in the Baus' apartment. I hold the book under my nose, breathing deeply. The musty scent reminds me of my days working at the library and of Jacob. It is my husband I miss, I tell myself. Only him. Being apart from him for so long is what has made me so irrationally upset about the Kommandant. I open the book and begin to read. Minutes later, my eyes grow heavy and I start to drift off.

Suddenly, I am jarred awake by a loud noise outside my window. I sit up, setting the book on the night table. How long have I been asleep? I wonder. The noise comes again. It is the sound of something hard hitting sharply against the glass doors. "What on earth…?" I mutter aloud, climbing from bed. I open the doors and, stepping out on the balcony, look down. The garden below is pitch black.

"Anna!" a voice calls in a loud stage whisper. "Anna!" It is the Kommandant, I realize in disbelief. "It's me, Georg. Please come down."

I hesitate. "One minute," I reply. I step back inside and dress quickly, then make my way downstairs through the darkened house. I open the front door. "What are you doing here?"

"I told the baroness I wasn't feeling well and took her home."

"Oh…" I am still confused. "What time is it?"

"Ten-thirty," he replies.

"It feels much later," I say, rubbing my eyes. "I must have drifted off."

"Anna." He takes one of my hands in his. "I'm sorry if I hurt you. I never wanted to be with anyone else." I am too stunned to pull away. "Anna, come home with me. Stay with me to-night. Please."

I am silent, a thousand thoughts running through my head. To dress and go home with him at this hour seems unlady-like. But at the same time, part of me wants to go. And it will give me another chance to search for documents. "All right," I say at last. "Let me get my coat." I race silently back upstairs and leave a scribbled note for Krysia on the kitchen table, then grab my coat and return downstairs to the Kommandant. As I climb into the car, I think I see an amused smile on Stan-islaw's usually expressionless face.

At the Kommandant's we are barely inside the door before he is upon me, and we are tearing each other's clothes off. Our passion is reminiscent of our first night together, except that this time we do not initially make it as far as the bedroom, but find ourselves lying spent on the sofa. Later, when his breathing has subsided, the Kommandant carries me to his bed. This time, it is I who am upon him, my legs straddled wide on either side of his broad hips. It is the first time I have ever been with a man in this way, and at first I feel strange and exposed. As the rhythm grows familiar to me, I feel a sense of power, and in his surrender, I release some of the hurt and re-claim some of the pride I have lost over the past few days.

"Will you stay?" he asks later in a sleepy voice. He tries to wrap himself around me from behind, but I shift onto my back. That position reminds me too much of how Jacob held me. "Be here in the morning, I mean?" I hesitate. I have always left the Kommandant's late at night or in the predawn hours before he is awake. But staying might give me more time to search for papers. I nod. "Mmm," he murmurs before drifting off to sleep.

My eyelids grow heavy. At first I fight the urge to sleep, afraid that I won't wake up until it is morning and too late to look for documents. I have to find something very soon, I know. I have been coming to the Kommandant's for more than two months and in that time Nazi plans for the Jews are moving forward, plans about which I have been unable to learn. I picture the inside of his study, wondering what I am missing. There are no important papers lying about, no safe. Perhaps, I realize suddenly, there is some sort of hidden compartment in one of the drawers. Finally, when I can fight it no longer, I close my eyes and sleep restlessly. I dream that I am in the park with Lukasz and we are playing hide-and-seek. Lukasz runs behind a bush. Suddenly, a small man in a black coat and hat appears beside me. It is the rabbi. "Where is my son?" he asks. He is gone, I lie. Gone, gone, gone...my words echo through the trees.

My eyes snap open. Beside me, the Kommandant has turned away and is snoring. Though the room is dark behind the heavy curtains, I can make out that the clock on his nightstand reads five-fifteen. The Kommandant is an early riser. There is not much time. I climb out of bed and tiptoe across the living room. The study door creaks loudly as I open it. I freeze, listening for any sounds of movement coming from the bedroom. Hearing none, I slip into the study and close the door behind me. Inside, I pull back the curtains slightly to let a shaft of pale gray early morning light into the room. I quickly scan the top of the desk but see nothing of significance. Slowly, I open the top desk drawer. I slide my hand under the papers along the bottom, but the surface is smooth. I close the drawer and drop to my knees to open the middle one. On the bottom, under my right index finger I feel a break in the wood. I clear back the papers. The drawer has some sort of fake bottom. I press my fingernails into the break, trying to lift up the panel.

"Anna…" the Kommandant calls. I jump back, trying to close the drawer, but it sticks, refusing to budge. Frantically, I push again, harder this time. The drawer finally gives way with a loud banging sound. Cringing, I move quickly to the closed door of the study. I recall the sound of the Kommandant's voice, trying to judge his location. Let him still be in bed, I pray. I crack the study door slightly, peer out into the dark living room, but I can see nothing. Taking a deep breath, I prepare to open the study door and return to bed. Suddenly, I hear a footstep in the living room. The Kommandant is just on the other side of the door.

I've got to get out of the study, I think frantically. I notice a door at the far side of the room. Hurriedly, I tiptoe across the study and open the door. As I suspected, it connects to the kitchen. I reach for a glass from the cupboard over the sink. "Anna," the Kommandant calls again, his voice closer this time. My heart pounding, I step out of the kitchen into the living room, still holding the glass. The room is dark, illuminated only by a faint beam of early morning light coming through the far window. "Yes, Georg?" I manage to say, fighting to keep my voice even.

"Oh, there you are." The Kommandant's voice is scratchy, his face heavy with sleep. "I thought maybe you'd gone home…."

He wasn't checking up on me, I realize; he wanted to make sure I hadn't left him. Part of me is almost touched by his concern. "No, of course not," I reply gently. "I told you I would stay until morning. I was just getting a glass of water. Why don't you go back to bed and I'll bring you one, too?" He nods, almost childlike in his grogginess.

When he has turned and padded back to the bedroom, I look once more in the direction of the study. I need to get back in there, though of course doing so now is out of the question. It is too risky. It may be nothing, I remind myself, as I pour two glasses of water. The hidden compartment may be empty, or the papers may have nothing to do with the Jews. But still…my heart races as I remember the feel of the secret panel beneath my fingertips. Something tells me this might be what Alek and the others have been looking for. Forcing myself to calm down and breathe normally, I carry the water glasses back to bed with the Kommandant.

In the bedroom, the Kommandant is sprawled on his stomach, one arm flung across my pillow. "Mmm," he mumbles, as I slide in beside him, rolling over and enfolding me in his arms. Trapped now in his warmth, I find myself studying his face. It is relaxed and peaceful, almost boyish. There is no sign of the intensity or the pain he wears like a mask in the daytime.

I drift back off to sleep then. Again, I fall into the dream where I am in the park with the rabbi. This time he is holding a baby. For a moment, I wonder if it is Lukasz when he was younger. "Where is my son?" the rabbi demands. I do not answer. The baby in his arms is not Lukasz, I realize, but the unborn child that died when his wife was shot. "Where is he?"

Just then, a rustling sound comes from a nearby bush. Lukasz bursts forth, giggling. *"Tata!"* he cries, running to the rabbi. The rabbi picks up Lukasz with his free arm, embracing both of his children joyously. But when he spins toward me there is a look of recrimination on his face. Without speaking, he begins to walk away, carrying the children. A deep scream rises within me. "No, no," I cry as they disappear into the fog.

"No, no," I say again. Suddenly, I open my eyes. I am still in the Kommandant's bed. He is awake now, lying on his side, watching me.

"Are you all right?" he asks, his face concerned.

"Just dreaming," I reply, hoping that I have not been speaking aloud.

He brushes away a lock of hair that has fallen onto my face. "About what?"

"Lukasz," I reply truthfully. "I worry about him sometimes. He has been through a great deal. Losing his parents, moving…"

"You care about him very much."

I nod. "Sometimes he's more like my child than my little brother. Because of the age difference, I mean."

The Kommandant rolls over onto his back, hands clasped behind his head. I cannot help but look at his naked torso. Though I have calculated that he must be nearing fifty years old, he is as trim and fit as a man half his age. His chest is muscular and his stomach has no sign of a paunch. "I have always regretted not having children," he says.

"Perhaps you still may," I offer. "It's not too late."

"Perhaps," he agrees. "Do you want children, Anna?"

"Of course," I answer quickly. But not with you, I think. I want them with my husband.

He places his arm around me again, drawing me close. I rest my head on his shoulder. "Thank you for staying last night. It's nice to wake up with you here."

"Well, with the competition and all. I mean, I'm sure the baroness would have stayed." I mean the words as a joke, but they come out sounding jealous, insecure.

The Kommandant turns toward me again, his face inches from mine. "I'm sorry about that," he says. "I never meant to hurt you. There's no one else." His eyes are wide and sincere. "When Margot died, I thought I could never feel anything for anyone ever again. And I didn't, until you. For the first time in two years, I am glad to wake up in the morning, and it's because of you. You are the only person I can trust. I love you, Anna."

I am stunned. I do not know what to say. "And I, you," I manage to say finally, swallowing hard.

"Oh, Anna," he says, drawing me close and kissing me. Several minutes later, we pull apart again. "I can make us coffee," he offers, sitting up. "I have some bread and cheese for breakfast, or I can order something in."

I shake my head. "I'm sorry, but I really must get home. It's late. There are chores to be done for Krysia, and Lukasz will be missing me."

"I understand," he replies, his eyes warm. "Stanislaw will drive you home." I dress quickly and kiss him goodbye. Outside, I slip gratefully into the Kommandant's car. I had considered declining his offer and taking the bus, but I am too embarrassed by my tousled hair and the fact that I am wearing the same clothes from yesterday.

A few minutes later I walk through the front door of

Krysia's. She is in the kitchen, trying to feed Lukasz a bowl of cereal as he plays in his high chair. "Good morning," she says without reproach.

"I'm sorry to have left without telling you," I say. "It was… unexpected."

"It's okay. I got your note. You made up with Richwalder, I take it."

"Yes."

"Good." I told you he would not stay mad, I can almost hear her thinking. "Would you like some breakfast?"

I shake my head. "No, thank you. I should get dressed."

She studies my face carefully. "Did everything go all right?"

"Sort of…" Krysia shoots me a questioning look and I hesitate, wondering how much to say. "I was able to get around after he was asleep and I found a drawer with a false bottom. It may be nothing," I add quickly, not wanting to get her hopes up. "The Kommandant woke up before I had the chance to see what was inside."

A look of concern passes across Krysia's face. "You're lucky you weren't caught. Are you going to try again?"

I drop to the chair beside Krysia. "Yes, as soon as possible."

"Good." She stops feeding Lukasz long enough to pour some juice into an extra glass that is sitting on the table. "I know that Alek will be very glad to have whatever you can find," she adds, handing me the glass.

"Have you spoken with him?"

Krysia shakes her head. "Not directly, only through intermediaries." She turns to face me directly. "Emma, listen. I don't want to worry you, but you need to know for your own protection—there are troubles in the resistance right now."

My hand, still holding the glass, freezes midair. "What is it? Is Jacob okay?"

"He's fine, and so are Alek and the others whom you know," she replies quickly. Relieved, I set the glass down, forcing myself to swallow the mouthful of juice that seems to have stuck in my throat. Krysia continues, "But a group of resistance fighters were picked up by the Nazis at a train station just south of Kraków a few nights ago. Alek and the others now believe that there is a leak in the resistance."

"An informant?"

"Yes. There is no other way the Nazis could have learned of the location of that group, the exact time they would be meeting. Whoever gave out the information had inside knowledge of resistance operations. Which means that he or she likely knows everything."

"Everything," I repeat, swallowing hard. My true identity, the work I am doing. All of us—not just me, but Krysia, Lukasz, Jacob, my parents—are in jeopardy.

"I'm telling you this so that you will know to be careful, even more so than usual. You must be on your guard at all times." She takes Lukasz from his high chair and sets him on the ground. He runs to me and I scoop him up and place him on my lap. As he babbles, I run my fingers through his tangled blond curls, thinking about what Krysia has said. A leak. I picture in my mind the faces of the resistance members I know. It seems unfathomable that any of them could be traitors. Krysia stands and begins to clear the dishes from the table. "Perhaps you should hold off on looking for anything further right now, while things are so dangerous."

"Perhaps," I reply, not wanting to worry her. The truth, I

know, is exactly the opposite. If there is an informant in the resistance, it is only a matter of time before my identity is revealed to the Kommandant—before this elaborately constructed charade implodes beneath us. My mission has become more urgent than ever. I have to find the information for the resistance and get out before it is too late.

CHAPTER 16

Krysia's warning echoes in my head as I make my way into the office the next day. *Be careful.* But time is of the essence. The resistance needs whatever information the Kommandant has. And if my identity is about to be betrayed by an informant, I do not have much time. When will I be able to get into the Kommandant's study again? I wonder. Our rendezvous after he left the baroness last night was impromptu and we do not have any dates planned. As I work, I try feverishly to come up with a plan to get into his apartment once more.

The Kommandant is in meetings all day and I do not see him until nearly five o'clock when he calls me into his office. "Here," he says in a businesslike tone, handing me a large stack of papers and files without looking up. There is no indication of the intimacy we shared the night before. For a moment I worry that he has learned, or suspects something. But then, remembering the genuine affection in his eyes as he held me the night before, I know that things are not likely to have changed so soon. Rather, I decide, he is just preoccupied with work.

I linger awkwardly by the side of the desk as he works, hoping that he will say something about the previous night or perhaps suggest getting together again. "That will be all," he says a moment later, as though he had forgotten I was there.

He's not going to ask me out, I realize, my heart sinking. I start for the office door, then stop. There is no time. I must be bold. Taking a deep breath, I turn back toward the desk. "Herr Kommandant..." I venture softly.

He looks up. "Yes, Anna, what is it?" he asks. His voice is gentle, but I detect a note of impatience.

"About last night..." I move closer to the desk, dropping my voice even lower.

"Yes?" A look of surprise crosses his face. We have seldom spoken of our affair at the office and I certainly have never brought it up. I wonder if he will be suspicious if I say too much.

I decide to press on. "Last night was very nice," I manage to say.

He smiles. "I agree. I'm very glad you finally decided to stay." He reaches out and touches my forearm. A jolt of electricity shoots through me.

I continue, "I know this may be rather forward of me, but the orchestra is playing a program of Bach tonight and I was wondering..." I allow my voice to trail off, drop my eyes.

"I would love to take you to the symphony, Anna," he replies, his voice sincere. "I'm flattered that you would ask. But I have an official dinner tonight, and I have to travel to Warsaw tomorrow morning first thing for a day of meetings. Perhaps over the weekend…?"

"Of course." I try to keep my voice even. How foolish of me not to have checked his schedule! "I understand."

"I will be thinking of you the entire time," he promises, raising my hand to his lips. I nod and carry the stack of papers from the room.

As I walk from the castle that evening, my mind races. My attempt to get back in the Kommandant's apartment failed. Was I too bold? Did he suspect something? No, I decide, he was genuinely pleased that I asked. Something else is nagging at me, though. It is a sense of rejection, I realize with surprise. I am actually a bit hurt that the Kommandant did not accept my invitation. Don't be ridiculous, I scold myself as I board the bus for Krysia's house. Your asking him out was simply part of the mission. But even as I tell myself this, I am unsettled by my feelings. It's like the baroness all over again, I think, remembering my jealousy of a few days ago. Why am I letting him affect me in this way? You've got to get your head out of this. Anyway, he had a good reason for declining: the dinner and the trip to Warsaw.

My head snaps up. The Kommandant is going to Warsaw tomorrow. He'll be out of town all day. Perhaps I can get into his apartment while he is away and look around for the information in the daytime. It would be the perfect opportunity. My mind races. I need an excuse to get inside the apartment. I consider offering to drop off papers at the Kommandant's apartment again, as I did the first time we were together, but there won't be any real need to do so while the Kommandant is gone. No, if I'm to get into the apartment, it will have to be without anyone knowing. The key, I remember suddenly. There is an extra key to the Kommandant's apartment somewhere in his office. I've seen Diedrichson give it to one of the office messengers in order to drop things off during the day sometimes. If I can obtain the key, I can enter his apartment.

I get off the bus and begin walking up the road to Krysia's house, still devising my plan. I'll go to work early, take the key out before Malgorzata arrives and sneak over to the apartment during lunch. Diedrichson will be with the Kommandant in Warsaw, so he won't notice the key is missing. At the front gate, I pause, the weight of what I am about to do crashing down upon me. This is taking the mission to a whole new level, not just sneaking around the Kommandant's at night, but actually breaking and entering. If I am caught, or even seen…I shudder. There is no other choice.

The next morning I arrive at work at a quarter to eight. I have calculated my arrival exactly early enough to beat Malgorzata in, but not so far ahead of my usual schedule as to arouse suspicion with the guards at the gate. The corridors are largely empty, except for a few officers who seem not to notice me. I unlock the front door to our office, then the anteroom. I pause at my desk to put away my bag, picking up some papers so as to look like I have reason to be in the Kommandant's office in case Malgorzata arrives and sees me. I am hoping not to be in there that long. I race into the Kommandant's office and walk quickly to the desk. I pull open the top drawer, searching for the key among the well-ordered rows of pens and other office supplies. It's not here, I think, panicking. I reach deeper into the drawer. Suddenly, my fingers close around a small piece of cool metal. Sighing with relief, I pull out the key

There is a sudden creaking noise outside the office. I jump. Malgorzata, I think, recognizing her heavy, plodding footsteps in the anteroom. I shut the drawer quickly and tuck the key into the pile of papers just as the office door opens. "Oh, Anna, it's you," Malgorzata says, sounding disappointed.

"Who were you expecting?" She does not answer. "I thought I'd get an early start today with the Kommandant out of town," I continue, reciting the alibi I had rehearsed. "There's a lot of correspondence to be done and I need to run out for some errands at lunch."

"Oh, okay," she replies matter-of-factly. "Why don't you let me help?" She takes a step toward me and points to the stack of papers I am carrying.

"N-no, thank you," I stammer, drawing the papers closer to me. I envision her trying to take the papers from me, both of us watching as the key drops to the ground. "The Kommandant asked me to handle these letters personally." I watch her face fall at this lie. Immediately, I feel a stab of guilt. Malgorzata already knows that she is a distant second to me in the Kommandant's eyes, that she does not share in his confidence and trust. Reminding her of that fact is hurtful of me, but I have no choice. "It would be great if you could handle some of the filing, though, today," I offer quickly.

"Certainly." She smiles, her posture straightening. As she turns and leaves the office, I think, not for the first time, that she really just wants to feel useful.

At noon I take my bag and walk from the anteroom to reception. "I'm off for my errands," I say brightly.

Malgorzata nods. "I'll stay here and go to lunch when you return, in case the Kommandant or Colonel Diedrichson should phone from Warsaw."

"An excellent idea." I knew that Malgorzata was going to suggest this. Though no one had ever asked her, Malgorzata considered it her duty to make sure the phone was manned at all times when the Kommandant was out of town. I suspect that she secretly fantasizes about him calling on an urgent matter while I am away, and that it will be her shining moment, possibly leading to her replacing me. Her zeal, in this case, is actually helpful, since I know she will not be able to man the phones and follow me. "I'll be back soon."

Walking as quickly as I can without attracting attention, I walk from the castle to the market square, stopping at the fruit stand to buy oranges to make my errands look real. Then, checking carefully to make sure I haven't been followed, I circle back around to the Kommandant's apartment building and slip through the front door. Inside, the building is deserted. I climb the stairs quickly to the second floor. My hands shake so badly that I can barely manage to put the key in the lock. I pause. Breaking into the Kommandant's apartment is the most dangerous thing I have ever done. Perhaps this is the wrong key, I think hopefully, and I won't be able to get in. But the key turns smoothly in the lock. I turn the doorknob and slip inside.

I close the door behind me, my heart pounding. I scan the room and my eyes lock on the door that leads to the bedroom. I almost expect the door to open and for the Kommandant to stride into the living room, to have to explain what I am doing here. But the apartment remains silent. I eye the low table, covered with newspapers and dirty glasses. He needs a good housekeeper, I think, not for the first time. But I am sure he would not trust anyone to come in here. Perhaps I could help him by…I shake my head. There is no time for such ridiculous thoughts. It must be my nerves, I decide. Taking a deep breath, I make my way hurriedly to the study. I walk to the desk and pull on the drawer handle, but this time it refuses to open. It is locked, I realize. My stomach wrenches. Why would he lock it now? Perhaps this is a setup. I half expect the Gestapo to come bursting through the office door. *Get out,* a voice in my head says. *Give up now and leave, before it is too late.* Then I think of my parents in the ghetto on the far side of the river. I have to save them. This is the reason I have done what I have done, why I have defiled myself and made my marriage a farce. A wave of fatigue overwhelms me suddenly.

No, I must get into the drawer. But how? I consider breaking it open, but that is out of the question. Even if I were able to do it, the Kommandant would then surely know someone had been here. I look across the top of the desk for something with which I could pick the lock. Something shiny catches my eye. A paper clip. I pick up the metal clip and unbend it, then insert the end in the lock. It turns, but does not catch on anything. I try again. Nothing.

I am breathing heavily now and I can feel the perspiration running down my back. This is impossible. I should just leave, I think again. Then I shake my head. I can do this. I turn the paper clip in the lock once more. It catches on something and turns. Holding my breath, I pull on the drawer handle and it opens readily. I drop my hand to the bottom of the drawer underneath the stack of papers, wondering for a moment if I had imagined the panel. But the crack is still there. Easy, steady, I think as I push the papers aside and pry open the panel. I inhale sharply. As I had suspected, the drawer has a false bottom and in the compartment beneath there are papers with a letterhead I have never seen before. *Directorate of Special Operations,* the first sheet reads in German across the top. It is dated November 2nd, just a few days ago. I lift the papers from the drawer, scan them quickly. There are some technical words I cannot comprehend, but the word *Juden* is everywhere. I gasp. This is what Alek was looking for.

I continue reading, oblivious now to my situation and the need to get out of the apartment. The ghetto is to be liquidated, I make out, and the Jews removed. My stomach twists. The papers speak of a change in policy: unlike the Jews which have been taken from the ghetto thus far, those removed from now on will not be sent to the labor camp Plaszow, but directly to Auschwitz or Belzec. Ground has been broken for the new barracks needed to hold Jews at these camps, the report says, and the barracks will be ready by early January.

I stop reading and look up, my hands shaking. My parents are going to be sent to the camps. Don't think about it now, I tell myself, knowing that if I do I will not be able to function. I reread the text, trying to memorize the key portions to report to Alek. I quickly realize that there is too much detail for me to remember. There are dates and names of places and numbers that mean nothing to me but could be significant to the resistance. I hesitate. Originally, I had planned just to read the papers and report to Alek on what I had seen. That was all he asked me to do. But looking at the papers once more, I realize that this will not suffice. I am going to have to take them.

Or at least a copy. Holding up the papers, I see that they have been typed on carbon paper. I lick my thumb and work at the corner of the first page. The back sheet, a thin carbon copy, separates from the main page. I hesitate. Do I dare take it? The chances of the Kommandant noticing the carbon copy missing are slim, but if I am caught with such a document it would cost my life, not to mention putting those around me in grave danger. Still, the opportunity is too good to pass up. The actual document will be of much greater value to Alek than just my memorization of it. Gingerly, I separate the back copy from the front, then do the same with each of the remaining four pages. I return the original document to the secret compartment, then close the drawer. I look up at the clock on the wall. I have been gone from the office for nearly an hour. Malgorzata will be suspicious if I do not return soon. I fold the carbon copy twice quickly and put it inside the neckline of my blouse. Then I close the drawer. Taking a last look to make sure I have left the chair and desk exactly as I found them, I back out of the study and hurry through the living room. I did it, I think, a wave of relief washing over me as I exit the apartment and close the door behind me.

"*Dzien dobry,* Miss Anna," a male voice says from behind me. I freeze, a wave of dread washing over me. I have been caught. It is over. I turn slowly to face Stanislaw, the Kommandant's driver, holding a bag of groceries.

I try to breathe. "*Dzien dobry,* Stanislaw," I manage to say. "Didn't you drive…"

He shakes his head. "Because of the snow that is expected to the north, Herr Kommandant thought it best to take the train to Warsaw. He decided only this morning."

"Oh." I knew that Stanislaw sometimes came to the apartment on errands during the day when the Kommandant was at the office and did not need him to drive. But with the Kommandant traveling, it had not occurred to me that he might be here today. An awkward silence passes between us. "I—I was just dropping off some papers the Kommandant needs when he comes home tonight," I offer at last.

He nods. "Of course," he says evenly. His face is expressionless and I cannot tell if he believes me. Suddenly, his head stops mid-nod and his eyes freeze on my midsection. I look down. Sticking out of the top of my blouse are the carbon copies of the papers.

"Oh…" I raise my hand to my blouse. Stanislaw has seen the papers that I have taken from the Kommandant's apartment. Frantically, I try to think of an explanation. If only it were raining so I could say that I had been picking up papers for the office and did not want them to get wet. At last I give up. "I need these papers," I say helplessly. I can think of nothing else.

Stanislaw stares at me for several seconds, not speaking. I wonder if he is trying to decide what to do. Then a small smile appears on his lips. "Of course," he says again. He reaches over and tucks the edge of the papers back under the corner of my shirt so it is no longer visible. Then, without speaking further, he walks past me into the apartment with the groceries.

I stare after him, too surprised to move. He's letting me go, I realize with amazement. It had not occurred to me that the Kommandant's driver might have anti-Nazi sympathies. He is a Pole, I think, but still… Not daring to linger further, I check once more to make sure the papers are hidden, then turn and start quickly back to the office.

CHAPTER 17

That night after work I race back to Krysia's house. She sits on the parlor sofa, knitting, Lukasz sleeping soundly in her lap. "I need to see Alek right away," I say softly. I do not show Krysia the papers and she doesn't ask what I have found. It is better that she know as little as possible.

Krysia nods. "I will try to make contact first thing tomorrow."

The next morning after breakfast, she asks me to watch Lukasz. She returns several minutes later, wearing one of her Sunday dresses.

"You are going to church?" I ask, surprised.

"Sometimes I can make contact that way." After she leaves, I reflect on the irony of the Jewish resistance using church as a means of communication. I suppose it makes sense, I conclude. It is one of the few places in town that there are no Nazis.

Several hours later, Krysia returns home. Her face is grave. "They're gone," she says, breathing heavily as she walks into the kitchen and falls into a chair.

"Gone?" Frantic, I kneel in front of her. "What do you mean?"

"I went to church to meet my contact, but he did not appear at his usual time. I waited there as long as I could, but I didn't see him or any of the others. So I went to…to a secondary site where I know I can usually make contact." I notice for the first time that Krysia's fine leather boots are caked with mud and wonder where the secondary site might be. "I saw a friend who told me that there was a raid on resistance headquarters. No one was there at the time," she adds quickly, seeing my expression. "And no one was arrested. The Gestapo didn't find any papers or things of significance, either." I nod, relieved. Alek is much too careful for that, I think, remembering the night in the ghetto he gave me the note from Jacob, then insisted on burning it. Krysia continues, "But Alek has moved headquarters to an even more secret location and has ordered all communications to be temporarily suspended. The resistance has gone dark."

"Dark?"

"Yes," Krysia replies. "No contact in or out until they are sure that it's safe." She bends over and loosens the laces on her boots.

I try to process what Krysia has said. No more contact with Alek, or Marta, my only links to Jacob. "But I have critical information," I persist. "There has to be a way."

"I've tried every way I know to make contact. I'm afraid it's impossible." Krysia stands and starts from the kitchen, then stops and turns back toward me. There is a faraway expression in her eyes and I can see her mind working.

"What is it?"

She shakes her head. "Nothing. It's too dangerous."

"What is?" I stand and walk over to her. "Krysia, if you have an idea, tell me." I pick up her hand and squeeze it. "Please."

She hesitates. "It's probably nothing. But before the invasion and in the early days of the war, Alek and the others used to frequent a bar on Mikolajska Street called the Dark Horse." I nod. I have walked past the place a number of times but have never been inside. Krysia continues, "The owner, Francisek Koch, was somewhat sympathetic to their cause. I am wondering if he might know something. But I cannot go there. It would attract too much attention."

"True," I agree. For an old woman to go to church was one thing, but to walk into a bar full of young people was quite another. I, on the other hand, could go. I open my mouth to start to tell Krysia this, then close it again.

"What is it?" she asks, studying my face.

"Nothing," I reply. There is no point in telling her my idea; she would only forbid it. "I understand. It's too dangerous."

Krysia studies my face, unconvinced. "Why do I think that you will be going to the Dark Horse this evening?"

"I'm not…" I start, but she raises her hand.

"Never mind, don't bother denying it. I don't want you to lie to me and perhaps it's better if I don't know. I think it's too risky, but it's your decision." She presses her lips together, smiling slightly. "You've earned that right." She turns and walks slowly from the room, shoulders low.

That night after we've put Lukasz to bed, I make my way downstairs to the foyer. Krysia follows me, watching silently as I put on my coat. "I won't be late," I promise, tucking the papers inside my coat.

"Here." Krysia reaches in her pocket and pulls out several coins and bills. "Take these. Pan Koch may talk more easily if you leave a large tip with your drink."

I take the money reluctantly. "Thank you."

Outside it is bitterly cold for November and now snow has begun to fall. I start down the road toward the city. Ahead, I see a bus and hesitate. If any of our neighbors see me, they may question why I am going to the city at such an hour. But I do not have a lot of time and it will save me nearly an hour of walking. I run toward the bus and board it. It is nearly empty, but I sit toward the back, hunched over, my coat drawn high around my neck.

Fifteen minutes later, I get off the bus two stops before the market square. It is snowing more heavily now and the ground is slippery as I make my way to Mikolajska, a small, winding street not far from the market square. The Dark Horse is one of the many bars in Kraków that is located in a brick cellar underground. I stand at the top of the stairs, hesitating, listening to the music and voices coming from below. I have never been in this, or any other bar, in the city, except to retrieve my father from the small café in Kazimierz where he used to play bridge with some of the men from the neighborhood. Taking a deep breath, I walk down the stairs and through a heavy door at the bottom. Inside the bar, the air below is thick with the stench of cigarette smoke and beer. It is emptier than I expected from the noise outside. A few older men huddled in a far corner of the room look up and eye me curiously. I do not return their gazes, but move quickly to the bar. "A coffee, please," I say to the large, bearded bartender, climbing onto one of the stools. He looks to be about thirty and I wonder if he is old enough to be the owner.

He sets down the steaming drink. "Anything else I can get you?"

I take a deep breath. "Is Pan Koch here?"

He eyes me suspiciously. "Who wants to know?"

I hesitate. "My name is Anna Lipowski," I say softly. "I am the niece of Krysia Smok."

A flash of recognition crosses his face. He moves closer. "I'm Koch. What do you want?"

"I am looking for Alek and the others. The resistance."

His expression hardens and he takes a step back. "I'm sure I don't know what you're talking about."

"Please, it's very important that I find them." I reach in my pocket. "If it's a question of money—"

"Don't!" he snaps. Then he lowers his voice. "It isn't safe. Those men over there are informants. If they see or hear anything, we'll both wind up in prison."

I chill runs through me. "Krysia didn't tell me…"

"She didn't know." His eyes are dark. "Those cretins only began coming here a few weeks ago."

"So you do know Alek, then?"

"Not by name. I think I know the man you're talking about, though. Tall, light hair, goatee?" I nod. "He and some others used to come in here and sometimes meet in the subbasement. I haven't seen them in a long time. I heard maybe they gave up after the last arrests, fled into the woods and abroad."

My heart sinks. "Thank you." I start to stand up.

"Wait," he says. "Finish your coffee. Act normal. You don't want any of those men getting suspicious." I nod and sit back down again. Koch turns and walks to the far end of the bar where he begins drying glasses. I watch his back, processing what he has said. He doesn't know where Alek and the others are. Maybe they really have disappeared. That's ridiculous, I think. Jacob would never give up, never leave me. But doubts fill my mind, overflow. What if the cause takes him to another country? What if another girl really has stolen his heart? No. I stop myself. I cannot think these thoughts, not here. I have to concentrate on getting out and back to Krysia's safely.

I finish my coffee and put some coins on the bar. I consider leaving all of the money Krysia gave me for the tip, then decide against it; Pan Koch has told me all that he knows. He looks over and nods slightly as I stand up and head for the door. Upstairs, I pause in the doorway, wrapping my coat and scarf more tightly around me. I step out into the street. The snow is still falling heavily and the wind has picked up. It is the first real storm of the season. As I start walking toward the market square, I hear footsteps scurrying behind me. I freeze. One of the men from the bar must have followed me. Perhaps the informants overheard my conversation with Koch. There is no point in running, I decide, turning around. In front of me stands an older, bald man. "Excuse me," he says quickly, blinking behind his glasses. His voice is gruff. "I didn't mean to startle you."

"What is it that you want?" I ask.

"I could not help but overhear your conversation with Pan Koch." His breath is smoky in the cold night air.

I hesitate. Is he one of the informants Koch mentioned? I do not recognize him from inside the Dark Horse. "I—I was only…" I start to explain, but he raises his hand.

"Save your explanations. There is no time. Koch doesn't have what you are looking for, but I do. Follow me. Quickly."

He starts walking in the opposite direction down Mikolajska Street. I hesitate. It could be a ruse, a trap leading me right to the Gestapo. Trust him, a voice deep inside me says. I have no other choice. I set off after him down the street. He does not speak as we cross the southwest portion of the city. We are going toward the river, I realize a few minutes later. The buildings here are dilapidated, industrial. Then the road gives way to an uneven, snow-covered path that slopes down toward the water's edge. "Mind your step," he says as we make our way down it. At the end of the path, close to the river's edge, sits a lone shack, not visible from the main road. The man leads me to the front door. "Wait here," he orders, disappearing inside. I stand alone in the dark and cold staring back and forth between the river and the road.

A moment later the door reopens and the man grabs my arm. "Inside, quickly." He pulls me into the cottage and shuts the door behind me. I blink, trying to adjust my eyes to the dim lighting. It is a tiny room, freezing cold and unfurnished except for a table and lone chair. A tattered brown leather glove lies on the table.

"What are you doing here?" a familiar voice demands.

I spin around. "Marek," I gasp. He is barely recognizable in a thick coat and ski hat pulled low over his face.

He glares at me. "You should not have come here. It isn't safe."

"I need to talk to you. It's important." I hesitate, uncertain how much I can say in front of the stranger.

"Thank you, Avi," Marek says to the bald man.

"Thank you," I echo.

The man nods and walks out of the cottage. Marek goes to the window, then draws the tattered curtain back and peers outside. "Do you think we were followed?" I ask.

Marek shakes his head. "Avi is too good for that." He lets the curtain drop once more. "Now, what is it?"

I look around the small, dank room for any sign of the others. "Where's Alek?" I ask, my teeth chattering from the cold.

"He is not in the city. It is too dangerous for him right now. So what's the emergency?"

I hesitate. I had envisioned talking only to Alek. I know, though, that Marek is one of his closest allies. He can be trusted. "This." I hand him the paper.

He takes it from me, scans the first page. "My German is not good. Tell me what it says."

I take a deep breath. "It says that the Nazis are going to liquidate the ghetto and send the Jews either to Auschwitz or Belzec instead of to the Plaszow labor camp."

Marek appears unfazed. "Yes, this is nothing new. We have heard it before." I stare at him in surprise. The resistance has known about the liquidation all along. I realize once more how little I know about what they are doing, this group for whom I risk my life daily. He continues, "The question is when."

"January," I reply.

He does a double take. "What?"

"They are going to start moving the Jews when the new barracks are finished being built at Birkenau in early January."

A look of revelation flashes over his face. "January!" He grabs the papers from me.

"Yes. It's all in there." I cannot help feel a bit pleased with myself. "The memo is less than three weeks old."

"That is what we needed to know. It's much sooner than we thought." He folds the papers and tucks them into his coat. "I need to get this to Alek." He opens the door to the cottage and I follow him outside. Perhaps he will take me with him to the others, I think. Surely I have earned the right to go with him by finding this information. But he points to the path from which Avi and I had come. "If you go back that way, you can pick up the road to Krysia's," he says.

I open my mouth to speak. I want to ask him about the others, whether he has had any word from Jacob. How will I find him and the others if I need them? "You are not to come here again," he says, reading my mind. Then he turns and starts walking in the other direction. Watching his back as he strides off into the night, I realize that he had not even said thank you.

I look back at the cabin once more. Has it been a resistance hiding place for some time? Suddenly I remember the brown glove on the table. A flash of hope surges through me. Jacob had gloves like that. Perhaps he has been here recently… I shudder, thinking of him staying in the cold, unheated room. Anyway, if he had been this close by, surely he would have found a way to come and see me, wouldn't he?

Enough, I tell myself. I have done what I set out to do, delivered the papers. I have to get back home. It must be close to ten o'clock, the city curfew, and Krysia will be worried. I start up the riverbank, trying not to slip on the slick slope. I think of Marek. His expression was so strange when he received the information. He was almost smiling. Then I remember the conversation I overheard at the apartment on Josefinska Street after my last Shabbes dinner in the ghetto. Marek is one of the more hawkish leaders of the resistance, he wants to strike the Nazis hard and often. This information about the ghetto liquidation probably supports his position. Now they will try to do something, I realize, my stomach twisting hard. Suddenly, I am seized with the uneasy feeling that even as I had provided information helpful to the resistance, I may have also placed Jacob in grave danger.

At the top of the hill, I pause, surveying the deserted street. I set off quickly across the city center in the direction of Krysia's house. A siren wails in the distance, signaling curfew. I quicken my pace, the soles of my shoes resonating against the slick, wet pavement. Mind your step, I think, as my toes begin to slide outward.

I press on, my chin buried deep against the wind. As I round the corner onto Starowislna Street, I run smack into a wall. My feet slide forward and to the side, and I land rather ungracefully on my backside in a dirty snowdrift.

Looking up, I realize quickly that it is not a wall I've hit, but a man coming from the other direction. I scramble to stand up, but before I can regain my composure, he slides his hands under my arms and lifts me to my feet. I am too surprised to resist. As I blink the snow from my eyes, I feel the stranger's hand press down on my brow from behind, like a mother checking her child for a fever. His coat gives off a spicy smell that was somehow familiar.

"*Dzienkuje…*" Now able to see again, I turn to thank the stranger, but he has already continued onward, the back of his dark overcoat receding well down the street.

Strange, I think, peering back around the corner from where I had come. The street is empty. But there is no time to stand and wonder. Brushing the remaining snow off my coat, I continue onward.

Suddenly, a loud wailing siren cuts through the silence. About fifty feet ahead at the intersection, a Gestapo car comes to a stop.

I leap back around the corner, pressing flat against the brick wall and willing myself invisible. In the distance, I hear car doors slamming, then the thud of heavy boots against the pavement. The glow from a flashlight licks the wall of bricks beside me. My heart pounds and sweat pours from my brow.

The Nazis stand in silence, searching and listening for what feels like an eternity. At last one says something in a low voice and I hear them climb back into the car. The engine starts and I cringe, waiting for the car to pass by and reveal in its headlights a pathetic, snow-covered young woman trying vainly to disappear into a brick wall. I hold my breath and count: one-one thousand, two-one thousand...

The tires screech, as the car reverses and drives off in the other direction.

As the sound of the engine fades, I collapse against the wall, shaking. If that man hadn't knocked me down, surely I would have run right into the Gestapo. If I had been caught violating the curfew, I could have been arrested or worse. I inhale deeply, thanking my good fortune for the stranger as I start walking again.

The dampness from the snowdrift has begun to soak through my clothing. I remove my wet gloves and place my hands in my coat pockets. Deep in the right pocket, my fingertips brush against something unfamiliar and hard. My hand closes around it and I stop again. I draw forth a smooth brown stone that had not been there an hour earlier.

A small yelp escapes my lips. It is a piece of amber! I knew then that the collision hadn't been an accident and the man hadn't been a stranger. It was Jacob who had bumped into me. He had left the stone for me as a sign that it was him. My stomach leaps. Now I know that Jacob isn't far away, saving the world with some other girl. He is close by, looking out for me. By bumping into me and knocking me over, he had stopped me from running into the Nazis. He was loving me from afar, the only way he could.

Suddenly I feel warm, the air around me gone electric. At this moment, nothing else matters—Jacob is alive, and he still loves me. I place my hand back in my pocket, the cool stone gripped tightly within, and race swiftly toward home.

CHAPTER 18

The brown stain on Lukasz's bowl refuses to budge. I dip it once more in the warm, soapy water and rub at it harder with a cloth. If it was any other dish, I would leave it to soak overnight, but this is the bowl with the rabbits on it, the only one Lukasz seems to like. The prospect of seeing the picture on the bottom provides motivation for him to finish his breakfast cereal. Without it he sometimes refuses to eat. It has to be clean and dry by morning.

I set the bowl in the water once more and lean against the countertop. It is nearly ten o'clock on Friday night. Lukasz has long since been put to bed and Krysia, usually so helpful around the house, begged off to bed with a headache, leaving me to clean up. I don't mind; it's easier to stay up knowing that I do not have to rise at dawn for work the next morning, and the evening hours provide rare quiet time. Still, the stress

of my situation, of keeping up pretenses, is wearing on me—
I am simply exhausted.

It has been more than two weeks since I gave the papers to
Marek. I have heard nothing further from the resistance. I
reach into my pocket to touch the amber stone I found there
the night I went to the cabin. A few times since then, I have
had the sense that I was being watched while walking down
the street. I spin around quickly each time, hoping to catch
some glimpse of Jacob, some sign that he is near. But I have
seen nothing and I wonder if I am imagining things.

If only I had some more information for the resistance,
some excuse to go to the cabin again, I think wistfully. I continue to go to the Kommandant's apartment when he calls for
me and to search for documents when he is asleep, but I have
found nothing new. In recent days, I have had fewer chances
to look because I have seen the Kommandant less often. The
war is not going as well for the Germans, I know, not only from
the official telegrams that cross my desk but also from the
hushed whispers and dour faces of the Nazi officers in the corridors of Wawel. As a result, the Kommandant has been working longer hours and frequently has meetings that last well into
the night. The few times we have spent the night together, he
has slept little, rising before dawn. I hear him pacing the floors
and poring feverishly over papers in his study as I lay awake
in his bed. Even when he does sleep, he is restless, and I do
not dare to try to look for papers for fear he will awaken.

With each passing day that I have been unable to search,
my frustration has grown. Perhaps I should try to contact
Alek and talk to him about terminating the assignment, I
think as I stand before the kitchen sink. There is little point

in continuing this game if it produces nothing further. Still, I have not contacted Alek to make such a suggestion. I try to tell myself that it is necessary to continue in case I can learn something new. In truth, I am not sure that I want my visits with the Kommandant to end. I look forward to our dates and his warmth has become comforting to me. I have stopped telling myself that my attraction to him is purely physical. The truth is, I also enjoy his company, a fact that has become more apparent since our nights together have become less frequent.

Anyway, even if I wanted to get out, how could the situation possibly end? One does not simply "break up" with a high- ranking Nazi official, especially not the Kommandant, and I can tell from the loving way he looks at me that he does not envision our relationship ending. We have agreed that it must be kept secret for the present time, since it would not do for him to be seen cavorting with his assistant, and such information would only be ammunition for his enemies. But in private, he has often spoken of a future together. "After the war we will be married," he has promised more than once, "and you will come back to Germany, you and Krysia and your brother, and live with me on our estate in Hamburg."

I do not respond when he speaks of marriage, but inwardly, I cringe. Any other young woman who was involved with her boss would likely find great comfort in promise of marriage. But I am already married and find such notions ludicrous, if not terrifying. How would I escape the Kommandant and return to Jacob in the end? If the Germans were defeated, it would not be a problem. But if the Nazis won…well, I cannot allow myself to think of such a scenario.

The windowpanes rattle noisily. It is early December and

bitterly cold. We have managed to keep Krysia's house warm with the firewood and coal we stockpiled last autumn. But I worry constantly about Jacob and my parents, who surely cannot have such comfort. I miss them more now than ever. Hanukkah starts tomorrow night, I know, by the Hebrew calendar that my childhood had permanently installed in my head. If only we could all be together to celebrate the holiday. Earlier that evening, I looked at Lukasz as he played with his blocks on the floor, thinking how he does not even know about Hanukkah. I longed to take him in my lap and tell him the story of the brave fighters that had saved the temple, and the miracle of the light that had burned for eight nights, as his father surely would have done. But even though I feel as though I am failing Lukasz by not carrying on the traditions of our religion, I do not dare. He is three and a half years old now, by our estimate, and becoming more talkative by the day. If he were to repeat the Hanukkah story to a neighbor, we would all be in danger. For the same reason, we will not give him Hanukkah gelt, the coins or small presents I had received on the holiday as a child. Nor will I fashion a dreidel, a small wooden top, and teach him to play Hanukkah games. Instead, Lukasz will get presents a few weeks later at Christmas, the holiday we pretend to celebrate in order to keep up appearances. But tonight, Krysia, in a wordless concession to our faith, made latkes, the fried potato pancakes with sweet applesauce and sour cream that are traditionally eaten on the Jewish holiday. The taste brought visions of my mother and tears to my eyes. I vowed that someday I would tell Lukasz all of this, why we had eaten the pancakes and who our own brave fighters had been.

In the hallway, the floor creaks. It must be Krysia going to the water closet, I think as I drain the dishwater and wipe off Lukasz's now clean bowl. I press my hands on a dry towel. Suddenly, I hear footsteps behind me in the kitchen doorway, heavier than those of any woman. Someone is in the house. I freeze at the sink, my hand wrapped around the handle of a frying pan that rests in the dish rack. I lift my arm, but before I can turn to wield the pan at the intruder, he presses up behind me and grips both of my forearms.

"*Shabbat shalom,* Miss Emma."

My heart leaps. "Jacob!" I cry, dropping the frying pan into the sink. I spin around. Standing there in the kitchen is my husband. For a second, I wonder if it is a dream. I throw my arms around him, expecting to close around empty air, but he is there, real and solid and safe. "Oh, Jacob!" I cry as his arms close around me. I cling to him as hard as I can, kissing him over and over again on his forehead and cheeks.

A moment later, he pulls back slightly and we look at each other, not speaking. My mind races. Jacob is here. He has come to me. I have dreamed of this moment so many times that it is hard to believe it is real. "Emma," he says, taking my face in his hands and bringing his lips to mine.

"I can't believe you're here," I say when at last we break. I study his face. It is thicker and tanner now, almost like a boy who has passed through adolescence to manhood, though of course that had happened years ago. I touch his cheek, which is ruddy and weathered from the outdoors. "It's been so long."

"I know. I'm sorry…" he begins, but I bring my finger to his lips.

"Don't," I say, shaking my head. "It's okay. As long as I know that you're all right."

"I am now that I'm here with you," he replies solemnly. "But…"

"Shh," I whisper, pressing my lips to his. Wordlessly, I lead him up the stairs to my bedroom. Closing the door behind us, I kiss him again. Our lips do not part as I take off his tattered coat and shirt and pull him down onto the bed. Our bodies fit together as though the past year had been an awful dream and we had never been apart.

"I should have offered you something to drink," I say sometime later when we lay spent on the bed.

Jacob shakes his head. "I'm not thirsty," he replies, reaching for me again. For a moment, I hesitate. In the heat of our initial lovemaking, I had forgotten about the Kommandant and all that has transpired since I last saw Jacob. Now I remember my betrayal and my shame crashes over me in waves. As Jacob moves above me, his torso pale and thin, an image of the Kommandant, large and muscular, flashes through my mind. No, I think, trying to block out the image. Not here, in this precious moment with my husband.

Closing my eyes, I force myself to concentrate on Jacob's movements, his touch. But as my passion rises, the Kommandant's face appears in my mind once more. Suddenly a horrible thought races through my mind: what if Jacob notices? For some time now, I have realized that I am different in bed with the Kommandant than with Jacob. My rhythms have changed in response to the Kommandant's and I find myself moving with more confidence and strength. Panicked now, I wonder if I am behaving as I should with Jacob. I try to remember how I acted when we used to be together, before he went away.

Jacob cries out above me, jarring me from my thoughts. I open my eyes as he collapses beside me, lost in his own passion. A wave of relief crashes over me. He has not noticed anything different.

"Mmm," he mumbles, his arms circled around me tightly, eyes closed. His breath grows long and even. I do not sleep, but lay on my side, eyes open, drinking in his presence. There is so much I had forgotten: his warmth, his breath, how our bodies fit together like puzzle pieces. We had both traveled great distances since our last meeting, me through the ghetto and my work at Wawel, Jacob through God only knew what.

A few hours later he wakes, and for the rest of the night we lay together, talking endlessly as we had when we were newlyweds. He tells me that he has been in the forest, and traveling between Warsaw, Lodz, Lublin and other major Polish cities, trying to coordinate the efforts of various resistance groups. "There are non-Jewish resistance groups, too," he says, "but efforts to coordinate between the Poles and the Jews have largely been unsuccessful. That's enough about my work for now, though." He strokes my hair. "Tell me what happened after I left you."

I hesitate, uncertain how much to tell. "Well, I tried to go back to my parents like you said," I begin slowly, my head resting on his chest. Being guarded with Jacob is an unfamiliar sensation. "But they were gone."

"And then you were in the ghetto." I can tell from the sound of his voice that he knows what we went through there, and that my suffering caused him pain.

"It was not so bad when I was there," I lie. "Alek and the others were wonderful to me."

"I heard you met Marta." I can hear him smile in the darkness and a flash of jealousy passes through me.

"Yes." I pause uneasily. Though Marta was my friend, I do not want her presence in the bedroom with us.

"She's quite a girl."

I am glad to hear him speak of her as a child. "There were many friends in the ghetto," I say.

Jacob presses his lips to my forehead. "Still, I know it could not have been easy."

"My parents…"

"I understand they are still there. We have tried, but it is so hard to get the older ones out."

I consider asking him if there is some way to help them, but he sounds like Alek, and I know that talking about it further is pointless. "I've heard of people escaping over the border to Czechoslovakia," I say instead.

"It's risky. The mountain passage is difficult and it is just as risky once you are there. The Slovaks can be so brutal to the Jews as to make the Poles look kind."

"The Poles are kind," I respond quickly. "Look at Krysia."

"Some are kind like Krysia, some are indifferent, others are as bad as Nazis. Most are only doing what they have to in order to survive."

"I suppose." Even after all we have been through, I have trouble accepting that the non-Jews I had known all my life had turned on us so willingly.

We fall back to sleep, waking late the next morning and making love again before rising. Krysia has left a note saying that she and Lukasz have gone into town to market. She has also left a fixed lunch for two. "So Krysia knew you were coming?" I ask, placing the bread, fruit and hard cheese onto plates.

Jacob rummages through Krysia's cabinets to find two glasses and fill them with water. "She knew there was a chance I was coming."

We carry the food into the parlor and settle on the floor in front of the fireplace. "How long do you have?" I ask, cutting a slice of apple and feeding it to him.

"I have to leave as soon as the sun goes down," he replies between bites. I silently curse the fact that the days are short and it will be dark by late afternoon.

We eat in silence for several minutes. My mind races with the many questions that I want to ask him. "Jacob…" I say at last. I hesitate, setting down the knife. "How is it that you are here?"

He stops eating and looks at me. "What do you mean?"

I take a sip of water, swallow. "I mean that for over a year, it has been too dangerous for you to come to me. In the ghetto, even here, you haven't been able to do it. But now?"

"I have been traveling between the other cities, mostly," he replies. "I came back to Kraków only recently."

"So a few weeks ago, on Starowislna Street, the amber stone…that was you, wasn't it?"

He nods. "I had been at the cabin with Marek just before you arrived. I didn't dare come out with Avi there, but I followed you when you left to make sure you were okay."

"And when you saw the Gestapo car coming, you knocked me down to keep me from rounding the corner and being caught?" He nods. "Thank you for that," I say. "But even then, you left me a stone, rather than actually letting me see you."

"It was too dangerous," he says.

"But now you are here," I persist. "So my question is, what's changed?"

"Nothing. It's still dangerous. But I came now because things..." He looks away from my gaze. "Things may change soon..."

"What do you mean? No..." I say, answering my own question as the realization slowly comes to me. Ever since I gave the information to Marek about the Nazis' plans for the Jews, I have sensed that Alek and the others were planning some kind of major action against the Nazis. I haven't known when or what, but my instincts have told me it is serious. Jacob has come now, I realize, because of this. Whatever they are planning, he is worried that he might not see me again. "No!" I cry again, flinging my plate aside and throwing myself into his arms.

"Shhh," he soothes, holding me tightly and stroking my hair. Several minutes later, my sobs subside. "Emma..." He sits me up and spins me around onto his lap, rocking me like a child. "Hanukkah starts tonight. Do you remember the story of the Maccabees?" I nod. "What do the four letters on the dreidel stand for?"

"Nes gadol vaya sham," I recite in Hebrew.

"Right, and what does that mean?"

"A great miracle happened there."

"Exactly! A great miracle happened in Israel when the Maccabees restored the temple and the tiny drop of oil burned for eight nights. A great miracle. This is the season for miracles. It will happen for us here, too. It has to." I look up then. His eyes are illuminated, as though a fire burns behind them. It is the look I fell in love with when we first met, only now it burns a thousand times brighter. For the first time, I understand: Jacob believes. He believes in Alek and the resistance, believes that this is the only way to deliver not just the Jews, but all of Poland, from the Nazis. The struggle has made him a warrior.

"You are so brave," I say, wiping my eyes.

"We are Maccabees, Emma. You and me and Alek and Marta and the rest." I start to protest, embarrassed even to be mentioned in the same breath as the others, but he continues. "Yes, you are brave, too. I know all about how you have helped the resistance by working for Richwalder." I cringe; he did not, could not, know everything. Jacob continues, "And how you have saved and hidden the rabbi's child. You, too, are a fighter."

"And Krysia, too," I add.

"Especially Krysia." As if on cue, I hear the front door open downstairs. Lukasz is babbling to Krysia as they climb the stairs. I gather from his words that, despite the cold, they had stopped by the duck pond on the way home. Jacob releases me and we stand up.

At the top of the stairs, Krysia freezes. At the sight of Jacob, her eyes grow moist. Then she looks down at Lukasz, hesitating. "Lukasz, this is my cousin, Michal." Lukasz, red-faced from the cold, stares up at Jacob with large eyes as Jacob goes to Krysia and kisses her cheeks three times. Both Krysia and Jacob fight to exercise restraint in their reunion and not become overly emotional in front of the child.

"Hello, Lukasz." Jacob kneels and chucks the child's chin playfully, but in his eyes I can see reverence—he knows who the child is and how he has come to be with us.

"You knew?" I say to Krysia over their heads.

She nods. "I didn't want to disappoint you in case it didn't happen."

"I understand." I look down. Jacob is speaking to Lukasz—in Hebrew. I remember suddenly Lukasz trying to speak Hebrew in front of the Kommandant. "Don't!" I exclaim. The three of them turn to stare at me. I, too, am surprised by the sharpness of my voice. "I'm sorry, Jac—Michal," I stammer, correcting myself. "It's just that…" I hesitate. I cannot explain my concern to Jacob, not without telling him that the Kommandant was here. Suddenly, a wave of fatigue washes over me. It is too much. For months, I have strained to keep the truth about my identity from the Kommandant, all the while dreaming of seeing Jacob. I hadn't focused on the fact that when I saw my husband again, I would have to lie to him as well.

Jacob stands and comes to me. "It's okay," he says, bringing his hand to the back of my neck and drawing me in close to his chest. "I understand." We should not be this affectionate in front of the child, I know, but in this moment, I do not care. Enveloped in the safety and warmth of his arms once more, I am gripped by a sudden urge to come clean about the Kommandant, tell him everything. He would forgive me, Krysia said once. He would understand. Out of the corner of my eye, I catch Krysia staring at me, her eyes burning. She knows exactly what I am thinking. Do not tell him, her stare implores. Do not crush him with the knowledge of your unfaithfulness to unburden yourself. Not now, while he has to go back into the darkness and cold to fight.

She's right, of course. There may be time for confessions and forgiveness in the future, but today is not that day. I straighten, pulling away from Jacob. "Lukasz, come, you are filthy from the woods," I say. "You need a bath." Reluctantly, Lukasz allows himself to be torn away from the stranger. I hate to leave Jacob for even a moment of his precious visit, but Krysia and he were kin long before I had come along. They would want to talk privately, and I wanted to afford Krysia the same courtesy she has given me. Jacob winks at me over Krysia's shoulder as I lead Lukasz upstairs.

As I run the bathwater, my mind reels. Jacob is here. The reality has not entirely sunk in, nor has the fact that in just a little while, he will be gone again. When I turn off the water and soap Lukasz's blond curls, I can hear Jacob and Krysia speaking in low, urgent voices below. Krysia clearly has some idea of what the resistance is planning, and I can tell from the terse sound of her voice that she is not in favor of it. I strain to hear more, too worried to feel guilty about eavesdropping, but I can make out nothing further.

When I have dried Lukasz and set him down for his nap, I return to the parlor. Krysia and Jacob break midsentence when I enter, and I wonder what is so secret and terrible that I cannot be allowed to hear. I, too, undertake important work for the resistance movement, yet I sometimes feel like an outsider.

My resentment is cut short when I look out the window. It is only three-thirty in the afternoon, but the sky is already turning dusky. Krysia follows my gaze and realizes the time. "I think I shall go have a bath, too," she says abruptly. "I've packed a basket for you, Jacob. Food and some warm clothes. It's on the table." With Lukasz out of the room, there is no need for restraint. She throws her arms around his neck. "Good luck, my darling. God be with you." As she pulls away and hurries from the room, his cheek glistens with the wetness of her tears.

Jacob and I stand in the center of the room as awkwardly as we had when we first met. "Having you here has been wonderful for her," he says.

"I'm glad to hear it. I worry that we've been a burden."

"Not at all." We stand facing each other in silence. I blink several times, determined not to cry in front of him. He wraps both arms around me, his chin pressing into the top of my head. "I will come for you, Emma. No matter what happens. We'll be together soon."

"I am with you always," I reply. He nods, then kisses me hard. When his lips leave mine, I keep my eyes squeezed shut, trying to hold the moment forever. But when I open my eyes, he is already halfway down the stairs, his boots thudding heavily below. I hear the door open, then shut with a soft click. I race to the front window and look down the street but there is no trace of him.

I return again to the spot where we last embraced, inhaling deeply, hoping to capture whatever scent he has left behind. The air around me has grown cold. For a few hours, I had been Emma again. Now Jacob is gone and I am just Anna, the Kommandant's girl.

Several minutes later, Krysia descends the stairs in a robe, her hair damp. She comes to the spot where I still stand motionless. "He is gone?"

Before I can answer, there is a knock on the door. "Jacob!" I exclaim, racing for the stairs. Perhaps he forgot something, or even decided that he would not leave tonight.

"Emma, wait!" Krysia calls after me. "Jacob wouldn't…"

But it is too late; I am already down the stairs and crossing the foyer. I grab the handle and throw open the door. "I thought you…" I freeze midsentence. There, standing in the doorway, are two Gestapo police officers.

CHAPTER 19

I stare at the Gestapo officers, unable to speak. Panic cuts through me. Did they see Jacob? He could not have gotten that far away. Perhaps that is why they are here. I take a breath. "G-good evening," I manage to say over the rock that has formed in my throat.

"Were you expecting someone?" the older of the two men asks.

I hesitate, searching for a response. "Our gardener, Ryszard, was supposed to be dropping off some supplies," Krysia says from behind me. She has come halfway down the stairs, still in her nightgown and robe. She steps past me, opening the door wider and extending her hand. "I am Krysia Smok."

The older man, who is thin and tall with glasses, takes her hand. "I am Lieutenant Hoffman and this is Sergeant Braun." He gestures to the younger man, who is short, with a thick build.

Krysia shakes his hand then turns to Sergeant Braun, who

merely nods. "Won't you gentlemen come in?" She sounds calm and polite, as if she is inviting one of her society friends for tea. Shutting the door behind them, I shoot Krysia a puzzled look. "Come upstairs," she says. "It's much warmer there." I suddenly realize that Krysia wants to get the policemen inside and off the street so they would not spot Jacob. She should be the one working for the Nazis under an assumed identity, I think, as I follow her and the men upstairs; she is a much better actress.

Krysia invites the men into the parlor. "Make tea, will you, dear?" she asks me. I hesitate, not wanting to leave her alone with them, but her voice is calm and firm. In the kitchen, I fill the kettle, my mind racing. Why have the Gestapo come now? What do they want? A few minutes later, I carry the tea tray to the parlor, forcing my hands not to shake. I set down the tray on the low table by the sofa. As I pour, I study the policemen furtively. Lieutenant Hoffman is standing by the fireplace, scrutinizing the photograph of Marcin on the mantel. I remember the night I arrived at Krysia's, my sadness at her insistence that we hide the photographs of Jacob. Now I am grateful for her foresight. My eyes dart around the room, searching for some sign of Jacob's visit just minutes earlier, but there is none. Sergeant Braun is staring out the window into the trees of Las Wolski. I shoot Krysia a nervous look. Is it possible that he could see Jacob fleeing in the darkness? "Gentlemen, please, come have some tea," she urges. Slowly, almost reluctantly, the men come and sit in the chairs across from us. "You'll have to forgive our using the everyday dishes," Krysia says, handing each man a cup of tea. "And my not being properly dressed to receive you. You see, we aren't used to having such distinguished guests arrive unannounced." She stresses the last word, subtly rebuking the Gestapo for their intrusion.

"We apologize for the inconvenience," says Hoffman, sounding like a chastised schoolboy. "It's just that we—"

"Nonsense!" Braun interjects with a blustering tone that reminds me of General Ludwig, our obnoxious dinner party guest on the night I met the Kommandant. "The Gestapo is not in the habit of scheduling appointments, madam."

"Of course," Krysia replies evenly. She is speaking slowly, stalling for time. "Our home is always open to you. What brings you out on this cold evening? How can we help?"

Hoffman speaks. "We've had reports of fugitives in this area." I know he means resistance fighters, though of course the Nazis will not call them by that name. "Operating out of the forest in the hills."

"Las Wolski?" Krysia asks. Her voice is filled with surprise that nearly convinces me.

He nods. "Have you seen anything?"

"Nothing," she replies with conviction. "Of course, we don't go walking in the woods this time of year."

"Of course," Braun replies. There is a hint of sarcasm in his tone. He faces Krysia squarely. "Have you heard from your nephew lately?"

I inhale sharply, stunned by the question. There is a moment of complete silence and I hope the policemen have not noticed my reaction. "I have several nephews, sir," Krysia replies, a slight tremor in her voice. "To which one are you referring?"

"Your nephew on your husband's side. You have only one: Jacob Bau." My blood runs cold. They know about Jacob.

"Oh, you mean Marcin's nephew, Jacob." Krysia pronounces my husband's name as though she has not heard it in years.

"Yes." Braun's voice is impatient.

"Has he done something?" she asks.

Braun hesitates. He is surprised, I think, by the boldness of her question. "He was a troublemaker before the war, publishing lies about the Reich. And he hasn't been seen since it started. We'd like to speak with him."

"That boy always was getting into scrapes," Krysia replies, trying to sound light.

"These are not 'scrapes,'" Braun replies with a scowl. "We're talking about treason."

"Yes, of course." Krysia's expression turns serious, as though she has only just grasped the gravity of the situation. "I understand. But I haven't seen Jacob in years. Not since before the war. Even then I only ran into him a few times in the city." I am amazed at how Krysia manages to lie so easily. "I haven't had much to do with that side of the family since Marcin died, you know." Her voice is even, her tone conversational. "And I don't get a lot of visitors since I moved out here." She directs her last remark at Hoffman.

"I find that surprising, Pani Smok," the older man replies quickly. "You are a gracious host, even to unexpected guests. And you have a beautiful home."

Krysia dips her head slightly to the left, sweeping her hair from her eyes. "You are too kind, sir." She is flirting, I realize, to buy time and throw the Gestapo off Jacob's trail. It seems to be working with Hoffman.

The younger man, however, is having none of it. "I noticed a cabin in the back garden," Braun interjects. "What's in there?"

Krysia turns to him. "Nothing," she replies quickly. "It's been empty for as long as I can remember."

Braun studies Krysia's face. "You won't mind if we take a look there, then?"

Krysia hesitates. Out of the corner of my eye, I see the quickest flash of panic. I can read the dilemma in her mind. Did Jacob leave? she is wondering, or is he hiding? "The lock is rather old and I'm afraid I don't have a key," she says at last, meeting the younger officer's eyes.

"If the lock is as old as you say, it should break easily," he counters. It is clear he is not going to back down.

I can see a thin line of perspiration forming on Krysia's upper lip. "Very well," she replies at last. "Give me just a moment to get dressed and I'll escort you."

Krysia walks from the parlor and up the stairs slowly, stalling as long as she can. I sit motionless, terrified of the questions the men may ask me. But they do not speak. Instead, they walk around the room once more, lifting and inspecting photographs and other items. Braun walks to the piano and fingers the keys in an awkward manner that tells me he has never played. Sitting helplessly as they rummage through our lives, I feel more violated than I ever have with the Kommandant.

The Kommandant. For a moment, I consider mentioning that I work for him; perhaps the mention of such a high-ranking official would persuade them to leave us alone. But if the officers decide to verify my story with him, they might explain why they came calling at Krysia's house in the first place, which would highlight my connection to Jacob. I cannot risk it.

A few minutes later, Krysia reappears in the dress she had been wearing earlier when Jacob was here. As she passes me,

I can smell the faintest hint of his scent, which still clings to her clothing. Run far, Jacob, I pray. Be safe. "Ready?" she asks the officers brightly, as though we were going on a picnic. We make our way down the stairs and Krysia opens the front door. Before we can step through, however, another uniformed man appears in the doorway.

"You were told to stay in the car," Braun admonishes.

"It's okay," Hoffman interjects. "What is it, Klopp?"

"We've been radioed by headquarters, sir. An urgent matter requires our return."

Braun hesitates, looking in the direction of the cabin in the backyard. "This should take just a minute—"

"I'm sorry, sir, but the message said we're to return at once."

Hoffman turns to Krysia. "It appears your cottage door is to be spared tonight. Thank you for your cooperation." The men disappear into the night.

Krysia locks the door behind them. Outside a car engine starts, then grows faint in the distance. I exhale sharply. "That was close."

Krysia does not answer but sinks to the bottom step, clutching her hands to her chest. Her face has gone gray. I kneel beside her. "Krysia, what is it? Are you okay?"

"Yes," she manages, her voice barely a whisper. Krysia is normally so strong and capable, I forget that she is nearly seventy. I wonder if the strain of the Gestapo coming here has been too much.

"Let's go upstairs." I put my arm around her and gently help her to her feet. Together, we make our way up the stairs into the kitchen and I guide her into a chair. From the upper floor, I can hear Lukasz crying. "Wait here," I tell Krysia.

Upstairs, I find Lukasz standing in his crib, his face red and wet. I lift him up and draw him close. "Good boy," I whisper, grateful that he had not cried earlier.

I carry him downstairs to Krysia, who sits where I left her, not moving. "Here." I place Lukasz in her lap. She clutches him tightly and rocks back and forth. "I'll make some tea."

Krysia shakes her head. "No tea," she says, still rocking. "Vodka." I remember the bottle I have seen stored in the back of the ice box. I pull out the bottle and pour some in two glasses, over ice. Then, I pour a small cup of milk for Lukasz. I rejoin Krysia at the table with the drinks. As Krysia reaches for her glass, Lukasz wriggles free of her arms and scampers to the floor, taking the cup of milk from me.

"Feeling better?" I ask Krysia, studying her face. Some of the color seems to have returned to her cheeks.

"Yes. I'm sorry about that," she replies. "Sometimes I just get some…some tightness in my chest when things are tense."

A wave of panic rises within me. "Krysia, that could be your heart. You need to see a doctor."

She shakes her head. "What would a doctor do for me, even if we could find one? No, I'll be fine."

I start to argue but know that it is futile. "Well, at least that's over with."

"For now, anyway," she replies tersely. "I have a feeling that they'll be back."

"We were lucky that they got called back to headquarters."

Krysia looks at me, a small smile playing at the corner of her lips. "What makes you think that luck had anything to do with it?"

I realize then that Krysia had not just been stalling upstairs.

I remember a radio that I saw once, tucked in the back corner of her closet. "What did you…? How did you…?"

"Let's just say that the men were likely to find the call back to headquarters had been some sort of misunderstanding."

My mind reels. I cannot imagine the connections Krysia must have to be able to fabricate such a call. I want to ask more, but the less I know, the better. "Were you worried that Jacob might be hiding in the shed?"

She shakes her head. "Not at all. Jacob, I knew, was long since gone. But there are things…well, let's just say that I need to get ahold of the resistance right away. That shed needs to be empty when the Gestapo returns."

"You seem certain that they will."

"Definitely. I think I had Hoffman fooled—"

I interrupt, "Yes, you flirted very convincingly."

She manages a laugh. "I thought I might have gotten rusty, but I suppose it's one of those things you never forget. Anyway, Hoffman may have been distracted, but Braun was still suspicious. And he's tenacious, like a pit bull." I nod, knowing the type. "At least Lukasz stayed upstairs quietly." At the sound of his name, the child looks up and smiles. "We may not be so lucky next time."

I slump backward, the full reality of what has happened crashing down upon me. The Gestapo has been here looking for Jacob. We are lucky not to be in a prison right now. Stay calm, I tell myself. It is your turn to be strong for Krysia. I take a small sip of the vodka, trying not to grimace. "I considered telling them I worked for the Kommandant so they would leave us alone."

"It's better that you did not," Krysia agrees. "We don't want them drawing to the Kommandant's attention any connection between you and Jacob, even if it is just that you are both somehow related to me."

"I thought the same thing."

She pauses and takes a large sip of vodka. "I'm not sure what we should do about the child."

"Do?" I ask, alarmed. "What do you mean?"

"If the Gestapo comes back and sees Lukasz, they are going to have questions."

"But we were able to keep him quiet tonight…."

"Anna, it's not that simple. Do you think it was a coincidence that the Gestapo came here asking about Jacob just moments after he left? No," she says, answering her own question. "I think someone told them that he was here."

I gasp. "An informant?"

"Yes. Perhaps one of my neighbors with Nazi sympathies who saw him arrive, perhaps a traitor within the resistance. I've been worried about this ever since we heard about the earlier leaks. There may be someone who knows, or suspects, that you and Lukasz are not who you appear to be. It may not be safe for him to stay with us much longer."

"No!" I cry, picking up the child. "He's only just gotten used to us. We can't uproot him again."

"We may have no choice, Anna. Our first priority has got to be his safety, keeping him alive."

I stand up, still holding Lukasz. "But…"

"I know you've gotten attached to him. We both have. But he's not our child. He may not be with us forever. You understand that, don't you?" I do not answer, but bury my head in Lukasz's curls.

"Where would he go?" I ask at last.

Krysia pauses. "I don't know," she concedes. "I can't imagine there is anywhere safer for him right now. So I will hold off on saying anything to the resistance about it. But you need to accept that it may happen."

"Maybe I could…" I start to suggest that I could speak to the Kommandant, get him to ask the Gestapo to leave us alone. Then I stop. He is not our friend in this. Asking his help would only draw his attention to the fact that Krysia has ties to the resistance. "Never mind."

"Here." Krysia sets down her glass of vodka and stands unsteadily. I can tell that she has not fully recovered from our run-in with the Gestapo. She holds out her arms. "I'll put him to bed."

"No." I turn away from her, not wanting to let go. Even though I know it is irrational, I am afraid that if I let go, she will take him away and I will not see him again.

"Anna, please." She tries to pull him gently from my arms, but I pull back, holding on. As I do, Krysia's foot hits the cup of milk that is still sitting on the ground. The liquid shoots in all directions. I see Krysia fall backward, as if in slow motion. "Oh!" she cries, landing on her backside on the hardwood floor with a yelp.

I rush to her side, still holding the child. "Krysia, are you okay?"

She does not answer and I can tell that she is shaken. "I'm fine," she says, though I know that her pride, at least, has been wounded. I hold out my hand to help her up, but she ignores it, slowly standing on her own.

"I'm sorry," I apologize, embarrassed. Krysia has been our protector and I am treating her as if she is the enemy.

"It's this war," she says, taking Lukasz from me. "No one is herself anymore."

Suddenly I remember my conversation with Jacob, my sense that he had come because something terrible was about to happen. Something that might hurt Jacob, keep him from ever coming back to me again. My stomach tightens. "I need to see Alek." I am surprised by the cold, forceful voice that comes from within me.

Krysia stares at me, surprised. "That may be impossible. You know the resistance has gone dark."

"I know that there are ways," I reply insistently. "I'll go out and find him myself if I have to."

She hesitates. "Fine. I'll try to send word that you need to see him this Tuesday."

I start to say that this is not soon enough, that I needed to see him now. Then I stop; there are even limits to what Krysia can do. "Thank you. Only Alek," I add. "It must be him personally."

"Anna, I know you are worried," Krysia says. "But you can't stop the resistance. They will do what they need to do." I do not answer her. Krysia is like Marta in the way that they both treat the resistance leadership with so much deference. A year earlier I might have, too. But I have seen too much these past few months to stand by and watch. Attacking the Nazis is suicide. I have to try to stop them.

Time seems to crawl for the next few days. Tuesday after work, I race to the market square and enter the café where I have met Alek and the others previously. Inside, it is nearly deserted, except for a lone couple smoking at a table in the corner. Alek is not there and I wonder if I am just early or if he is not going to show. Trying to remain calm, I sit down at an unoccupied table and order a glass of tea.

Several minutes later, Alek appears. His cheeks are icy from the cold as he kisses me hello. "It's been a long time," he says, gesturing to the waitress for coffee. He sits down.

"Yes. Did you receive what I gave to Marek?"

He nods. "It was tremendously helpful. Exactly what we were looking for." He does not speak until after the waitress has brought his coffee and left again. "You have something else for me?" he asks eagerly, turning to me.

I hesitate. I knew that the urgency of my message would mislead Alek into thinking I had obtained some additional information for him. I hated tricking him, but it was the only way. "No, I'm sorry, I don't."

Alek looks puzzled. "Then why did you summon me? Is something wrong? Did someone find out about you?"

I shake my head. "No one has found out. But there is something wrong…Alek, this is madness!"

A look of understanding crosses his face. He slams his hand down on the table so hard the dishes rattle. The couple at the table across the room looks over at us. "I knew I never should have let Jacob go to see you," he whispers harshly. I am stunned. I have never seen Alek angry before.

"He didn't tell me anything. I guessed."

"You guessed what?" he demands.

I falter. "Th-that you are about to do something dangerous."

"Dangerous? Emma, this whole war has been dangerous. Sending you to work for the Kommandant was dangerous. Hiding Lukasz is dangerous. Sending our fighters into the forests is dangerous. And for all of these dangers, these risks, our people continue to suffer and die." His eyes burn with anger, not at me, but at the evil the resistance is fighting. I recognize it as the same expression I saw in Jacob's eyes three days earlier. They are united in their determination to go through with whatever it is they have planned.

"But…" I start to protest.

Alek raises his hand. "This is none of your concern."

"None of my concern?" Now it is my voice that rises. The woman at the other table looks over again, raising her eyebrows in our direction. "None of my concern?" I repeat, lowering my voice. "Alek, I have risked my life for this movement. I have abandoned my parents, shamed my marriage. It is more than my business." I meet his eyes squarely. "It is my right."

We glare at each other without speaking for several moments. "You have gained great strength these last few months," he says at last, his face softening. I detect a note of surprise in his voice. "Very well, what do you want to know?"

"Why now?"

He lowers his voice. "There is great danger afoot for our people, Emma."

"The ghetto…"

"I am not talking about the ghetto. I'm talking about the camps!" I blink, not comprehending. "You've heard about Auschwitz, haven't you?"

"Yes, it's a labor camp." My stomach turns. I can still picture the haunted look in the Kommandant's eyes the night after he visited Auschwitz with the delegation.

"That is what the Nazis have told the people, what they would like the people to believe. It's a death camp, Emma. The Nazis have begun gassing our people to death, and burning their bodies in ovens. Thousands of Jews every day. Soon there will be no ghetto, no labor camps. Only Auschwitz, and Belzec and the other death camps. The Nazis will not stop until every Jew has gone up the pipes in smoke!"

"No…" I turn away, sickened. Surely it cannot be true. Yet I trust Alek, and the sincerity of his words makes them impossible to ignore. I did not realize until this very moment that the Nazis mean not merely to enslave us, but to exterminate every single Jew.

"We believe this is a critical time," he continues. "The Germans are entering their second winter in Poland. The war is not going well for them. They are getting desperate. The information you provided to us demonstrates that they are planning to liquidate the Kraków ghetto and send the Jews to the death camps very soon. So you see why it is essential that we act now."

"Yes," I reply weakly. Alek is right. Despite my love for Jacob and all of my concern, there is nothing more that I can say.

"Good. Emma, there is one other thing." I look at him quizzically. "It's about Richwalder. I know you have wondered about his past, his wife." I nod; Krysia must have told him this. "I have long thought the less you knew, the easier it would be to work for him. But now…" Alek pauses. "Well, I don't know for how much longer our meetings will be able to continue. It is essential that you know everything.

"Richwalder's wife was named Margot," he begins.

"I know that," I reply.

"But what you do not know is that her maiden name was Rosenthal. You see, Emma, her father was a Jew." My jaw drops. Alek continues, "When the war first broke out, Richwalder thought that his wife's heritage, the fact that she was

half-Jewish, might be kept a secret. But shortly after Richwalder was appointed to a senior position in the Ministry of
Defense, Margot's father, who had been a prominent political activist in the Communist Party, was arrested and sent to
a camp, Bergen-Belsen. Margot pleaded for her husband to
intervene to save her father, but Richwalder knew that to do
so would only expose his wife's ancestry. To protect her, or perhaps to protect his precious career, he refused. Friedrich Rosenthal was executed before a firing squad. The next day,
Richwalder came home to find his wife dead—she had shot
herself in their bed with his own revolver."

My stomach twists. "Oh, no…"

"She was six months pregnant when she died," he adds. I
can barely hear him over the pounding in my ears. "You can
see now why we felt it best you not know the truth. But,
Emma, no matter what you think and no matter what happens, you must go on pretending with Richwalder. Many lives
depend upon it."

I am frozen, unable to move or speak. "I'm sorry, but I really have to go," Alek says. He stands and throws a few coins
down on the table.

I look up. "How, I mean when, will I see any of you again?"

He places a hand on my shoulder. "Have faith, Emma. As
the great American President Lincoln once said, 'And this, too,
shall pass away.' I look forward to one day sitting openly in
an outdoor café with you and our friends, having a beer and
looking back and remembering."

I look up at him. His words are brave, but I know from the
troubled look behind his eyes that he suspects in his heart such
a day will never come to pass. At the same time, there is a clar-

ity to his eyes that tells me he is unafraid of whatever will come. I stare up at him, awed by his bravery. "God bless you, Alek," I whisper, squeezing his hand. "And thank you." He turns without speaking and is gone.

CHAPTER 20

"Good night," I say to Stanislaw as I step out of the car in front of the Kommandant's apartment onto the snow-covered pavement. As he drives away, I pause to look around. It is late December, and the snow has just stopped falling. Though it is six o'clock in the evening and the sun has set, the sky seems illuminated. The ground is covered in unbroken white, making it impossible to distinguish between sidewalk and street. I pause and scoop up a handful of snow, touching the coldness to my cheek, breathing the wetness in deeply. The city feels empty and silent.

It has been nearly three weeks since my conversation with Alek. At first I thought it would be impossible to continue with my charade, knowing about the Kommandant's past, the Nazis' plans for the Jews and the fact that the resistance was about to do something very dangerous. I remember how once, as a young girl, I had read a book in which the protagonist was able to see the future. I had remarked to my father how wonderful a gift that would be, but he had only shaken his head. "Unpredictability is the best part of life," he had said. "The surprise of who or what might be around the corner, it's what keeps us going. It is hope. Such foresight of the future, without the ability to change anything..." He shook his head ruefully. "What a curse."

What a curse is right, I think now, as I let the snow fall from my gloves and start toward the entranceway of the Kommandant's apartment. Despite all I've learned, I have somehow managed to lift my chin and continue working for the Kommandant—there is no other choice. I look at him differently now, though. My head is no longer buried in the sand about who he is and what he is doing. I have managed to hide my conflicted feelings about him in the office, and fortunately, I have not had to see him in the evenings because he has been so preoccupied with work.

Until now. Earlier today, as I was taking dictation from the Kommandant, he stopped speaking midsentence and reached over and took the stenographic pad from my hands.

I looked up in surprise. "Yes, Herr Kommandant?"

"Anna, is something wrong?" he asked, his brow furrowed.

Yes, I want to say. *You ran a prison camp for Jews. You keep my parents locked in the ghetto. You let your wife's father be killed and would kill Jacob, too, if given the chance. Your wretched Gestapo came to our house, and now Lukasz might have to leave us. Let me count the ways.* Of course I did not dare to say any of this. "No, Herr Kommandant," I replied, managing to keep my voice even. "Everything is fine."

He reached out and placed his hand over mine. "You seem distracted and it isn't like you." As I looked down at his hand and thought about all of the harm it had done, I had to fight the urge to pull away.

"It's nothing. Everything is fine," I repeated quickly.

"Are you sure?" he pressed. He stared at me deeply, searching for an answer.

"Yes." I paused, searching for an explanation. "It must be the nearness of the holiday."

"Of course," he replied, not sounding entirely satisfied with my explanation. His hand lingered on mine a moment longer, then retracted. "Well, that will be all for now." I stood, relieved to escape from his penetrating gaze. But as I turned to leave, he caught my arm. "May I see you tonight?" he asked.

His question caught me by surprise. He has been so busy with work, I assumed an evening with me would be the furthest thing from his mind. I studied his face. The affection is his eyes was genuine and I felt a momentary surge of warmth toward him. In that moment, I wished desperately that we were not who we were. This would have been so simple in another time and place. If I were not married and he were not a Nazi, we might actually have had a chance together. But, as my mother used to say, if wishes were horses, beggars would ride. This was exactly who we were.

I hesitated. Spending a night with the Kommandant was the last thing I wanted to do tonight. It has been hard enough pretending all day in the office setting without having to then mask my distaste when we are alone, just the two of us. But even as I wrestled with his invitation, I knew that I had no choice. Another visit to the apartment meant another chance to find something else useful for the resistance, perhaps even some information that might convince Alek to cancel whatever dangerous mission he was planning. "Yes, that would be lovely," I said at last to the Kommandant, who was still looking at me expectantly.

His face broke into a wide smile. "Good. We can have a quiet dinner, just the two of us. Here," the Kommandant said, fishing in his pocket and pulling out a key and some money. "I have some work that needs to be finished this evening, but I won't be very late. Why don't you leave now and pick up some food on your way to my apartment? You can make yourself comfortable, have a nap if you're tired. I'll be along as soon as I can."

I nodded and took my leave from his office. Seeing the heavy snow falling outside the windows of Wawel, I had asked Stanislaw to drive me to the store and then the apartment.

The snow has stopped now. Looking down the street, bathed in white, I think of Jacob. He always loved snow. During our one winter together, the months before we were married, he would coax me out to the woods to play every time a fresh snow fell. At first I had looked at him as if he was crazy. Having been raised an only child in the city with not many friends, I had done little more with snow than catch a few flakes on my tongue. Having snowball fights and building snowmen were foreign concepts to me, and I could not believe he actually wanted me to lie down beside him in a patch of snow and wave my arms and legs back and forth to make the shape of an angel. But he had persuaded me, and as I lay in the snow beside him laughing, the freezing wetness seeping through my clothes, I had looked up at the white sky and breathed in the crisp air and felt truly alive for the first time.

Still standing in the street, I bend down and lift another handful of white flakes to my face, inhaling the wetness and remembering. I can see his face so clearly. But snow does not bring only happy thoughts of Jacob now. Is he warm enough wherever he is? I do not even know if he is indoors. We will play in the snow together again one day, I vow silently, touching the snow to my cheek. I brush the snow from my gloves and watch it scatter in the wind.

I wipe my boots on the mat before making my way into the apartment building, a small basket of groceries in my hand. Upstairs, I enter the apartment and look around. I have not been here in almost a month. The apartment is more unkempt than ever, with newspapers and drinking glasses scattered everywhere. How can the Kommandant live like this? He is otherwise so neat and precise. Probably because he has been here so little, I decide, between working late in the office and traveling frequently to Warsaw. I set down my basket on the low table in front of the sofa and begin to clear the mess so I can put out supper there.

As I carry the glasses to the kitchen, I can feel the picture of Margot staring at me from the mantelpiece. I stop and turn to meet her dark eyes. The picture, I know, was taken before her father was killed. But there was still a sadness in her eyes, a foreshadowing of her own tragic end. How much of the horrible truth had she already learned about who the Kommandant really was, or had become? I think then of the earlier photograph of Margot, the one the Kommandant keeps on his desk. She looked so happy and in love in that picture. I study her face for some clue, wishing she could tell me about the man the Kommandant used to be. But her expression remains impassive, her voice muted by time. Poor Margot. The two of us are not so very different. Both Jewish, at least in part. Both of us trapped by love for men kept from us by a sense of duty to a cause. And both of our loves had gotten shipwrecked by this wretched war. I only hope that my story will end differently.

I turn toward the Kommandant's study. I could go in there now and look around. Perhaps there is something I missed the last time or maybe some new development. I shake my head. Not now. It is too risky. There is no telling how soon he will be home. No, I will have to look later, after he is asleep. A chill runs through me. I have not been intimate with the Kommandant for some time now, not since before I learned of his terrible past. Not since before Jacob's visit. The idea of being with the Kommandant again after making love to Jacob seems like I am breaking my marriage vows all over again. There is a part of me, though, that welcomes the chance to be held by him. I wish I could ignore that part, or did not know that it exists. I shiver and, forcing these thoughts from my head, carry the dirty glasses into the kitchen.

The Kommandant arrives a short while later as I am setting out our supper, a light meal of bread, delicatessen meats and cheese. "Hello." He bends and kisses me hello in an absent-minded manner. His face is stormy, and though I do not dare ask, I wonder what happened at the office after I left to change his mood so markedly.

Not speaking further, he sets down a briefcase that I imagine to be full of work and goes to the water closet to wash up. Maybe he will be too busy to be with me that night, I think as I pour two drinks, a glass of brandy for him and a much smaller one for me. If that is the case, I will not be able to get into his study at all. My heart sinks.

I bring the drinks to the table and sit down. A few minutes later, the Kommandant comes back into the room, his jacket off and shirtsleeves rolled up. "Come sit," I urge, patting the space beside me on the sofa. He nods, but he does not join me. Instead he walks to the mantelpiece. For a moment I wonder if he is thinking of Margot, but he does not seem to be looking at her picture. Rather, he is staring into the fireplace, his mind somewhere far away.

"Christmas is coming," he says at last. He sounds as if the realization has only just occurred to him, though I had mentioned the holidays in his office earlier in the day.

"Just a few days away," I reply. I might have forgotten the holiday myself, but for the sprigs of fir and red bows that Krysia has placed around the house in lieu of a tree. The city, usually festive with displays in the window shops and the aroma of holiday treats, was virtually unadorned this year.

"Christmas was such a grand affair in our house," he says. For a moment, I wonder if he is speaking of his life with Margot, but he continues, "Our father would take us on a midnight sleigh ride through the woods to search for the Weinachtsmann, whom we believed would bring the Christmas gifts." He walks over to the sofa and sits down beside me. "We never found him, of course, but would come back to the house to find that he had sneaked in while we were gone to leave us wonderful presents. And the next morning, the breakfast table was always piled high with cakes." He smiles, his expression almost childlike.

"That sounds lovely," I say. My mind races to come up with a story about my childhood Christmases, in case he asks.

"We should do something special for Christmas," he says abruptly. "Go away somewhere for a few days, just the two of us."

I stare at him in disbelief. It is as if he has forgotten the war, his role in the administration. "Herr Kommandant, with all that is going on, I wouldn't think it possible…"

His smile fades. "No, of course not," he says quickly. I watch the heaviness return to his eyes, regretful that I have taken his moment of escape from him. "It's this damn war," he adds. He touches my cheek. "I'm sorry, Anna. You deserve so much better."

I do deserve better, I think, but not in the way he means. I deserve to be with my husband. "Not at all," I reply, my stomach twisting.

"I'll make it up to you someday," he insists. "Things will be different for us after the war. I promise."

I open my mouth, but before I can speak, he reaches for me, his lips pressing down thickly on mine. His embrace is tight, his kiss demanding. Caught off guard, I freeze momentarily. After so many weeks, his touch feels both strange and familiar at the same time. Then I find myself responding, my kisses matching the intensity of his. Despite all that has happened and all that I have learned about him, I feel at once the burn and the chill, the same thrill and disgust brought on as much by my own reaction as the touch that inspires it.

The Kommandant's hands drop to my torso. His weight begins to press on me, bending me backward against the arm of the sofa. There is an urgency about him that I have not seen before. It is as if he is running, trying to hide from something in my arms. I pull my lips back from his, cradling his face in my hands. "What is it?" I whisper. "What's wrong?" But he shakes his head and begins kissing me once more.

Suddenly there is a sharp knock at the door. The Kommandant hesitates, a look of concern crossing his face. He is not expecting anyone else, I know, and no one would dare call on him unannounced. He turns back to me, continues kissing me as though he has heard nothing. A moment later, the knock comes again, too loud to be ignored.

He breaks from our kiss and sits up. "Yes?" he calls out, irritated.

"Urgent message, Herr Kommandant," a thin male voice calls through the door. The Kommandant rises and straightens his collar as he walks to the door and opens it. A young soldier stands in the hallway, sweating and breathing heavily. "M-my apologies for the intrusion…" the soldier stammers.

"What is it?" the Kommandant demands. The messenger hesitates, looking at me over the Kommandant's shoulder. "Anna is my personal assistant. You may speak freely in front of her."

The messenger holds his arm out straight, a piece of paper caught in his shaking fingertips. "Warszawa Café," he gasps as the Kommandant snatches the paper and scans it. "There has been an explosion."

My stomach sinks. Warszawa Café, once a posh Polish establishment located directly across the street from the opera house, had become a popular Nazi bar during the occupation. Even in the early days of the war, we had learned to steer away from the area where the German soldiers were densely gathered and often drunk. This is the work of the resistance, I know it. "What sort of explosion?" the Kommandant asks.

"An incendiary device of some sort, sir."

"You mean a bomb?"

The soldier nods. "There are casualties among the officers, I'm afraid."

The slip of paper falls from the Kommandant's hand. His expression is one of surprise. The idea that someone has carried out an action against the Nazis seems more than he can comprehend. Both the messenger and I look at the Kommandant, waiting to see what he will do. Without a word, he retreats into the bedroom. I look at the messenger questioningly, hoping that he will be forthcoming with more details. He does not speak or meet my gaze, though, but rather shifts his weight from foot to foot. Outside, sirens wail in the distance.

The Kommandant reemerges from the bedroom wearing his jacket once more. He adjusts his belt and I can see the silver glint of a pistol in his waistband. He passes by me on his way out the door. "I have to go. Stanislaw will see you home," he calls over his shoulder, already halfway down the hall. The messenger slams the door shut behind him.

I rush over to the window that faces north and scan the skyline. In the distance, on the far side of the city center, I can see a red glow. Flames shoot toward the sky. So this is what they had planned. *Jacob,* I think. *Alek.* I press my head against the glass, seeing their faces in my mind. *Oh, my sweet, foolish boys, what have you done?*

I turn around. I am alone in the Kommandant's apartment, certain that with all that has happened, he will not be home for many hours. I am free to go into his study, to search through all of his papers and find more information, to tell Alek everything he and the others want to know. All of these months, everything I have planned and done, has been about getting to a moment like this. Only now it is too late. I laugh aloud at the irony, my voice echoing through the empty rooms.

Then I stop abruptly. The world has just exploded and

those I love most are undoubtedly at the center of the inferno. I have to do something. I grab my coat and run out of the Kommandant's apartment and into the night.

A few meters from the apartment building, I pause. Where should I go? Though I know it is dangerous, and the last thing the resistance would want me to do, I begin running wildly toward the city center and the scene of the explosion. At first, people on the street look at me strangely. But as I near the far corner of the market square, my hysteria seems entirely appropriate. Sirens wail, Gestapo police bark out orders and Poles, who for the past several years of occupation have learned to steer away from trouble, run directly toward the fiery scene. I follow the crowd west along Stolarska Street.

A bomb, I hear voices alongside me whisper as we draw nearer to the scene; Nazis killed. They sound almost gleeful. My heart lurches. The fact that a few Nazis were killed is irrelevant to me. I can think only of my beloved Jacob and brave, strong Alek. I am certain they are among those who set off the explosion. Are they okay? Alive?

Just above the square, a police barricade has been erected. "No entrance, miss," the guard says as I try to pass.

"But I live…" Lying, I point to the other side of the barricade.

The guard shakes his head. "No exceptions. Go around another way."

I make a left onto Tomasza Street, and then a right onto Florianska, which runs parallel to the street I'd been hoping to take. Though this street is just one block away from the explosion, the police had not thought to barricade it and it is largely deserted. I make my way up the street, staying close to the buildings, hidden in the shadows. As I near the scene of the explosion, thick smoke fills the air, burning my throat and making it difficult to see. Shards of broken glass crunch under my feet. I reach the end of the street where it dead-ends at the Florian Gate. It is here, by the medieval city wall, that Lukasz and I saw the soldiers that terrified him so on our first trip into town after coming to Krysia's house.

If I follow the wall, stay close to the buildings, I may be able to make it to the scene of the explosion. I start around the corner. Suddenly, an arm shoots out of a doorway and grabs my shoulder hard. "Hey!" I cry, as I am pulled into a dark alleyway by a stranger. Two arms grab me from behind, a hand clamps over my mouth. For a second I wonder if it is the Gestapo. They would not bother with secrecy, I quickly realize, struggling to break free. Desperately, I open my mouth and manage to bite the hand that has been covering it. Suddenly I am released.

"Ouch!" a woman's voice exclaims.

"What on earth…?" Breathing heavily, I turn to face my assailant. Her face is covered by a heavy wool shawl.

"Shhh!" The stranger pulls back the shawl and a familiar head of dark curls springs out.

"Marta!" I exclaim. Her face is scratched and covered in soot and I can tell she has been to the scene of the explosion. "How did you…?"

"You shouldn't have come here," she admonishes, as though speaking to a child. "It's dangerous. The Gestapo is rounding up anyone who looks like they do not belong here. You could have been arrested or worse."

"I'm sorry, but I had to come. I was out of my mind with worry. Jacob? Alek?"

"Both alive," she replies, a catch in her voice. She looks away.

I grab her by the shoulders. "What is it?" I demand, my voice rising.

"Shh!" she repeats, looking uneasily out into the street.

I drop my voice but do not release my grip on her. "Tell me what happened."

She hesitates and I can tell she is wondering how much to say. "Jacob was injured by the blast…."

My heart stops. "Injured? How?"

"During the explosion. I don't know the details. He was seriously injured, but he is alive." Her eyes are dark with concern. I have suspected since our first meeting after the ghetto that Marta has feelings for my husband. Now, seeing her face so heavy with torment and grief, I am certain of it.

"I have to go to him," I say. "Tell me where he is."

She shakes her head. "No, Emma, no. Jacob has been taken from the city. Alek has given orders that none of us are to go to him. It isn't safe. Not now."

White-hot rage sears within me. "But I am his wife! I have every right to see him!"

Marta's expression changes and her lips press together hard. "His *wife?*" she spits sarcastically.

I pull back. "What are you saying?"

"I know what you have done all of these months. What has been going on between you and the Kommandant."

"But…" I falter, stunned. How could she possibly know? Had Alek told her? Had she told Jacob as a way to come between us and get closer to him?

"Jacob doesn't know," she replies, reading my thoughts. "I thought about telling him, believe me. But Alek forbade me.

He said it would have hurt Jacob too much, been a distraction when the resistance most needed him to be strong. I wanted to tell him. He deserves to know what kind of woman you really are."

Her words cut through me, sharp and painful. "Marta, you can't think that…I've done what I was asked. What had to be done."

"Maybe." She looks me squarely in the eye. Her voice is icy. "But I wonder who it is that you really care for. If you even care for Jacob at all."

"How can you say that? I've done what I've done with the Kommandant for the resistance, because it was the only thing to do. I love Jacob! *Only* him!" My voice sounds too insistent, as though I am trying to convince her and myself. "You know that."

She looks away. "I don't know anything anymore." Me, neither, I think. Neither of us speaks for several seconds. Then Marta turns to me again, gripping me by the shoulders and shaking me hard. "Now, you listen to me—you cannot go to Jacob now. The situation is very serious. The Nazis are combing the city, looking for the perpetrators, and they have a pretty good idea who did it. There will be repercussions for what has happened tonight. Alek has risked much by sending me to find you and tell you that Jacob is alive. So you need to calm yourself and go home and say nothing, even to Krysia. And tomorrow you will go to work as though nothing has happened. Do you understand?" I nod. Marta softens a bit. "We care about Jacob, too." Though she used the plural, I know it is herself for whom she is speaking. "I will send word to you as soon as it is safe. Trust me." She hugs me quickly and disappears into the alley once more.

I step out of the doorway and, after making sure no one has noticed me, start back down Florianska Street. Crowds of people continue to rush in the direction from which I have just come. At the far side of the market square, I hesitate. I should go back to the Kommandant's apartment, I think. My basket is still there and I did not clean up the food. But I cannot face him now, not after all that I have learned. Hopefully he will be too preoccupied to notice, but if he asks, I will tell him that the news of the explosion was so shocking, I developed a headache and started feeling ill. It is an excuse not that far from the truth.

As I make my way through the back streets toward Krysia's, I think of Marta. Her expression was so hard and cynical. I remember then the laughing girl I had met in the ghetto last year, the one who had taken me under her wing and brought me to Shabbes with Alek and the others at Josefinska Street. What has happened to us? She's just jealous, I tell myself. She spoke out of her feelings for Jacob. Still, her words ring in my head over and over like a bell. *I wonder who it is that you really care for...* It is a question that, despite my best efforts to avoid, has haunted me a thousand times in recent months. I still love Jacob without question. He is my husband. But until his recent visit, I had not seen him in more than a year. The Kommandant...well, I see him every day. And I have been intimate with him many more times these past several months than I ever was with Jacob in our few short weeks living together as husband and wife. But I hate the Kommandant, or should. Sometimes, like after recently learning about Margot, it is easy to despise him. Other times, though, when we lay in the dark and his uniform is gone, he is just a man who brings me pleasure and comfort. I can almost forget who he is, who we both are. Almost. In those moments, I cannot help but wonder if in another life, where no one wore a swastika or wedding ring, I had met both men at the same time, which I would have chosen.

Enough, I tell myself. The point is a moot one. There is no choice to be made. Jacob is my husband and he is injured. Though we cannot be together right now, my loyalty is to him. The Kommandant is my lover, the man with whom I have to sleep for appearances. The truth is as simple as it is ridiculous. Laughing bitterly aloud in the cold night air, I draw my coat closer around me and hurry toward home.

"Are you okay? What happened?" Krysia rushes to meet me as I come through the door an hour later.

"I'm fine," I say, taking off my coat and boots.

"They said something on the radio about a bombing at Warszawa."

I do not reply as I follow Krysia up to the kitchen. I am going to tell her, of course, despite Marta's admonition to say nothing. Krysia is as much a part of this as any of us and she deserves to know. But I remember how Krysia nearly collapsed after the Gestapo came on the night of Jacob's visit. I must tell her carefully. I wait until we are both seated at the kitchen table with the water boiling for tea before speaking. "There was a bombing," I reply at last, my voice cracking at the end.

"The resistance?" she asks. I nod. "I feared something like this when Jacob came to visit." She shakes her head. "Those foolish boys. Many will pay for their bravado."

I am surprised at her reaction. It is the first time I have ever heard her question the resistance. "You don't think they should have done it?"

She pours steaming water from the kettle into two teacups. "I understand why they did it. I just don't think it was the smartest tactic."

"I think it was incredibly stupid," I say bluntly. She does not reply. I wait until she has set down the kettle before speaking again. "Krysia, there is one thing more." I take a deep breath. "Jacob was hurt in the explosion."

Krysia's face turns instantly gray and she grasps the edge of the counter. Fearful that she might faint, I jump up and guide her to a chair. "How?" she asks.

"Marta didn't say what happened."

"Is it serious?"

I hesitate. "Yes," I reply. I cannot lie to Krysia. "But he is alive," I add quickly.

Krysia inhales sharply, her face growing even paler. She is not a young woman and Jacob is like a son to her. I wonder if I have made a mistake in telling her, if the strain of receiving such news might be too much. "Jacob, Jacob," she moans softly, pressing her fingers against her eyes and rocking back and forth. It is the first time I have ever seen her cry.

"Shh, it's okay," I hear myself saying. The words sound foreign and untrue. Inside I am screaming. Jacob is badly hurt. I should be there with him. I look down at Krysia again. Jacob would want me to be strong for her. "It's okay," I repeat. I stand over her helplessly for several minutes, my hand on her shoulder.

When her sobs subside, she looks up and pulls out a handkerchief. "What else do you know?" she asks, dabbing her eyes.

I sit down beside her. "They've taken him somewhere outside of the city. That's all Marta would tell me. I wanted her to take me to him, but she wouldn't. Alek's orders."

Krysia breathes deeply, calmer now. "If Alek said it is too dangerous, then that's probably right."

Now it is my turn to become upset again. "But we can't just sit here, Krysia! Not if Jacob is hurt."

"I know you want to do something, Emma. We both do. It may be, though, that there is nothing to be done right now, other than to wait and pray Jacob is all right. But we need more information than what Marta has told you. First thing tomorrow, I will see what I can find out."

The next morning I leave for work to find the city transformed. As a result of the bombing, the Nazis have placed Kraków under a state of martial law. The streets teem with Gestapo: tanks sit at every major intersection, police and soldiers stand on the street corners, watching the passersby closely. Local residents, long accustomed to the presence of the Nazi occupation, walk with heads down, not speaking. I am stopped for identification and questioned about my destination three times before I reach Wawel.

As a result of these new security checks, I do not reach work until almost twenty past nine. The castle corridors are bustling with a new sense of seriousness and urgency. When I reach our office, Malgorzata, looking smug as a cat, informs me that the Kommandant has already left for emergency meetings, and will be gone the balance of the day.

I enter the anteroom. My desk is piled high with papers, each stack topped by a small note from the Kommandant. I set about following his instructions with each. Toward the bottom of the papers there is a classified envelope. Normally, I would set it aside as I had been instructed on my first day of work. Today, however, I do not care. These are telegrams from Berlin, I am sure, and I need to see what they say about the bombing. Reckless now, I open the envelope and begin reading the telegrams. Café Warszawa had been packed with Nazis celebrating the holiday early, I learn. Seven had died, and many more had been injured. The telegrams from Berlin order swift and immediate reprisals, both against the Jews within the ghetto and across the general Polish population. My blood runs cold as I read this last sentence and think of my parents.

I read until I have almost reached the bottom of the folder. The last telegram consists of just a single sentence:

Leader of resistance movement, Alek Landesberg, shot and killed while resisting arrest at his apartment last night at 0200 hours.

The paper drops from my hands. The telegram had been sent to Berlin that morning. It was signed by the Kommandant.

CHAPTER 21

I am making *choulent* for our midday meal, the thick beef, potato and bean soup that I had eaten every Sabbath lunch and dinner of my life until the war began. Of course we don't dare to call it that now. I overheard Krysia telling Lukasz that we would be having "beef stew" for dinner, and I had cringed inside to think that the child of a great rabbi is growing up not knowing about this Jewish Sabbath dish. I have not had it for over a year, but now, in the deepest part of winter, it is the one food I crave.

It is mid-February, almost two months since the resistance bombed the Warszawa Café. "An act of great heroism," I heard a man remark under his breath on the street. I could not have disagreed more. So a few Nazis had died. It was a drop in the bucket. And at what cost? Alek, the very backbone of the resistance, is dead, shot in his apartment the day after the bombing. My eyes burn as I picture his face the last time we met, resolute, unafraid of the danger that lay ahead. The Nazi-controlled newspapers portrayed Alek as a criminal, claiming that he was shot while trying to escape. I knew, though, that nothing could be further from the truth. Alek had died a hero, struggling for the cause of the resistance even as he was killed. Of that much I am sure.

As for Jacob, Krysia's inquiries have turned up little other than what we already knew, that he was injured in the bombing and has been removed from Kraków. One of Krysia's contacts thought he might be recuperating in the mountains. Apparently his is not a bullet wound, but rather heavy shrapnel from the explosion. But there is no news about the seriousness of his condition, the extent of his wounds. With Alek dead and a number of other fighters, including Marek, arrested and imprisoned, the resistance is in tatters and it is nearly impossible to get information. I do not even know what has become of Marta since our encounter on Florianska Street the night of the bombing. Surely she would find me, or at least send word about Jacob if she could. I wonder if she has seen him. Jacob. His face appears in my mind. I think of him constantly now. Some of my thoughts are happy ones, of our days in the apartment on Grodzka Street and the last night we spent together here. But there are other images, too: I imagine him lying in a bed in a cabin somewhere, bloodied and bandaged and alone. As hard as I try, I cannot force these images from my mind. Be strong, I pray. Come back to me. Since Jacob went underground, I have been able to endure it all—the ghetto, working for the Nazis, even being with the Kommandant—because I knew Jacob was out there somewhere and would find a way for us to be together again. I do not know how I will go on if he does not survive.

The attack has had larger consequences, too: Kraków remains under a state of martial law. Gestapo are stationed on every corner and ordinary citizens continue to be subjected to frequent stops and searches, as well as a curfew from dusk until dawn. It is not the Poles, though, for whom I am most concerned; surely the brunt of the Nazi wrath and revenge is being felt by the Jews in the ghetto. My parents, I think as I stir the *choulent*. I have heard horrible stories, whispered on the streets and in the corridors at Wawel, of groups of randomly selected Jews being lined up against a wall and shot.

Malgorzata was the latest to repeat the rumor to me as I passed through reception the previous morning. Her face was sad as she told me, and there was none of the usual smugness or self-importance in her voice. It occurred to me for the first time that perhaps she had secret relatives in the ghetto, too. Unlikely, but maybe she had Jewish friends from before the war. I wanted to ask her how she knew: was this just one of the typical secretarial rumors that spread through headquarters, growing each time it was told, or had she seen an official telegram detailing the incident? More likely the former, I decided. Though meticulous in planning, the Nazis seldom put the atrocities they committed in writing. It was as if they subconsciously knew that someday they might no longer be in power and might be called upon to account for their crimes. Of course I did not dare ask Malgorzata or seem too interested in her gossip, but rather nodded and hurried into the anteroom, nauseous.

I had wanted to ask Krysia about the rumor. I decided against it, though; the strain of recent events had taken its toll on her and I did not want to add to her worries. In any event,

I knew what she would say, that the story was probably exaggerated, that even if it was true there were thousands of people in the ghetto, that my parents would not be among those selected. Such words would be of little comfort.

Hadn't the resistance thought about the repercussions they would bring on to others? They seem not to have cared, I think for the hundredth time, as I remove the *choulent* from the burner and turn off the gas. More so than my grief at the loss of Alek or even my frantic worry for my husband, I seethe with anger at this foolish act of heroism.

Yet despite all that has happened, we are forced to go on. Our charade does not stop just because my world seemingly has. Every day, I get up and go to work at Wawel as though nothing is wrong. Occasionally, Malgorzata or one of the other secretaries comment that I am quieter than usual, or ask if I am feeling well. For the most part, though, I have been able to keep up appearances.

I lift the heavy pot from the stove. Suddenly, my body weakens. I become very hot, then chilled. A cold sweat breaks out on my forehead and a wave of nausea sweeps over me. The pot of *choulent* drops from my hands and crashes to the floor, shards of porcelain and gravy spraying in all directions.

"Oh!" My hands rise to my mouth. The pot had been one of Krysia's favorites, a wedding present from many years ago.

Krysia, who has been waiting at the table with Lukasz, comes swiftly to my side, stepping over the remnants of our meal and her beloved crockery as though they aren't there.

"I'm so sorry," I say, starting to cry.

"It's okay," she replies, her voice sincere.

I shake my head. "No, no, it's not," I sob. The broken pot,

it seems, is the final straw. I remember suddenly the morning I learned of Alek's death. I had forced myself to replace the telegram in the folder and continue working, not to react. Even that night as I told Krysia the news in the safety of our home, I had not cried. Now suddenly all of the frustration and worry and grief of recent weeks seems to come pouring out of me at once. I cry for Alek, who had led the resistance so bravely and brought me a connection to Jacob once more. For the wounded husband whom I cannot be with, for my parents, and for the nameless strangers shot in the ghetto. I cry for Margot and her father. For me, Krysia and Lukasz. For all of us.

Krysia wraps her arms around me. "There, there," she murmurs, rocking me gently from side to side as she might Lukasz when he scraped a knee. I place my head on her shoulder and melt into her warm embrace.

"I'm sorry," I repeat, still bawling. I can feel my tears soaking the shoulder of her dress, but I do not care. "It's just that…"

"I know," she soothes. "Let it out, just let it—" Krysia suddenly stops rocking me. She freezes midsentence.

I look up through my tears. "What is it?"

She places one hand on my stomach, the other on my cheek. "Emma, are you…pregnant?"

I straighten and pull away, wiping my eyes with my sleeve. I am stunned by her question. "Pregnant?" I repeat as though the word is a foreign one. An image leaps into my mind of Lukasz's mother, lying on the ground after she had been shot, her lifeless arm draped across her full stomach in a gesture of futile protection. Pregnancy meant life and there was no bringing life into this dark world now. "No…"

"Are you sure?" Krysia presses. I shake my head. Pregnant

is something that happens to married women with normal lives, those blessedly lucky ones who get to go to sleep each night beside their husbands. Margot had been pregnant. Krysia continues, "Because you have not been yourself lately and there are dark circles under your eyes. I've heard you in the water closet…" I can see Krysia's mouth moving but I can no longer hear what she is saying over the buzzing in my ears. For weeks now, I realize, I have been trying to avoid asking myself this very question. I haven't had my period in more than three months. I have tried to tell myself that my cycle has been thrown off by the stress of everything that has happened, all of the pretending and worrying and grieving. But there are other signs, too, the nausea and dizziness and a stomach growing rounder despite our modest food supply.

Now, hearing Krysia say it, I know it is true. I nod, unable to speak the words.

She does not appear surprised. "How long?"

"I only suspected it a few days ago," I lie quickly, not wanting Krysia to think I have been hiding something from her. "I wasn't even sure until now."

"No, I meant, how far along do you think you are?"

I shrug. "I don't know…."

"A doctor could tell us, if there was a decent one to be trusted still left in this town," Krysia laments. "When was your last cycle?"

I blush, unaccustomed to speaking of such things. "Three months ago, give or take." I can see her doing the math in her head, trying to see if the timing coincides with my husband's only visit. It does not. "I don't know if it is Jacob's," I add softly.

She looks at me sharply. "I didn't ask."

"Oh, God…" The full reality of what is happening begins to sink in. I am pregnant, and the child is likely the Kommandant's. I feel my knees start to wobble once more.

Noticing, Krysia takes my arm and guides me to a chair. "Breathe deeply," she instructs, placing a glass of water on the table in front of me. "Drink this."

I obey, taking sips of water in between my sobs. "I'm so sorry."

"Don't say that. It's not your fault." Krysia walks to the cupboard and pulls out a whisk broom and dustpan. Not my fault, I think as I watch her clean up the mess I made. I feel stupid, as though I should have known better. But how? I knew so little about having a child. My mother had not spoken to me about such things, even before my wedding to Jacob. In our religious community, a married woman did not try to prevent pregnancy, at least not openly; it was her duty to bear as many children as God saw fit to bless her with. I had heard whispers from some of the girls in my neighborhood about being less likely to get pregnant at certain times of the month, but I had not really understood what they were talking about and had not dared to ask. I should have thought about it when this business with the Kommandant began, I realize. Perhaps Krysia could have helped me be more careful. But everything happened so quickly and I was focused on getting the information for Alek. And now it is too late.

Krysia returns to the table a few minutes later, having managed to save some of the *choulent* that has not touched the floor. She sets three small bowls of the stew on the table and puts Lukasz in his chair. Food is precious, I realize. Even in a catastrophe, one must be practical. She scoops a spoonful of *choulent* and blows on it to cool the temperature before feeding it to Lukasz. She alternates spoonfuls between the child and herself. Numbly I eat my stew, trying not to think.

When Krysia's bowl is empty, she pushes it away from her and begins speaking. "Emma, I was pregnant once, too. In Paris. Before Marcin." I look up, stunned by her admission. I had no idea that Krysia had ever been pregnant, and certainly had not imagined her having lovers other than her husband. I think of all of the times these past several months that she has comforted me about my illicit affair with the Kommandant, how she tried to assuage my guilt about my confused feelings about him. She understands, I realize, because she had an affair of her own as a young woman.

"Who was he?" I ask. Though I know him only from the photographs, it is difficult to picture Krysia with anyone but Marcin.

Krysia smiles. "His name was Claude. He was a writer, or wanted to be, anyway. He lived in a tiny room above a café. The landlord let him wash dishes in the kitchen and sweep the café floor because he could not afford to pay rent." She pauses and studies her fingers. I can see a thin line of blood where a shard of porcelain cut into the pale, smooth back of her hand. "I never thought it would happen. I was young and carefree and in love. We both were, or so I thought. I was prepared to leave my family to be with Claude, but he said it was impossible, that he had no money for a family. That a child would interfere with his art." I can see the sadness now in her eyes as she remembers going to her lover with dreams of a future together, only to be rejected. "I would have kept the child and raised him or her alone, scandal be damned. But my parents would not hear of it. The nineteen-year-old daughter of the chargé d'affairs studies art and music at the Sorbonne. She does not have an illegitimate child. They threatened to cut me off entirely. I would have been penniless."

"Oh, Krysia," I say.

She stares straight in front of her, unblinking. "I could have chosen to make a go of it on my own with the child. I could have gotten by somehow. But I was young and afraid. So I did what they wanted. I asked if I could go away and have the child then put it up for adoption. They refused, said the scandal would have been too great." She rises and walks to the sink, her back to me, turning the faucet until the cold water sprays hard on her hand, flushing out the wound. "I let my parents decide for me, and it is a decision I have paid for all my life." Krysia shuts the water off and wraps her hand in a clean towel. She turns to face me again. "Do you understand what I am telling you?" I nod. Whatever they had done to Krysia to end her pregnancy must have left her unable to have children. "Good. A child is a blessing." As if on cue, Lukasz toddles across the room and tugs at Krysia's skirt.

"But what if it is the Kommandant's?" I ask. "I mean, what would Jacob…?" The sentence catches in my throat.

Her hand still wrapped in the towel, Krysia lifts Lukasz with a groan, then sinks into a chair; he is getting too big for her to carry. "Your child has a Jewish mother. He or she will be Jewish. A Jewish child. And it will be Jacob's child." She raises her eyebrows for emphasis. "No matter what." I know then that the secret would be ours, and that she will never tell anyone.

"Jacob's child," I repeat hesitantly. Does Jacob even want

children? There were times before the war when I was not certain. Once before we were married, when discussing politics, Jacob had said that the world population was growing too quickly, that he wasn't sure if he could bring a child into this world with all of its problems and political injustice. His words had been a blow to me. I had always wanted a family. I did not react outwardly or argue, though. I told myself that he would change his mind after graduation when we were married and he had settled down from his student causes into a job. But that had never happened; the war broke out and he became more politically involved than ever. We never discussed the matter again. I wonder what he would say now, whether the war has strengthened his view that this world is no place to raise a child. He might be unhappy with my pregnancy, even if he thinks the child is his. Then I remember him the day of his visit, kneeling down to speak to Lukasz. Perhaps he will see the importance of carrying on the Jewish faith through our children.

I do not share these thoughts with Krysia. I am sure she presumes that Jacob wants children, that he will be a good father. "You must assume that the baby is Jacob's," Krysia adds, mistaking my hesitation as being about the paternity. "You can say that he or she was born prematurely, if you need to."

I look at her, puzzled. "I don't understand."

"It's a way to make the dates fit respectably. Women who have accidentally gotten pregnant before their wedding day have been doing that since the beginning of time."

"Oh," I reply with surprise, realizing again how much I do not know.

The corners of her mouth turn up slightly. "How ironic it

is that one of the Nazis may have helped to put another Jewish child on this earth."

"If the Kommandant finds out..." I stop midsentence, shuddering.

Her slight smile fades quickly. "Richwalder can never know about this baby. We have to find a way to get you out of Kraków before the truth becomes obvious."

"Okay," I agree. Keeping up appearances has been hard enough without this. And there is no telling how the Kommandant will react.

"I will try once more to get in touch with what is left of the resistance, Marek or possibly Marta, to let them know we need to get you out." Inwardly, I cringe. Marek will surely blame me for getting myself into this predicament and inconveniencing the resistance at such a desperate time. And Marta...somehow I know that she will suspect that the baby is the Kommandant's and see this as evidence that I do not really love Jacob. Krysia continues, "Thankfully, you aren't showing yet, but that won't last. We will need to get you some fuller clothing so no one notices. Because even if I am successful in getting through to the resistance, I suspect it may take several weeks or even months for an escape route to be devised. Can you manage to keep up appearances until then?" I nod. "Good. This will not just be a question of getting you out of Kraków. You need to leave the country. Somewhere that Richwalder will not be able to find you once he realizes you are gone." I shudder, picturing myself hiding in the woods as Nazis fan out across the countryside, hunting me like an animal.

"What about Jacob?" I ask.

"Good question. We need to find out where he is and when

he will be healthy enough to travel, so the two of you can go together. In the early spring, when the snows thaw, I think. I am sure you will have to go over the mountains."

"And Lukasz?" Hearing his name, the child looks up.

Krysia bites her lip. I can tell that she is remembering our earlier fight about the child having to leave us. "I don't know. Let me try to get some information first and we will cross that bridge when we get there."

"My parents…?"

Krysia hesitates. I know I am bombarding her with questions to which she does not have answers, but I cannot help it. "I'm afraid that getting them out of the ghetto now will be impossible," she replies gently.

Though I already know what she is saying, my heart sinks at her words. "I understand," I reply. "But I need to know whether they are all right before I leave."

Her brow furrows. She will not, I know, make promises that she cannot keep. And getting information from inside the ghetto, like everything else, has gotten harder in the weeks since the Warszawa bombing. "I will try to find out." She stands up.

"Thank you." I reach up and grab her hand. "For everything."

She pats my shoulder. "I'll clean up. You get some rest. And try not to worry too much."

I stand and walk from the kitchen to the base of the stairs. Behind me, I hear Krysia placing dishes in the sink, followed by the sound of water running. I turn back. Her hands are washing a plate, but her gaze is fixed on the wall in front of her. I know that she is lost in memories of Claude and Paris in her younger days. It must have been so painful keeping the truth secret from her beloved Marcin all of those years, not being able to tell him why she could not have children, about the horrible choice she had made. Will I someday be like Krysia, alone with my secrets, regretful of the choices I made to survive? The thought is almost too much to bear. A wave of nausea overcomes me then, and I turn and hurry up the stairs.

CHAPTER 22

We do not speak of my pregnancy again after that night. A few weeks later, I find a new skirt and two new sweaters lying across my bed. They look much the same as my other work clothes, except that the sweaters are a bit longer and fuller and the skirt has an adjustable waistband. They will hide the growing roundness of my stomach, at least for now. I wonder where Krysia got them.

At least no one will question why I am wearing such heavy clothes, I think as I leave the house for work in one of my new outfits for the first time. Though it is early March, the weather remains bitterly cold, the ground still covered by a thin coating of ice and snow. As if on cue, a sharp gust of wind blows down from the hills. I draw my winter coat closer and make my way to the corner. A few minutes later, the bus arrives, and as we board, I eye the other passengers surreptitiously: do they notice anything different about me, these people with whom I ride nearly every day? They do not, I decide as I make my way down the aisle. A few nod, most barely look up or make eye contact. Each is preoccupied with his or her own day-to-day life, with survival. That has not changed just because my world has.

The morning after my conversation with Krysia, I had been awakened by Lukasz standing at my bedside, patting my face with his tiny hand to let me know he was hungry. Downstairs, I found that Krysia was gone. Though she had not left a note, I knew that she had gone to try to make contact with the resistance. I fed Lukasz his cereal, too nauseous to eat anything myself. As I finished drying the breakfast dishes, I heard the front door creak open. I set down the dish towel and walked to the top of the stairs. Krysia, who was stamping the snow from her boots in the entranceway, looked up at me. "I sent the message," she replied to my unspoken question. "Now we just have to wait."

Wait, I think now, as the bus lurches forward, its wheels skidding slightly on the icy road. How long can I wait? Krysia's words from our conversation the night she learned of my pregnancy echo in my head: the Kommandant must never know. Fortunately, I only have to keep it from him in the office. He has been so absorbed with work that he has made little effort to see me outside of work in recent weeks. I accept his rushed apologies only too willingly. If he tried to touch me now, he would surely know the truth.

My mind turns to Jacob. Krysia had said that there is a possibility I will be reunited with him, that we will leave Poland together. Of course, she cannot know this for sure, but the very thought, a long-held dream, nearly forgotten, fills me with warmth. And questions. Where would we go? How would we make a living? There are few jobs for scientists and library workers now, I suspect, though I have picked up good secretarial skills working for the Kommandant this year. I allow myself a small, inward smile at the irony of this, but my amusement quickly fades to nervousness. Even if we are able to escape and survive, what will our life together be like? I had not wanted to admit it, but there was some awkwardness between Jacob and myself during his visit. On some level, we were strangers to each other. That will improve, I tell myself, when we are together permanently again. But a part of me is not convinced: the war and all that has come with it has changed each of us so, how can we expect to be the same together as we were before?

I am hesitant for other reasons as well. I think of Krysia and Lukasz. As I have dreamed of a future with Jacob and free of the Nazis these many months, I have always imagined them being with us. Krysia had said that Lukasz might not be able to go with me, and she has not spoken of her own future or escape at all. The notion of leaving them behind to face the questions and consequences that would surely follow my sudden disappearance is unthinkable. I must persuade Krysia that she and the child go with me, refuse to leave if they do not. We are a family now.

Family. I shudder, thinking of my parents, whom I have not been able to see or speak to in nearly a year. Krysia promised to try to check on them, but I could tell from the look in her eyes that she did not think it would be possible. How can I leave town and abandon them even further?

The bus lurches to a sudden stop, jarring me from my thoughts. A tense murmur arises from the passengers. Recently, the Gestapo has established new security checkpoints at all major entry points into the city, including the spot where our road bisects the Aleje. Vehicles are subject to random stops and searches. I have seen cars and horse-drawn wagons pulled over, ordinary citizens forced to stand by the side of the road and answer questions about their identities and destinations. This is the first time, though, that I have seen or heard of them intercepting a bus. For a second, I wonder if they are looking for me. Perhaps someone from the resistance talked after being arrested and named names. A chill runs down my spine. Don't be silly, I tell myself; if the Gestapo wanted you, they could just as easily find you at the Kommandant's office or at Krysia's house. It is just a routine stop.

Two brutish police officers climb aboard the bus, shouting for everyone to get off. Hurriedly, we gather our belongings and obey. I avoid eye contact with the men as I pass them. Two more Gestapo police stand outside the bus, each with a large German shepherd on a thick leash. I stand huddled with the other passengers on the street corner in the freezing cold while the Nazis inspect the bus. We do not speak. Ten minutes pass, then fifteen. I am going to be late for work. I picture the Kommandant looking at the clock and pacing his office impatiently, wondering where I am. I briefly consider leaving the crowd and walking the last few blocks to Wawel; it would be much quicker than waiting. Then I decide against it, not wanting to draw attention to myself.

Twenty minutes pass. Finally, the policemen emerge from the bus and wave us back on board. They stand by the bus door as we enter, demanding identification papers from several passengers, seemingly at random. I brace myself as I pass, but they do not stop me. When everyone is reseated, one Gestapo officer stands on the steps of the bus by the still-open door. "Klopo-wicz, Henrik!" he barks. There is silence. The officer repeats the name, his face reddening. Out of the corner of my eye, I see the man across the aisle from me slowly raise his hand. His face is ashen. I do not turn toward him, but remain facing forward. *"Schnell!"* the officer shouts. The man rises and makes his way forward reluctantly. As he reaches the front, the officer grabs him by the arm and drags him off the bus. The doors slam shut behind them. I have seen that man on the bus every day since I started work. He appeared unremarkable, a manual laborer of some sort. I wonder what he has done, or was thought to have done, that caused him to be arrested. There must have been something; it did not appear to be a random selection. I shudder as the bus lurches forward once more.

Some fifteen minutes later, I reach the base of Wawel Castle and race up the ramp. Malgorzata is already seated at her desk when I enter the reception area. The clock over her desk says that it is eight-thirty. The Kommandant will be waiting.

"Dzien dobry," Malgorzata says smugly. Her greeting is a reproach: you are late and I am not.

"Czesc," I reply hurriedly. She opens her mouth to say something, but I am already through the door to the anteroom.

I shut the door behind me with a click. The anteroom is warm, a cozy fire burning beneath the furnace grate. Malgorzata must have made the fire for me. She tries sometimes, I think, removing my hat and gloves. I really should be more kind to her. I remember asking Krysia after the dinner party where I met the Kommandant how she could be so pleasant to those we despised. "Keep your friends close and your enemies closer," she had replied.

As I start to remove my coat, the door to the anteroom opens. It is Malgorzata.

"Yes?" I say, looking over my shoulder at her.

"The Kommandant went to a meeting at Pomorskie," she says.

I turn toward her. "Did he say when he will be back?"

She shakes her head. "He said to tell you that..." Malgorzata stops midsentence. Her eyes grow wide.

"What is it? What's wrong?"

She does not answer. I follow her stare, then freeze. Her eyes are fixed on my midsection, her mouth agape. As I'd been taking off my coat, my sweater had pulled from the waistband, revealing the fullness of my belly.

"Malgorzata..." I say, then stop, uncertain how to continue.

She turns hastily to leave, nearly tripping on a corner of the rug that has turned up by the door. As she stumbles, I catch her by the arm. "Malgorzata, please wait..." She pulls her arm from my grasp. "I can explain," I add, though I have no idea what to say.

She does not meet my eyes. "I have to go. There is much work to be done before the Kommandant returns."

"Malgorzata," I try again, but she is gone, slamming the door behind her.

Oh, God. I sink to my chair, a wave of nausea overtaking me. Malgorzata saw my stomach. She knows that I am pregnant. I consider racing after her, pleading for her silence. It would do no good. Malgorzata has sought my favor for months, hoping to be my ally because I occupy a favored position with the Kommandant. Now she no longer needs to be nice. She has all of the information she needs to unseat me. And it is only a matter of time, I am certain, before she tells the Kommandant.

"I made contact with the movement," Krysia tells me a few days later after we put Lukasz to bed. We are sitting in the parlor sorting clothes that she had washed earlier that day.

I look up in surprise from the towel I had been folding. My breath catches. "Really, with whom?"

"Jozef. He was the boy who brought you here from the ghetto."

I nod, picturing his face. I have never heard his name before. "Did he say anything about…?"

She interrupts me gently. "I asked him about Jacob first thing. He didn't have any information beyond what we already knew. I'm sorry."

"Oh." My heart sinks.

"But the good news is that I was able to speak with him about getting you out of Kraków. He thinks he can arrange an exit route for you during the last week of March. Do you think you can manage until then?"

I hesitate, doing the math in my head. Three weeks. Three more weeks of pretending and praying that the Kommandant would not find out my secret. My mind flashes back to my encounter with Malgorzata. Maybe it was my imagination and she did not notice anything, I think now. She and I had not spoken again that day and I have avoided her ever since, arriving at work early and remaining at my desk each day until after I knew she had gone. I do not want to face another confrontation. Or maybe she does know but will not tell the Kommandant. No, I realize suddenly, the ridiculousness of this last thought snapping me back to reality. I saw the look of astonishment on her face, quickly followed by smug triumph. She knows my secret, and is poised like a cat, waiting to strike. I am sure that she would have told the Kommandant already, had he not been out in meetings all week.

"Emma…" Krysia says gently, interrupting my thoughts. "Are you listening to me?"

I pause uncertainly. I should have told Krysia about my encounter with Malgorzata, but I did not, in part because I did not want to worry her further, in part because I am ashamed I had been so careless as to be caught. I do not know how to tell her now. It feels awkward, like I have hidden something that should have been disclosed much earlier. "I'm listening," I reply at last.

"Can you manage three weeks?" she repeats.

I swallow hard. "I think so."

"Good. That is probably the optimal time, anyway. Hopefully the weather will have let up, but you will not be too much farther along. Jozef said he can arrange an escort for you then."

My heart sinks. An escort likely means that I will not be going with Jacob. I start to ask Krysia, then stop. She has already said there is no further news about Jacob and I do not want to be difficult. "What about you and Lukasz?" I ask instead. She cocks her head, puzzled. "I mean, if I disappear, there will be questions, especially from the Kommandant."

"I have thought about that, of course. If I stay behind, I can make excuses. That you went to visit another relative or something."

I shake my head. He will never believe that I just left without saying goodbye. "But, Krysia, it won't be safe once I am gone. When the Kommandant realizes what has happened, there will be repercussions," I persist. "I can't leave you two behind to face that."

"It is a chance we have to take. We cannot all disappear at the same time. It would be too difficult—you cannot escape through the woods with an old woman and a child, and all of us traveling together publicly would attract too much attention." I search desperately for a response, but cannot find one. Krysia is right. She continues, "Anyway, I can't leave. I'm an old woman. This is my home." Her eyes are stormy.

I think of all the older people who have been ripped from their homes by the Nazis. They were not given the choice to stay, and her comment seems self-indulgent in light of all that has happened. I know, though, that this is not the principal reason for her refusal to leave. She is trying to do what is best for all of us. If that meant leaving, I have no doubt that she would be packed and at the door in an instant, ready to take on an escape through the woods in her cashmere coat and fine shoes.

I walk over to the chair where she is sitting, determined to try once more. I kneel beside her and take her hand. "Krysia, come with me," I plead. But she shakes her head and I know there will be no further debate. "What about Lukasz?" I ask. "He really shouldn't be here if the Gestapo comes looking for me."

She does not answer right away and I can see her mind working, considering what I have just said. It is not an easy dilemma. The child must be kept safe, and it is hard to know which would be riskier, keeping him here and facing questions when the Gestapo comes or taking him with me to face possible capture as we escape. "Taking the child would slow you down," she says at last. "And be riskier for you."

"I can manage," I insist.

"You have more than yourself to consider now. You have your own child."

"But…" I want to tell her Lukasz is my child, too, but Krysia raises her hand.

"Let's not argue. We don't have to decide now."

"Okay," I reply. I return to the sofa and pick up the towel I had been folding. A moment later, I look up again. Krysia is staring out the window into the darkness, the pile of clothing in front of her untouched. "What is it?" I ask.

She turns to me and I notice for the first time a deep sadness in her eyes. "After Marcin died, I found the loneliness unbearable. I became used to it after time, but it's a dull ache that never really left me. Until the night you arrived." Her eyes are moist now. "I just realized how much I have enjoyed this time, having you and Lukasz with me. How much I will miss you when you are gone."

"Oh, Krysia." I walk back over to her and put my arm around her shoulder. I had not considered until that moment how my leaving might affect her. I wanted to tell her that things would not change, that we would always be close. But I could not. The three of us living together had been an unexpected arrangement, strange and lovely and born out of necessity. By necessity it would all soon end.

"He's already asked for you twice," Malgorzata informs me smugly as I enter reception the next morning. Surprised, I look quickly at the clock behind her desk, wondering if I am late.

But the clock reads seven-forty-five, a full quarter of an hour before I am scheduled to arrive. The Kommandant is early. My stomach plunges.

Stay calm, I tell myself as I enter the anteroom hurriedly. He probably just has a lot of paperwork to catch up on or an early meeting. But even as I think this, I know that something is wrong. The Kommandant is as precise about time as he is about everything else; he always leaves his apartment at exactly eight o'clock and enters the office approximately fifteen minutes later, unless there is traffic. The Kommandant being early is as unthinkable as him being late.

My heart racing, I take off my coat and grab my notebook from the desk. The door to the Kommandant's office is ajar. I knock softly. "Herr Kommandant?" I call through the opening. There is no answer. I repeat the words, louder this time.

"Come in."

I open the door a few more inches and slide through. The Kommandant is standing at the far side of the office, looking out the window. "Malgorzata said you wished to see me." The door clicks shut behind me.

"Yes, sit down." I perch on the edge of the sofa, pen poised. The Kommandant does not look in my direction, but continues staring out at the river.

I take a deep breath, fighting the urge to turn and run from the room. Another minute of silence passes, then two. Finally I can stand it no longer. "Is something wrong, Herr Kommandant?"

"Wrong?" he repeats softly. He turns and begins walking toward me, his face stormy. He exhales hard through his teeth. "Everything is wrong. Partisans blow up cafés at will, killing our men. We are losing the war." I am surprised by his last statement; it is the first time I have ever heard the Kommandant, or any other German, admit that the war is going poorly for them—until now, it had only been a rumor, whispered by Polish staff in the corridors of Wawel or heard on the street. The Kommandant continues speaking, just feet away from me now. "And my enemies would like to blame both of these matters on me in order to see me ousted."

A wave of hope arises within me. Perhaps political matters are all that are troubling the Kommandant. "These are difficult times," I offer, trying to sound supportive.

"Yes." He sits down in the chair beside me, still looking away. "And then there is you."

My stomach drops. "M-me?" I stammer. My heart is pounding so loudly I can barely hear my own voice.

"Yes, Anna. You." He turns to face me then. "Is there something you would like to tell me?"

I hesitate, feeling the heat rise to my cheeks. He knows something. But what? In my despair over my pregnancy these past few weeks, I had almost forgotten that I have a much larger secret. Now I wonder if my true identity has been revealed. "No, Herr Kommandant," I reply at last, looking down.

"Anna." He reaches down and lifts my chin with his fingers, forcing my eyes to meet his. "Call me Georg." Though he had given me permission some time ago to use his first name when we are alone in his apartment, it is the first time he has ever bade me to do so in the office. His eyes are soft, I realize, without any sign of anger toward me. He would not look at me this way if he had discovered who I really am. Suddenly, in that moment of attempted intimacy, I know exactly which secret he has learned.

So he knows about my pregnancy, I think, and he does not seem angry about it. I am still not sure what to say. "Georg…" The name feels heavy and strange on my tongue. "How did you find out?" I know the answer of course, but I am stalling for time in order to figure out what to say.

"Malgorzata told me."

"Oh?" I try to sound surprised at this.

"Yes, she came to me with the news, thinking that I would be angry that you were unmarried and with child and cast you out from this office." I look up. "Oh, don't worry, I know she has long had designs on your job. Of course, she had no way of knowing that the child is mine." His face turns serious. "I wish I had heard it from you, though."

"I'm sorry," I say, shifting uncomfortably.

"No, Anna, it is I who needs to apologize." He takes both of my hands in his much larger ones. "I have been so preoccupied with this war business, I did not notice, and I did not give you a chance to tell me. Anyway, it doesn't matter how I found out. I know now." He takes my face in his hands and kisses me on the forehead.

"You mean you aren't angry?" I ask, my surprise genuine.

"Angry?" he exclaims, smiling broadly. "Anna, I couldn't be happier! You know that I always wanted children." I nod. "And with Margot, well, we never got the chance…" A picture flashes through my mind of Margot, lying on the floor, blood from the self-inflicted gunshot wound covering her pregnant, full stomach. I feel suddenly nauseous. Concentrate, I think, forcing the image from my mind. "I would have liked things to happen for us in the traditional sequence, of course— marriage, then children," he replies. "But it is no matter."

"But what will people think? I mean, your career…"

I watch the Kommandant's face as he considers for the first time the stigma of having a baby with his unmarried assistant, the ammunition it will give his political enemies. "Yes," he says slowly. "We must get you out of Kraków before anyone else notices." How ironic, I think; that is exactly what Krysia said when she learned of my pregnancy. The Kommandant leaps up and begins pacing the floor, as though dictating a memorandum. "I would like to send you to my home in Hamburg," he says, thinking aloud. "But that's impossible right now. The enemy bombings make it too dangerous. I know…" He stops and turns to face me. "My sister Hannah lives in the countryside near Salzburg. I will send you there."

My stomach drops. Austria is even deeper into Nazi territory. How will I ever find Jacob or my parents again if I am sent there? He is watching me now, waiting for a reaction. "Herr Kommandant, I mean, Georg, that is very kind of you." I hesitate, searching for the appropriate response. "But I cannot leave my family…."

"No, of course not," he replies. "And you cannot travel alone. Krysia and Lukasz shall go with you." I marvel at how he thinks he can rearrange the lives of so many with just a few words, though of course he has been doing that to the Jews for years now. "Colonel Diedrichson will escort the three of you as far as Vienna and I will have my sister's driver meet you there. How does that sound?"

It sounds like a death sentence. I cannot let him send me away. "Georg…" I try again.

He sits down in the chair beside me. "What is it, Anna?" I can hear the impatience in his voice.

I take a deep breath. "What about you?" I ask.

A look of realization crosses his face, followed by a smile. "About us, you mean?"

"Yes," I say quickly, running with the lie. "I would hate to be so far from you."

"And I, you," he replies, touching my cheek.

"Perhaps I can remain in Kraków, hidden from sight...."

He shakes his head. "I'm sorry, but it is impossible. The chance of someone finding out would be too great. And with the way the war is going..." He hesitates, looking away. "Well, I don't want you and the baby here if something should happen in the city." I want to ask what he means by this: does he think that Kraków will become under siege, a battleground when the Allies advance? He continues, "Anyway, the medical care is much better in Austria. No, it is for the best. You are leaving tomorrow." He takes my hands once more. "And then after the war, as soon as I can arrange it, I will join you there and we will be married. Okay?"

I start to open my mouth to raise another point, then close it again. The Kommandant is like Jacob in that regard—there is no point in arguing further once his mind is made up. "Good," he says, taking my silence as agreement. "Then it's settled. I'll make the arrangements. You will leave tomorrow morning at nine."

I look up at the clock. Twenty-four hours. I need to get out of the office and tell Krysia immediately. "Georg," I say, standing up. "I apologize, but I am feeling rather weary. If there is nothing pressing, would you mind if I go home?"

He rises. "Of course, of course. It is your condition, I am

sure. Go home and rest for the day. You will need your strength for the journey."

"Thank you." I start for the door.

"Anna," he calls after me. I turn back. "There is one other thing."

Reluctantly, I walk back to where he is standing. "Yes?"

"Will you see me tonight?" He looks away, runs his hand through his hair. "I mean, it's been so long since we've had any time alone together, and now, with you leaving tomorrow, it may be some time…" He turns back to face me again. "What do you think?"

I stare at him, puzzled. With everything that has happened, he cannot possibly be thinking of romance. "I—I don't know," I reply.

"Please," he persists. "Just for a little while."

I pause, considering his request. The last thing I want is to spend the night with the Kommandant. But I cannot afford any suspicion, not now after all that has happened. Seeing my hesitation, the Kommandant looks quickly at the door to make sure that no one is there, then draws me into his arms and looks into my eyes intensely. My heart beats hard against my chest as it always does when I am close to him. I wonder if he can feel it. He presses his lips against mine, quick and hard. A moment later, he releases me. I step back, smoothing my dress. "What do you say?" he asks, as though his kiss should have magically persuaded me.

"Okay," I relent quickly. Anything that will get me out of the office and back to Krysia's house.

"Excellent. Stanislaw will come for you tonight at eight. Do you want him to drive you home now?"

I shake my head. "No, thank you. I have some errands to run on the way."

"Very well, then I will see you tonight." He turns and begins walking toward his desk. "Send Malgorzata in on your way out, will you?" he calls over his shoulder.

"Yes, sir." His request is routine, as though it was any other workday and our exchange had not taken place. But I can tell from the Kommandant's tone that this day would be Malgorzata's last at Wawel, because she had tried to betray me, and because she knew too much.

In the anteroom, I put on my coat and scarf quickly. Taking only my bag with me, I step into the reception area. "The Kommandant wishes to see you," I inform Malgorzata coldly. Avoiding my eyes, she leaps from her chair and scurries into the Kommandant's office. I realize that, seeing me leaving the office in my outerwear so early in the morning, she probably thinks I have been fired, and that she is being called in to replace me. I am almost too weary to pity her. I try not to run as I leave the office and walk out of Nazi headquarters for the last time.

CHAPTER 23

"You are leaving at dawn," Krysia announces at two o'clock that afternoon.

Four hours earlier, I had entered the house, breathless from running, with the news that the Kommandant knew of my pregnancy and wanted to send us all to Austria. "I was afraid that might happen," Krysia said when I had finished the story. "Stay here with Lukasz." Krysia had thrown on her coat and boots and raced out into the street. A few minutes ago, she had returned and, without saying where she had been, told me breathlessly that I was leaving.

Now, walking up the stairs, she briefly outlines the plan for me. "Someone will come here to escort you to Myslenice." I nod; I am familiar with the small town, thirty kilometers south of Kraków. "You will be hidden there until tomorrow night when it is dark and then smuggled by wagon over the border to a safe house in the mountains of Czechoslovakia. It's a risky plan, not nearly as good as the one we would have had if we had been able to wait another month, but there is no choice."

"I'm sorry," I reply, following her into the kitchen and dropping into a chair.

She waves her hand. "There is no point in worrying about what can't be changed. We just need to get you out of here." She carries the empty teakettle to the sink and turns on the water. "Lukasz is napping?"

"Yes. What about Jacob? I mean, will he be going with me?"

She stops filling the kettle and turns to me, a helpless look crossing her face. "Emma, I'm sorry, I don't think so. There's been no further word about his whereabouts or his condition. I had hoped you would be able to go together, but with having to get you out of here so unexpectedly, it's just not possible. Perhaps in a few months he will be able to follow you," she adds.

So I will be going without Jacob. For a moment, I consider refusing. "You have to go," Krysia says, reading my mind. She puts the kettle on the stove and then turns to face me once more. "I know my nephew, and above all else, he would want you and your child to be safe." If that is true, then why hasn't he been here with me, I wonder for the hundredth time, instead of fighting with the resistance? If I mattered most, we would be together. He would not be wounded and I would know the child I was carrying was his. But the truth, I know, is not that simple. If Jacob had not gone underground, I would never have escaped the ghetto. We would both be in a concentration camp by now, or worse. Krysia is right, of course; Jacob would want me to do what is necessary to survive.

"What about you and Lukasz?" I ask a few minutes later, as she places the cups of tea on the table.

She shakes her head, sitting down. "We cannot all go together. Making the journey now, ahead of schedule when the mountain snow is still deep, is dangerous enough for you. Lukasz cannot manage it and he would only slow you down. I've arranged with the resistance that, when you go, Lukasz will be taken from the house and hidden in the countryside."

"But why?" I cannot bear to think of Lukasz uprooted again and left with strangers.

"Emma, once you are gone, the Gestapo will surely come here again. I will tell them that you have gone to visit relatives back in Gdańsk, but we need to make it look like Lukasz has gone with you. So you see why it must be this way."

I do not answer. We drink our tea without speaking, the silence broken only by the ticking of the grandfather clock in the hallway. A few minutes later, I clear my throat. "Krysia, there's one other thing." I hesitate. "My parents…"

"Oh, yes." She smoothes her skirt, not meeting my eyes. "I asked about them just now while getting information about your escape plan. They are all right, surviving as well as can be expected. That is all I've been able to learn. I was hoping to find out something more before mentioning anything to you." I can tell by the uneasiness in her voice that she is not saying all she knows.

"I need to see them before I leave."

She shakes her head firmly. "I'm sorry, it is out of the question."

"Please," I implore. "I can't just leave without saying goodbye."

"Emma, be reasonable," she replies impatiently. "Podgorze

is not safe now. Security is tighter than ever since the Warszawa incident and there are checkpoints everywhere, especially around the ghetto. You would be risking your life by going there. And even if you went to the ghetto, what is it you would do? Go back inside?"

I hesitate. "I—I don't know," I admit. "I mean, no, of course not. But perhaps I can find a break in the wall, like the one I escaped through the night I was brought from the ghetto. I could speak with them at the wall, or at least send word."

"It's too dangerous." Her voice softens. "I will make sure the resistance has someone look in on them after you are gone."

I am not convinced. I do not doubt the sincerity of her words, but I take them in with the same distrust I have acquired of all those I had once believed in the most. No one would look in on my parents, not unless it was eminently convenient or in his or her own interest to do so. Our families had been collateral damage to the resistance. For the millionth time, I curse myself silently for trusting them, for not trying to do something to get my parents out of the ghetto months ago.

But I know this is not a fight I will win with Krysia. "And the Kommandant?" I ask instead.

"What about him?"

"I am not at all sure he will believe that I disappeared the very day I was to be going to Austria."

"You let me worry about the Kommandant," she replies, her eyes narrowing.

"You didn't seem surprised at his proposal," I remark.

"Of course not. He is in love with you."

I look away. "I know."

She looks up, surprised at my tone. "What is it? What's wrong?"

"Nothing." I do not know what I am feeling. Pity, perhaps, or regret.

Krysia pats my hand. "I understand. It is no fun to break a heart, even one like Richwalder's."

"I suppose not." I clear my throat. "He's asked to see me tonight."

Her hand freezes on mine. "Oh? What did you say?"

"I said yes. I had to," I add. I can hear the defensiveness in my own voice. "I had no excuse not to."

She nods. "That's right, of course. Although it does complicate things a bit, with you leaving in the morning."

"It will be fine. The Kommandant is a heavy sleeper." I can feel myself blush as I reveal this intimate detail. "And I've left before he's arisen many times."

"Still," Krysia says. "We need to be sure." Without speaking further, she rises and walks out of the kitchen. A few minutes later, she returns. "Here." She presses a small glass vial containing a white powder into my palm. "Sleeping powder," she said. "If you can slip a little bit of it into his brandy, it will make sure he doesn't wake up when you do."

I look up at her, puzzled. "How on earth…?"

"Pankiewicz gave it to me some time ago, before he was taken from the ghetto. It is normally used by doctors to sedate patients for minor procedures. I asked him for it because, well, you never know what you might need."

I think about all of the times I had waited for the Kommandant to fall asleep so I could search for papers. "Why didn't you give it to me to use earlier?" I ask.

"I considered it, but the powder is extremely powerful," she replies. "Even if you had used a small amount, he would have woken up feeling very sluggish, as if he'd had way too much to drink the night before. I thought it was too risky to use on a regular basis, when you had to keep going back there. I was afraid he might get suspicious. But now…"

"I understand." Tonight is the last night I will ever go to the Kommandant's. There is nothing more to lose. I tuck the vial into my skirt pocket and stand up. "Krysia, it's safe, isn't it?" Now it is her turn to look confused. "For the baby, I mean, if I have to go to the Kommandant's tonight…" My voice trails off—I am embarrassed.

A look of realization crosses her face. "Of course, you haven't been with him since you found out you are pregnant, have you?" I nod. "Don't worry. It should still be fine at this early stage."

From upstairs comes the sound of Lukasz, awake and babbling. "I'll get him," I say, suddenly eager to escape the conversation.

"Okay." She starts up the stairs to the third floor. "I'll gather some warm clothes for you and Lukasz."

Krysia and I spend the rest of the day preparing things for Lukasz's and my departure the next morning, packing two small bags tight with clothes and preparing foodstuffs that will travel well. We speak little as we work. That evening, Lukasz clings to me tighter than ever as I tuck him into bed, as though he somehow knows it will be the last time.

A few minutes before eight, I hear the Kommandant's car pull up in front of the house. "You have the powder?" Krysia asks, following me down to the foyer.

"Yes," I reply as I pull on my coat. "I'll be back before dawn."

"Good. Be careful tonight. We are so close now. We can't let anything go wrong." Her papery lips brush my cheek. "I will see you in the morning before you go."

When the car pulls up in front of the apartment building, I am surprised to find the Kommandant waiting for me downstairs by the front door. "You look radiant," he says warmly, taking my arm. As he escorts me upstairs, I notice that his face is freshly shaven and that he has put on cologne. Inside, the apartment looks transformed: the tables are cleared of clutter and the air has a faint lemon scent.

I turn to him in surprise. "You cleaned the apartment?"

"Yes," he says, helping me off with my coat. "Or had it cleaned, I should say. Squalor may be fine for a bachelor like me, but you can't raise a child in such a place." I start to reply that the child will not be raised, or even born here, then think better of it. He is trying to show me, I realize, that he will make a good father.

As I walk to the sofa, I notice another change: the photograph of Margot has disappeared from the mantelpiece; a vase filled with fresh flowers sits in its place. "Georg…" I turn back to him and gesture toward the mantelpiece.

He comes over to where I am standing and takes my hands in his. "You are my life now," he says. "It's time to let go of the past." I search his face for any sign of sadness or remorse, but find none. For the first time since I have known him, he looks completely happy. A wave of guilt washes over me suddenly. Tomorrow I will be gone and the charade of Anna will, too. What will happen to him then?

"Are you hungry?" he asks.

I start to shake my head, then remember the vial of powder. "A bit," I lie. "Perhaps something light. Why don't I pour
the drinks while you get it?"

He disappears into the kitchen and I walk to the glass-front
cabinet where he keeps the liquor. I take out two glasses and,
looking quickly over my shoulder, tap a small amount of the
powder into one of them. I hesitate uncertainly. Krysia had
not said how much to use. I add an extra pinch for good mea-
sure, then pour brandy into both glasses. "Here we are," the
Kommandant calls as he comes through the door of the
kitchen carrying two plates.

Trying not to panic, I stash the vial hurriedly back in my
skirt, then turn to him. "That looks delicious," I manage to
say, as I carry the glasses to the low table by the sofa.

The Kommandant makes small talk as we eat, as though
this was any other day and I was not leaving the country in
the morning. I watch carefully as he drains his glass of brandy,
hoping the powder has completely dissolved and will not leave
a telltale trace in the bottom of the glass. A few minutes later,
I study his face to see if there is any effect, but his eyes are clear
and give no indication of sleepiness. I wonder how long it will
take for the powder to work. When we have finished our meal
and had coffee, he starts to reach for me.

"Let's go to the bedroom," I suggest. If the powder takes
effect here and he falls asleep on the sofa, it will be harder for
me to sneak out of the apartment.

"Okay," he agrees. In the bedroom, I begin to see the effects of the drug. His pupils are dilated, and his kisses are slow,
his hands clumsy. A few minutes later, he falls away from me,
eyes closed. He is breathing heavily. The powder is really

strong, I think, rolling away from him. I hope that I have not given him too much. I look at the clock on the nightstand. It is after eleven. I had not realized we had been talking over dinner for so long.

I stare at the ceiling, wondering what to do. I would like to leave now, but I don't know how long the powder will last and I am afraid he will wake up and find me gone. No, I should stay at least for a little while. Though I had largely pretended to drink my glass of brandy, the few sips I took have made me drowsy and I have to pinch myself a few times not to doze off.

As I lay in bed, my thoughts turn to my parents. It has been so long since I have seen them, and now I am supposed to leave, without even saying goodbye. My earlier conversation with Krysia plays over and over in my mind. She is right, I know; by going to the ghetto I would be risking my life, and the safety of everyone around me. It would be a crazy thing to do, especially now, when we are so close to the end. And there is no guarantee that I would even be able to reach my parents. But even as I play the risks over and over in my mind, I know that I have to try. In a few hours I will leave Kraków, possibly forever. I had already walked out on my parents once the night I escaped from the ghetto. I cannot do it again.

I look over at the clock again, then back at the Kommandant sleeping. Krysia had told me that I needed to be back at the house by four o'clock. The Kommandant's apartment is only a short walk from the bridge to Podgorze. There is time, I realize; time to go to the ghetto, if I dare. My mind is made up. Silently, I slip from bed. The Kommandant snorts and rolls over. I freeze, terrified that he has awoken and that I will be unable to leave, but he continues breathing evenly, eyes shut. I dress quickly and start for the door of the bedroom.

Then I stop and turn to look at the Kommandant. This is the last time I will see him. I tiptoe back to the side of the bed where he is sleeping, fighting the urge to climb back into bed beside him, to wrap myself around him once more. A wave of sadness passes over me. There are so many things I want to tell him. That I'm sorry for deceiving him, for not being able to really be the woman he thought he loved. That I wish things could have been different between us. But there is no time for regrets. I bend over, touching my nose to his hair, and kiss him lightly on the forehead to say goodbye. He does not stir.

I cross the living room and pick up my coat from the chair where I had placed it earlier. As I start to put it on, I hesitate, looking down at the low table where our dinner plates still sit, half filled with meat and cheese. So much waste. I will take the food with me to give to my parents, I decide. I tiptoe hurriedly into the kitchen and grab a paper bag from the cupboard, then return to the living room and put the food inside. I make my way out of the apartment. Outside, the street is deserted, the air bitterly cold. I head toward the bridge, hugging the shadows of the buildings. My every nerve stands on end; I must not get caught. Soon, I reach the river's edge and cross furtively over the railway bridge.

The streets of Podgorze are silent and dark. I know, though, that the Gestapo could be hiding anywhere, lying in wait for someone to come along. When I reach the ghetto wall, I press myself against it, trying to hide in the thin shadows. I look at the wall, which seems to stretch endlessly in both directions. An urge to turn and leave washes over me. Perhaps Krysia was right.

I press myself flat against the wall as I inch my way along, feeling with my hand until I touch a small break in the stone, no larger than a loaf of bread. I peer through the hole. The streets inside are also deserted. This is the industrial side of the ghetto near the kitchen, I realize. It is unlikely that anyone will be here in the dead of night. Inhaling deeply, I continue along the wall.

Several meters farther down, where the wall turns and curves inward, there is another, bigger break in the stone. I look through the hole, relieved to see apartment buildings instead of warehouses. This street is not far from the street where my parents live, but it too is deserted. This is hopeless, I think, looking nervously over my shoulder at the empty street behind me. I should go now, before I get caught. But I cannot leave, not when I have made it this far. A few minutes later, I hear a faint scratching sound on the other side of the wall. I press my head through the hole, craning my neck in both directions, but I can see nothing. It's probably just a rat, I think, sinking back. Then I hear the sound again, louder and closer. I look again. An old man shuffles along the ghetto street toward me, head down. His back is hunched to the point he is almost doubled over as he takes his tiny steps. As he nears, I start to call him over to ask if he has seen my father. Then I stop, mouth agape. The old man is my father.

"Tata," I whisper loudly, pulling back my shawl. He looks up. Several minutes pass before the light of recognition crosses his face. He walks slowly toward me.

"*Shana madela,*" he rasps in Yiddish, stretching a bony hand through the hole in the wall. Pretty girl. The eleven months since I have seen him last have aged him beyond all recognition. His face is like a skull, barely covered with skin. Only a few patches of his beard remain. The few teeth that still remain of his once full smile protrude grotesquely from his sunken mouth.

"Tata, what...?" So many questions flood my brain, I do not know where to begin.

"I walk at night sometimes," he says, as though that explains everything. I remember, as though from a past life, the hunger pains that came at night in the ghetto, shooting through my stomach like knives, making it impossible to sleep.

"Here," I say, pulling out the bag of food I brought from the Kommandant's apartment. I push it through the crack in the wall. "It's not kosher, but..." He takes the bag and holds it limply, as though he does not realize it is there. My stomach twists. Something is horribly wrong. "Mama...?" I ask, not wanting to hear the answer. My mother never would have let him out alone at night. She never would have let his hair be unkempt, or his clothes dirty, even in the worst of times.

"Ten days ago," he says, his eyes turning to dark pits.

"What...?" I ask, not wanting to understand the meaning of his words. I notice then that the front of his shirt has been torn in the Jewish ritual of mourning. "No..."

"She's gone," he whispers with difficulty, tears springing to his eyes.

"No!" I cry loudly, oblivious to the danger that someone might hear. Suddenly I am five years old and in bed with the flu in our Kazimierz apartment. My mother had slept with me when I was ill, and rubbed grease on my chest and made soup and sung songs. "Mama..."

My father looks at me helplessly through the hole in the wall, a tortured expression on his face. He could never handle my crying, even as a child. The notion that something was wrong with me that he could not fix had always been an unbearable one to him. My grief, I know, is worse for him than his own. "She first became sick last autumn with a terrible fever."

"I know," I reply between my sobs. "I tried to get help." I cannot bring myself to tell him the resistance refused to help. "Krysia tried to do something."

"She sent Pankiewicz, the pharmacist. The dear man was a godsend. He tried everything, used his scarcest medicines on your mother, but the illness was like nothing he had seen before, a total mystery. Eventually, the fever broke and she got a little better but she was still very weak. She was never the same afterward and the winter…well, a few weeks ago the fever returned and that was it."

I swallow, my sobs easing. "Was she peaceful? At the end, I mean?"

My father hesitates. "She was at peace," he replies carefully, and I can tell from his expression that she suffered a great deal. "She was strong and brave. I was with her the whole time…"

"I should have been there, too," I say, my voice cracking.

He shakes his head. "She understood. All she wanted was to know that you were safe." But I am inconsolable. I picture my mother the night I left, sleeping beside my father. I did not have the chance to say goodbye, not even the casual goodbye I might have said when headed out the door to the bakery or the library, planning to meet again in a few hours. No, I had disappeared in the middle of the night and now so had she.

"I'm sorry I left you," I say.

"No, no, it wasn't like that," he protests quickly. "We were worried, of course, that morning when we awoke and found you gone. But we received word quickly that Jacob and his friends had somehow gotten you out. That you were okay. We were glad. In the end, your mother was sorry she didn't have the chance to say goodbye. But she understood why you had to go the way you did. I did, too."

I begin to sob openly again, oblivious to where I am and the danger that surrounds us. My father watches me helplessly from the other side of the wall, heavy with his own grief. *"Yisgadal, v yiskadash shmay rabah…"* he begins in Hebrew to chant the mourner's *kaddish*. In a choked voice, I join in. It is the Jewish prayer for the dead that does not mention death, but only praises God in the highest. How many times had my father said it alone these nights? I wonder.

I inhale, fighting to regain my composure. "We have to get you out," I say frantically. "I will come back in an hour with papers…." He shakes his head. We both know that it is impossible. No one is getting in or out of the ghetto these days. My father certainly could not pass as a messenger, or a gentile, and he could never survive the journey through the forest.

No, I cannot get him out. But I want to give him something, something that will linger where I cannot. "Tata, I am going to have a baby." A confused look crosses over his face. "Jacob was able to come visit us once last autumn," I add quickly. I do not tell him, of course, that the child might not be my husband's. In that moment, it does not matter.

He smiles weakly. *"Mazel tov,* darling." But his eyes look pained. I know in his mind he is seeing the grandchild he would never hold, never witness bar mitzvahed. Yet his family would go on. My words are both a wound and a gift.

"If it is a girl, I will name the child for Mama," I add.

"Emmala," he says. I shudder. It has been so long since I have heard him call me by his pet name for me. It feels like a warm blanket around my shoulders. I see in his eyes then a helpless look. It is the look of a father acknowledging all that he is unable to give to his child. His guilt at not having been able to protect me. Suddenly, his expression changes. "Wait," he says. "Wait right here." Before I can reply, he disappears. I press back against the wall into the shadows, seeing my mother's face in the darkness. Had Krysia known? I wonder. Did she lie and tell me my parents were all right, knowing I would not leave otherwise? Several moments pass. Finally, I hear my father's shuffling steps as he reappears. "Here." He thrusts his hand through the wall once more, pressing three items into my palm. The first two are my wedding and engagement rings, which I had long ago tucked under my mattress in the ghetto. The last is a piece of paper. I unfold it and gasp aloud. It is my marriage certificate to Jacob.

I hesitate, my hand still aloft. A Jewish marriage certificate and rings. Once these things would have meant everything to me. Now I see only the danger in taking them. If I am caught, they will surely betray my identity. I look at my father then, at the light that giving me these few things has brought to his eyes. I have no choice but to take them.

"Thank you." I wrap the rings in the paper and tuck them both in my pocket.

My father nods, content to be able to give me that much. "And when you see Jacob, you tell that boy your father said he is never to leave your side again."

"I promise."

My father nods emphatically. "Tell Jacob I said enough

with his political nonsense. He has my grandson to raise." I am amazed to see a small smile at the corner of my father's cracked lips. Even now, at his darkest hour, he can find some humor, some joy.

"Grandson," I reply, desperately trying to find the humor to match his own. "I knew you always wanted a boy."

He shakes his head, serious now. "I wanted you. You are my everything."

I fight back the tears that are starting to well up again. "And you are mine," I reply softly. "But, Tata, the ghetto…"

"Yes…" He is not smiling now. He, too, has heard the rumors of liquidation. Having witnessed two terrifying *akcjas* already, he surely knows what to expect, the horrors that lay ahead for him. Yet his eyes burn clear and unafraid. "The Lord is my shepherd," he says simply. There is a kind of radiance to his thin, starved face. I realize then that I am staring into the eyes of absolute faith. I think of all of the days spent in the tiny Remuh Synagogue on Szeroka Street, davening and chanting his prayers. Of candles lit and wine blessed. Even in the ghetto, I know he has spent these long nights reciting over and over to himself the Twenty-Third Psalm. Still, I wonder how he remains so serene. Perhaps he has walked God's path for so long that he has no need for the searching and fear that others do. Or perhaps he has lost so much there is nothing else to take. Most likely, he knows that my mother is waiting at the end of this path.

"Go now," he urges.

"I can't leave you again," I protest. "I won't."

He shakes his head. "You must." I do not reply. I know that he is right. I cannot free him, and staying here will mean certain death for us both. Still I linger, wanting to hold on to the last page of my childhood, a book that is about to close forever. I press my head through the hole in the wall, the cracked edges scratching my cheeks and forehead. My father tries to ward me off, not wanting to pass whatever germs and disease lay in the ghetto on to me and my unborn child. But I reach my arm through and draw him close to me. I am just able to graze my lips against the papery skin of his cheek.

"I love you, Tata."

"God be with you, my darling." I hold his fingers in mine for another second until he pulls away and, with great effort, turns from the wall. I watch as he walks away, grateful that he has gone first, knowing that I could not. I stand motionless as his figure grows smaller and then disappears into the darkness of the ghetto. I reach through the hole in the wall once more, but on the other side is emptiness. Finally, I can stand it no longer. I turn away from the ghetto wall and begin to run.

CHAPTER 24

Once away from the ghetto, my thoughts turn to getting safely back to Krysia's. I consider trying to find my way back through the forest, but I know from hearing talk around Wawel that the Nazis have long since identified the woods surrounding Podgorze as a potential escape route from the city. Since the café bombing, the forest is crawling with Nazi sharpshooters who will fire at anything that moves. No, I realize, I will have to chance going back through town.

I reach the foot of the railway bridge. The clanging of my shoes is painfully loud as I climb the bridge steps. When I reach the top, I hesitate, scanning the length of the bridge. It appears to be deserted, but the full winter moon shines down like a spotlight. The other side seems as far as another country and there is little cover, other than the shadows of the widely spaced columns. I draw my shawl over my head. As I start across, a fierce gust of icy wind cuts through me. I hunch over, nearly doubled in half, clutching the shawl under my chin as it threatens to blow away. My eyes concentrate on the ground as I try to walk softly and avoid the slippery patches and uneven metal seams.

Suddenly I hear the sound of a vehicle in the distance ahead of me. My breath catches. Someone is coming. I am almost halfway across the bridge, too far to turn back. I leap behind one of the steel columns of the bridge. Seconds later, a Nazi truck with a lone driver approaches, heading in the direction of the ghetto. I cower in the shadows, pressing myself into the column, not breathing. The truck continues past me, slowly, painfully. Don't stop, I pray, and it does not. A minute later, it disappears off the far side of the bridge.

I exhale deeply. I am safe, at least for the moment. Still standing behind the column, I bury my hands in my pockets. My fingers graze my marriage certificate. I wrap my fingers around the thin paper, feeling the hardness of my wedding and engagement rings wrapped within. I should not have these things with me, I think. I should get rid of them in case I am stopped. I picture myself throwing the items over the edge of the bridge, watching as the rings drop quickly to the water below, the paper fluttering behind it. Jacob would under-stand, even agree. He had instructed me to get rid of the cer-tificate the night before he left. But I cannot bring myself to part with them. They are my last connection to him, a prom-ise that we will be together again.

I look over the railing of the bridge. Even if I could do it, the point is a moot one. The river is frozen, unwilling to hide my secrets beneath its dark waters. The paper would blow away, the rings might be found. And I do not dare to move to throw them for fear of attracting attention. No, I have taken these things from my father and they are with me now.

I remain motionless behind the column for several more minutes, terrified of stepping out into the open again and risking being seen. I have to keep going, I realize at last. Krysia will awaken soon and wonder where I have gone. I listen carefully, and hearing nothing, I peek my head out and look in both directions. The bridge is clear. Taking a deep breath, I step reluctantly out from my hiding place. My legs shake as I continue across the bridge in quick, tiny steps. Just a few more meters, I think. I can see the end of the bridge, its shadows beckoning like a promise. I'm almost there.

Suddenly I hear a loud noise behind me. I jump. It is the sound of an engine, coming from the far end of the bridge. The truck, I think, panic seizing me. Its driver has seen me and turned around. I consider leaping behind a column once more, but it is too late. In the distance behind me, I hear the engine switch off. A door opens. "Halt!" a male voice shouts. "Halt!"

My blood runs cold. I know that voice; it belongs to the Kommandant.

"Hands up," he orders, his heavy footsteps growing louder as he crosses the bridge toward me. I obey, my mind racing. What is the Kommandant doing here? He is supposed to be asleep. The powder must have worn off too soon; perhaps I did not use enough. But how did he know I was here? Did he follow me to the ghetto? I can hear him coming closer now. He stops, just feet behind me. "Turn around," he orders sharply.

He does not realize that it is me, I realize. He thinks I am just a Pole who has broken curfew. I hesitate. For a moment, I consider revealing myself to him. My mind races to come up with some excuse why I am out, wandering the streets at night, but I can think of none. "Turn around," he repeats, a familiar impatience in his voice. Taking a deep breath, I turn to him, keeping my head low, my face covered. Don't let him recognize me, I pray. From underneath the shawl, I can see the Kommandant, now just a few feet away. His gun is drawn.

"Miss, what are you doing out alone at night?" The Kommandant's tone is somewhat softer now that he realizes that he has apprehended a woman. "Don't you know that you are breaking curfew?" I shake my head slightly, knowing that he expects an answer and that if I speak he will recognize my voice. He lowers the gun slightly, extending his free hand. "Your papers, please."

Oh, God, I think. There is no way out now. "Papers!" he demands, growing impatient once more. Hoping to stall for a few minutes, I reach into my pocket slowly, pretending to search for my papers. I feel once again the possessions my father returned to me, the cool metal of my wedding and engagement rings, the wrinkled marriage certificate. If I refuse to turn over my papers, I will be arrested and searched and these items will surely be discovered. Then my hand closes around my identity card, the one that names me as Anna Lipowski. I pause, wondering whether to reveal myself. Perhaps if I can come up with a plausible explanation for being on the bridge in the middle of the night, and if I tell it to the Kommandant with just the right smile and touch, he may believe and forgive me.

I lift my head an inch, trying to gauge his expression. As I do, my shawl opens slightly at the neck. Something flashes in the darkness. It is the necklace the Kommandant had given me, its brilliant blue stone caught by the moonlight.

The Kommandant gasps. "Anna," he exclaims, recognizing the jewel.

"Yes, Herr Kommandant," I say softly, too nervous to use his first name. "It is me."

He lowers his revolver and pulls the shawl back from my face. "Why didn't you tell me it was you? What are you doing here?"

"I can explain." He looks at me expectantly. "I—I…" I stammer.

"Why did you leave?" he demands. "I was so worried when I woke up and found you gone."

"I'm sorry. I just wanted to spend my last night at Krysia's." I study his face, but I cannot tell if he believes my explanation. "I missed Lukasz," I add.

"You could have told me, Anna. I would have understood. And Stanislaw would have driven you home. You shouldn't be on the street alone at night. You could have been arrested, or worse. Anna, this is very dangerous!"

"I know," I reply. "I'm sorry."

He looks out over the side of the bridge in the darkness. "But that's not all, is it?" he asks.

My stomach drops. "I—I don't understand…"

"I mean, that's not the only reason you are out here, is it?" He knows, I think, too paralyzed to respond. He knows everything. He looks back at me. "You were running away."

"No," I reply quickly. "I mean…"

"It's okay," he says. I look up at him, surprised. "I understand."

"You do?"

"Yes," he says without anger. "This all must be so scary for you. Having a baby, leaving Kraków. It is only natural that you should panic."

A wave of relief washes over me. He does not know the truth. "It is scary," I say nodding hard. "I am terrified."

"So you were running away…" He looks out over the water into the darkness. "Where were you going to go?"

"I don't know." I study his face as he processes what he has heard, wondering if he will believe me. "Are you angry?" I ask.

"No," he replies quickly, reaching out and taking my hand. "It's okay. When I woke up and found you gone, I realized how scared you must be. That's why I came to find you. I wanted to see you and reassure you that everything will work out."

"Oh…" I am uncertain how to respond.

"Anna…" He reaches down and lifts my chin gently with his fingers. "I don't want you to be afraid anymore. I'll do whatever you need to make this okay for you. If you want, I will leave my position tonight, if need be, and we can run away together."

"Georg…" I am stunned by his words.

"I mean it. All that matters to me is your happiness."

I do not answer. My mind whirls, overwhelmed by all that has happened. In an instant, I have gone from my secret nearly being discovered to the Kommandant pledging his undying devotion. I look up into his eyes, bewildered. This awful beast of a man, who has killed so many innocents, is offering me absolute, unconditional love. No, not unconditional, I remind myself. My identity is a condition that, if discovered, would change everything. In truth I know that it is Anna he loves, an imaginary woman who does not really exist. Or does she? It is my face and my voice, my words and touch that have engendered his feelings, perhaps the truest I have ever known from a man.

Suddenly, I begin to cry with great heaving sobs. The Kommandant steps forward and wraps his arms around me. "Oh, Anna," he says. "Don't worry."

"I'm sorry," I say through my tears, meaning it.

"No," he says softly, stroking my hair. "No more apologies for either of us. No more tears. Let's move forward with our life together, okay?"

I nod, taking a step back and wiping my eyes with my hand. "Okay," I say. I reach into my coat pocket and pull out my handkerchief. As I do, I feel the possessions my father gave me start to fly out. I try to stop the motion, but it is too late. The rings clatter noisily to the bridge, and the paper flutters softly behind them. I gasp involuntarily.

"You've dropped something," the Kommandant says, starting to bend down.

"No!" Forgetting my composure, I leap to the ground, trying to get to the items before he can.

But it is too late; the Kommandant straightens, the paper and rings in his right hand. "What are these?" he asks, holding the items up and studying them in the moonlight. I do not answer. "Wedding rings?" As the Kommandant scans the writing on the paper, I pray desperately that he will not be able to discern the meaning of the paper, written in Hebrew, but the illustrations around the border of the paper make the meaning clear. "A Jewish marriage certificate? I don't understand." For the moment he is more puzzled than angry, but I know that is only because he has not put all of the pieces together. I realize that he still does not understand the connection, or does not want to. Perhaps there is a chance.

"I—I…" I try to come up with a story. I consider telling him that Krysia asked me to pawn the rings, that we need the money. But the idea is implausible and it still does not explain the paper. "A friend," I manage to say at last.

He clicks his tongue, holding up the marriage certificate to try to read it in the moonlight. "Such friends you keep, Anna. I knew Krysia was amenable to the Jewish artists before the war, but really…" He freezes midsentence, the realization I dreaded coming to him at last. "Krysia was married to a Jew…" His arm drops, the paper still dangling from his fingers like a wet cloth. "You're Jewish?"

"I can…" I begin, but he cuts me off.

"Are you Jewish, yes or no?"

I take a deep breath. "Yes."

He takes a step back, looking as though someone has punched him. "Herr Kommandant…Georg… please let me explain…"

"There is nothing to explain. You are a Jew." He looks away, his eyes burning. Again, I can almost hear him thinking, *again, like Margot.* I eye the gun, which he holds low by his waist, pointed at the ground. I could try to run for it while he is distracted, I think in that instant, but I do not. He looks at me again. "I don't understand how…"

I hesitate. I know that I should say nothing, give nothing away to him, but part of me thinks that perhaps if I explain he will be more sympathetic. "My real name is Emma," I begin. I consciously avoid using either my married or maiden surnames, hoping he will not connect me to either my parents or Jacob for their safety. "I have been living with Krysia under an assumed name since the beginning of the war."

"So your being a schoolteacher from Gdańsk, your parents dying in a fire…all contrived?" he asks. I nod weakly. "What about Lukasz?"

"He's not my brother, but he is Krysia's nephew. From her Catholic side," I add quickly, desperate to continue at least part of the lie in order to protect the child. I can tell from the Kommandant's expression that he doesn't believe this, doesn't believe anything I say anymore. "That's it, the whole story," I conclude, though of course it is not. I have said nothing about Jacob or Alek or the resistance. He does not speak. "So now what?" I say after a few minutes have passed. I look up at him imploringly; my eyes scan his face for some sign that he has some feeling for me.

"You are a Jew," he says again, as though that in itself contains all of the answers.

"Does that have to matter?" I ask desperately. I reach out and touch his arm. "I am the same woman you loved five minutes ago."

He pulls his arm away roughly. "No, five minutes ago you were Anna. But she no longer exists. Everything between us was a lie."

"No," I protest. "My feelings for you were real. Are real," I correct myself. He looks down at me and I can tell there is a part of him that wants to believe me. I touch my stomach. "And our baby…"

He cuts me off. "The child is a Jew also." His voice is like ice, his eyes dark, hollow pits. He turns and takes a step away. "You lied to me, Anna. I mean Emma." He spits my real name bitterly. "You betrayed me. And you have broken more laws of the Reich than I can count." He pulls his revolver out once more. "I should shoot you here, instead of arresting you and sending you to the camps. Believe me, I would be doing you a favor."

"So now you are going to kill me?" I ask in a whisper. I take a deep breath. "Like…like you did with Margot?"

He looks as though I have slapped him. "I did not kill my wife." His voice is hoarse, about to crack. "She committed suicide."

"Because you would not save her father," I continue, reckless now about saying too much, not caring if he wonders how I know about Margot. He does not respond. "So what if you did not pull the trigger yourself? You killed her." I do not recognize this voice that comes from inside me now, forceful and bold. "Just like you killed her father. Just like…" I spin around recklessly, my arms flailing in the directions of the Jewish quarter and the ghetto. "You killed all of these people!"

"I did not!"

He lunges at me, but I step away. With his free hand he grips both of my wrists and pins me against the steel column of the bridge. His face is inches above mine, a wild look in his eyes. He shakes me hard. "Who told you about Margot?" he demands, his eyes bulging.

Alek! Alek Landesberg! I want to shout, the hero whom you murdered. But I do not; I will die before I betray the resistance. "It doesn't matter," I reply. "It's the truth."

"No!" he cries hysterically. "It's not true. I did it for us. You must believe me, Margot! I did what I had to do to save us." I look up in surprise. The Kommandant is staring at me, but he thinks he is talking to his dead wife. I have pushed him too far, I realize. He has survived the war on an elaborately constructed world of fantasy and delusion, separating his actions from their consequences. Discovering the truth about me has caused that world, and the Kommandant himself, to crumble.

"It's okay," I say softly, playing along. Perhaps if he thinks

I am Margot, he will release me and I may be able to escape. "I understand, my darling. And I forgive you."

He does not answer or move, but looks out over my shoulder into the darkness, lost in his memories. An eternity seems to pass with his weight bearing down on me, pressing the rail of the bridge into my back.

Suddenly the Kommandant releases me and steps back. I straighten, trying to catch my breath. "I didn't kill my wife," he says, seeming to realize to whom he is talking once more. His voice is strangely calm. He leans against the steel column of the bridge for support. "I loved Margot. I never would have hurt her." Now it is him begging me to understand. It is more than that, though; he is trying to make himself believe it, too. "I loved my wife. I even cared for her father. But I had no choice in the matter."

Choice. I hear Krysia's voice, as if in a long-forgotten dream. *There's always a choice,* she said after I had become involved with the Kommandant. *We have to take responsibility for our actions. It is the only way we can avoid becoming victims and keep our dignity.* I consider telling this to the Kommandant. Then, looking over at him, I shake my head inwardly. There's no point. He appears defeated, wholly unrecognizable as the strong and powerful man I once knew. His cowardice has made him the victim. No, I conclude, he will not understand.

"I was a good man once, Anna," he says suddenly. His eyes are looking off across the water, away from the ghetto. His face wears the same faraway expression I have seen so often when he stares out the window of his office, and I know that he is picturing Margot and himself in happier days before the war. "The change in me came about over time, so slowly I didn't notice." It is the first time I have heard him admit to wrongdoing.

"You still are a good man," I offer, moving closer to him and taking his hand in mine. Perhaps, now while he is vulnerable, there is still a chance for me to save myself. "You still can be."

He shakes his head, pulls his hand from mine. "It's too late for that."

"It's not too late. Georg, please," I implore, reaching out again and placing my hand on his arm. Get close, I tell myself. Close enough so that he can smell the scent of your hair. Close enough so that he can remember. "We can still go away together, you and I and our child."

He pulls away. "Our child?" he repeats, his voice bitter. "How do I even know it is mine?" He gestures to the marriage certificate and rings, still clutched in his palm underneath the handle of the gun. "You are married, Anna. The child could be his."

Emma is married, not Anna, I think. "I have not seen my husband in more than three years," I lie. "Not since the beginning of the war. I do not even know if he is alive." I move closer to him again. "The child is yours, Georg." I watch his face processing this information, wanting to believe.

"Perhaps…" He seems to be considering what I have said.

"You said you wanted a family and children," I continue, trying to keep the desperation from my voice. "This is our chance. We can leave here and start over. Please." He does not answer, but I can tell that he is considering the idea. I watch as he paces back and forth, his face twisting, as he wrestles with a torrent of conflicting emotions. It is the only time I have ever seen him uncertain of what to do. "No one has to know the truth," I add.

Suddenly, something within him seems to change. He pushes me away, steps backward. "I would know," he replies coldly. "You lied to me, Anna." Reading his stony eyes, I can tell that his heart is closed to me now. I understand then that it is my betrayal and lies, more so than my faith, with which he cannot live. There is nothing more I can say or do. His hands shaking with anger, the Kommandant lifts his gun.

For a moment, I consider begging him, pleading for my life. Then I decide against it. If my promises of a child and a new life did not soften his heart, groveling will not, either, and it will make him despise me even more. I look ahead toward the end of the bridge, which seems an eternity away, too far to run. Then I wrap one arm protectively around my stomach. I'm sorry, I apologize inwardly to my child for the life he or she will never have. I close my eyes and think of the bravery of those I love: my parents, Krysia, Lukasz, even Alek flies through my mind. Then there is Jacob. "Do not be afraid," I hear him whisper, and I can almost feel him squeeze my hand.

I hear a click as the Kommandant cocks the gun. I open my eyes, wanting to see the moment that is to be my last. The Kommandant stands before me, pistol aimed at my heart. "Goodbye, Anna," he says, tears streaming down his face. I close my eyes again.

A shot rings out, then another. I must be dead, I think, for I feel nothing. "Emma!" I hear my name being called out by a familiar voice in the darkness. My eyes fly open. I am not hit, I realize. The Kommandant has spun away from me, firing wildly in the darkness. He stands frozen now, his arm jerked high in the air like a marionette's, a twisted half smile on his face. The front of his uniform is dark and wet. He collapses to the ground.

"Georg!" I cry out. I run to him, kneeling. Has he shot himself instead of me? He reaches up to clasp my hand. "Don't move," I order, looking around desperately. "I'll get help!" But even as I say it, I know it is impossible. If I call the police, I will be arrested. I cannot risk my own life to save him.

The Kommandant shakes his head weakly, coughing. "It's too late for that. Stay with me, Anna," he says, still using my pseudonym, wanting to believe my charade to the last. "It's better this way."

"Don't say that!" I put my hand under his neck, lift him to me. His face is white. "You are going to be fine. We just have to get you to a hospital."

"No, I don't want it to go on like this. If we can't be together…"

"We can be," I insist. He is bleeding more heavily now, the dark red seeping into the snow underneath him.

He squeezes my hand tightly. "I'm so sorry. I love you. I never could have hurt you."

"I know," I whisper, though in truth I do not. He had loved Margot, too, but it hadn't been enough.

"I love you, Anna," he repeats.

"I love you, too," I say for the first time. I realize now that, for some part of me at least, it is true. I brush the hair from his sweat-soaked brow.

"Anna," he says again. His eyes flutter, then go blank.

"No!" I cry, bending my forehead to his. I freeze there, hoping to feel some hint of warm breath on my cheek. I press my lips to his eyelids, kissing them closed. His face is calm, relieved of all its intensity and torment, and in that moment I know that the Kommandant is gone.

CHAPTER 25

I kneel frozen beside the Kommandant's lifeless body, too stunned to move. "Emma," I hear someone call from behind me. The voice I had heard calling my name as the shots rang out had not been imaginary. Someone else is here. The Kommandant was not alone, I think, leaping to my feet and staring in the direction from which he had come, searching for another Nazi. "Emma," the voice calls again. A Nazi would not know my real name. I spin around. There in the shadows, holding a still-smoking gun, stands Marta.

"Marta!" I exclaim, walking toward her. "I—I don't understand…what are you doing here?"

"I followed you," she replies. "I was supposed to come for you at dawn to take you to Jacob." So she is the escort, I think. She continues, "I knew you wouldn't leave without seeing your parents, and I was afraid that when you found out about your mother…" Her voice trails off and she looks away.

I look at her in disbelief. "You knew?"

She nods. "I found out a few weeks ago. I wanted to come and tell you, but Marek forbade it." Damn him, I think. Damn them all. "I'm sorry," she adds. I do not answer. "I followed you to the ghetto, then here. When I arrived, I saw him…" she gestures toward the Kommandant's lifeless body. "He was going to shoot you. So I shot him first."

"Thank God! If you hadn't come…" I shudder. My anger toward her is quickly replaced by gratitude. Had she not been there, it might be me lying dead on the bridge. "Oh, Marta, thank you so much." I try to hug her, but she pushes me away.

"There's no time for that!" She rushes over to where the Kommandant lies. She must have seen me with him after he was shot, I realize as I follow her. I wait for her to reproach me for holding him and crying as he died, but she does not. Instead, she kneels before the Kommandant's lifeless body and pries the rings and paper from his already-stiffening fingers. "Here." She reaches up and hands them to me and I put them quickly back in my pocket. "The authorities will be here soon. We have to get rid of the body. Quick, let's push him over the edge."

The Kommandant's body. I look down at him. My stomach twists. An image flashes through my mind of him hovering above me in the darkness, his torso inches from mine. Fighting the urge to vomit, I look away from him and walk over to the railing of the bridge. "Impossible, the river is frozen. Let's just leave him, Marta. We need to get out of here. Come on!" I look down to where she kneels, not moving. "Marta?"

She shakes her head, sinking to the ground. "I can't." I rush to her. A red stain seeps across her midsection.

"Oh, Marta, you've been hit!"

She smiles ruefully. "I was faster than him, but not fast enough."

I kneel beside her. "Is it very painful?"

"It's not too bad." But I know she is trying to be strong. Her face is pale and there is a thin layer of sweat on her brow.

"We have to get you to Krysia's. She can find a doctor...."

She shakes her head. "There's no way. I can't walk."

"Here, I'll help you." I place my arm around her waist, trying to lift her to a standing position, but she pushes my hands away, falling to the ground once more.

"It's no use," she says, panting. "You can't carry me. No, you have to go without me."

"I'll go for help," I offer, looking around.

"Not for help. Just go. I will tell you the planned route for your escape."

I stare at her in disbelief. "But you can't stay here. The police will come soon and they'll find you."

"Exactly," she replies, a light growing in her eyes. "If they have me and think I did it, they won't be looking for anyone else. You'll be able to escape."

"I won't leave you here," I protest.

"You have to."

"No..." But even as I say this, I know there is no changing her mind. I hear in her voice the same courage, the same stubbornness that I had seen in Alek and Jacob. Still I persist. "I can't leave you like this. Not after all that you've done for me."

"Listen to me." Mustering all of her remaining strength, Marta reaches out and grabs my sleeve. "The resistance is about survival, the survival of our people. It always has been.

Those who can must go on. Alek knew it and Jacob does, too. Whoever can go on, must, and no sentimental nonsense about it. Do you understand?"

I take a deep breath. "Yes."

"Good." She releases my hand, then reaches over the Kommandant's body and grabs his gun. "Here," she says, holding it up to me. "Take this."

I stare at the weapon that was pointed at my heart just a few minutes earlier. "I—I can't," I stammer, recoiling.

"Just take it," she insists. "You may need it for your escape." Reluctantly, I take the gun from her. The cold metal is heavy and unfamiliar in my hand. She falls back to the ground.

I place the gun in the waistband of my skirt. "Where is Jacob?" I ask, realizing she might be the only one who knows.

"He is in Czernichow."

"But…" I stare at her in disbelief. Czernichow is a small village just on the other side of the forest, not ten kilometers from Krysia's house. All of this time, I had been led to believe Jacob was recovering far away in the mountains when in fact he was close by.

"Everyone thought he was in the mountains, Emma," she gasps. "We had to pretend. The leaks in the resistance have been even worse since Alek was killed. And even among those we trusted, we could not risk that someone might be captured and made to tell where he was." I nod. So many secrets. She continues, "There is an abandoned hut just behind the livery outside of Czernichow. Jacob is there. He may be hiding in the root cellar underneath. The property is owned by a farmer called Kowalczyk who can be trusted to help you if you need it. Take the forest path from Krysia's," she continues with short, labored breaths. "You can tell the Kowalczyk place by its blue roof." Sirens wail in the distance then. "Get out of here now! Go to Jacob." She rocks back and forth in a fetal position, nursing her pain.

I stand to go. She reaches up, grabbing my hand. "Emma, one last thing…about Jacob…" She hesitates. "I'm sorry." I know she is referring to the thing that had remained unspoken between us, her feelings for my husband. She had always had a crush on him, even before she knew me.

"It's okay," I reply, squeezing her fingers. And it really was. I could not judge her. You loved who you loved. She could no more help her feelings for Jacob than I could mine for the Kommandant.

"Go now," she orders as the sirens grow closer.

"God bless you, Marta," I say, bending to kiss her cheek. I release her hand and start running, making my way across the bridge. When I reach the end, I look back. Marta sits motionless by the Kommandant's body, gun still clutched tightly in her hand, looking off into the distance.

I climb down the steps of the bridge, then freeze. There is a large black sedan parked at the base of the bridge. The Kommandant's car. So he had not been in the truck after all. Through the tinted glass windows, I can make out Stanislaw's bald head. I consider running back up the steps of the bridge, but before I can react, the driver's door opens and Stanislaw emerges. We eye each other uncertainly, neither of us speaking. A long moment of silence passes between us. *"Dobry wieczor,"* he says at last, bidding me good evening as though it were entirely usual for us to meet under these circumstances.

"Dobry wieczor, Stanislaw," I reply, my mind racing. Did he

hear the shots? Is he wondering what became of the Kommandant? I keep my hands crossed to hide the bloodstains on my
dress, praying that he does not notice. There is another awkward silence. The sirens are getting louder now. It is a matter
of minutes before he realizes that the police are coming here.
For a moment, I consider running. Then I remember the day
I had encountered Stanislaw when taking the papers from the
Kommandant's apartment. Even after catching me in the act,
he let me go without question. Maybe he really is sympathetic
to the resistance. Then again, he is, or was, the Kommandant's
driver and probably a loyalist like Malgorzata. I cannot risk it.

"Perhaps you would like a ride?" Stanislaw asks, breaking
me from my thoughts. I look up. His face is impassive but
there is a glint in his eye that makes me think that he knows
what has happened and understands.

So maybe Stanislaw really is on our side. Or perhaps it is a
trap and he will deliver me to the Gestapo. Either way, I need
to get back to Krysia's right away and walking will take an hour
that I do not have. I have to take a chance. "Yes, please, Stanislaw. To Krysia's house as fast as you can." Stanislaw nods and,
moving more swiftly than I knew he could, opens the back
door of the car. I slide in and he shuts the door behind me.
The sirens are deafening now, the police almost upon the
bridge. Stanislaw slams on the gas and the car takes off. He
drives wildly through the streets, not stopping at the intersec-
tions and taking corners nearly on two wheels. He is going to
attract attention, I worry as I grasp the seat in front of me
tightly. We will be stopped by the police. Then I remember
we are driving in the car of a high-ranking Nazi official; no
one will dare to stop us.

I sink back in the seat, suddenly overwhelmed by all that has happened. The Kommandant's face appears suddenly in my mind. Don't, I think, but it is too late: suddenly I am back on the bridge. I see the Kommandant, his gun trained upon me, his face racked with pain. His eyes were so desperate when he realized he was in love with a Jew, that fate had played the same cruel joke on him not once, but twice. Finding out the truth about me was like losing Margot all over again. He simply could not bear reliving that pain.

I hear the shots in my mind and flinch as though they are real. Would he have actually been able to go through with shooting me? I wanted to believe that he could not, that he loved me too much. But he had loved Margot too, so how could I ever know for sure what might have happened if Marta had not arrived?

Marta. I should not have left her, I think, a wave of guilt washing over me. She saved my life and I abandoned her to die. But she was right: the resistance, everything we have done, has been about survival. I had to go on because I could.

My mind turns from all that has happened to the present situation. It will be a matter of minutes before the Gestapo realizes what has happened to the Kommandant and begins to investigate and will surely learn of our affair. I need to get out of Kraków as soon as possible. For a moment, I consider going directly to the forest to make my way to Czernichow and find Jacob, without stopping back at Krysia's. But I need to go there one last time, to pick up the clothes and food she packed for my journey and to tell her all that has happened. To say goodbye to her and Lukasz.

I look out the car window. We are almost at the roundabout

at the top of Krysia's street now. I lean forward to the front seat. "Stanislaw, stop here, please." He obliges and looks back, puzzled. "The engine will attract attention on the street this time of night. Let me get out here." He nods, then turns to open his door to get out and help me from the car. "No, it's all right," I say. "I can do this on my own."

He opens his mouth to start to argue. I realize that even after all that has happened tonight, it is this, not being allowed to do the simple duties of his job like opening the car door, that seems to trouble him most. Then his expression changes. "As you wish," he says.

"Thank you." I open the car door, then turn to him again. "Stanislaw, after tonight, there will be questions. It may not be safe for you here."

He shakes his head, a determined look in his eyes. "Don't worry, I'll be fine."

He would have made a good resistance fighter, I think. Suddenly, I remember Alek saying something about the resistance having other spies around Wawel. Surely Stanislaw is not... I open my mouth to ask, but he reaches back and extends his hand. "Good luck."

He is right, of course; some things are best left unspoken. I take his hand, then lean forward awkwardly into the front seat to kiss his smooth, full cheek. "God bless you." I open the door and leap out, then close it softly behind me.

Taking quick, silent steps, I round the corner onto the deserted street, then stop, eyeing Krysia's house with surprise. All of the lights in the house burn brightly through the windows, as though we had never gone to bed the night before. Even if Krysia had already awoken, she would have kept the house as dark as possible since I am supposed to be leaving in secret. Something is wrong. I race toward the house.

A few meters farther, I halt once more. There is a military car parked in front of the house. Someone is here, I realize, my blood running cold. The Gestapo has come again.

I hesitate, uncertain what to do. I have to help Krysia and Lukasz, but how? I cannot just walk into the house in the middle of the night with bloodstains on my dress; it will raise too many questions. For a moment I consider running away again. Those who can survive, must, Marta had said. But I cannot abandon Krysia and Lukasz. I have to do something. Desperately, I turn and duck behind the hedge on the side of the house.

Crouching low, I make my way around to the back garden, as I had the night Jozef had brought me here. I peek in the window at the foyer, but it is deserted. They must be upstairs. Stepping back, I crane my neck to look up at the second-floor window. I can make out the heads of at least two men through the parlor curtains, but I cannot see what they are saying or doing. I sink back into the bushes, my mind racing. Why are they here? For a moment, I wonder if they know about the Kommandant and have come for me? Impossible, I realize. There is no way they could have figured it out already and gotten here before me, not with the way Stanislaw was driving. Perhaps it is the two Gestapo officers who came last time, making good on their threat to return with more questions. I look over at the cottage that the one officer had wanted to inspect last time, but the door remains closed. Maybe someone in the resistance leaked the plan of my escape and they are here to stop me.

I should go for help, I think, then laugh inwardly at the notion. There is no help anymore. The resistance is all but gone. The one person who could have called the Gestapo off, Kommandant Richwalder, is dead. I picture Marta holding the gun on the bridge, ready to go down fighting. She would have known what to do.

The gun, I remember suddenly, my hand dropping to my waist. I had nearly forgotten about the Kommandant's pistol, still tucked neatly in my skirt. I pull it out. I have never fired a gun in my life. Would I even be able to do it properly? The Kommandant fired twice, which I imagine should mean that there are four bullets left. I turn the gun over in my hand, considering. Suddenly, a loud, crashing noise comes through the second-floor window. I leap up. Something has happened. I have to go in. I pull the lever back on the gun and start around the corner of the house, my finger on the trigger. Just before I reach the door, I hear footsteps. Someone is coming down. I leap back around the side of the house, out of sight.

Through the window, I can see three Gestapo policemen in the foyer. They are not the same ones that were here before. The front door opens. "The old woman was lying," I hear one of the men say as they walk out into the garden. Oh, God, I think; they were interrogating Krysia. I wonder if they saw Lukasz.

"I don't think she knew anything more," another replies. His voice is fainter and I can tell they are walking away from me toward the front gate.

The first voice speaks again. "It doesn't matter now." Panic shoots through me. What have they done? I fight the urge to leap up before they have gone. A moment later, when the car doors have slammed and the car has sped away, I race into the house.

"Krysia," I call, sprinting up the first flight of stairs. There is no response. "Krysia!"

I reach the first-floor landing. The house is in complete disarray. Broken glass and porcelain dishes litter the kitchen floor. In the parlor, the sofa pillows have been ripped open, scattering down feathers everywhere. I cross the room to the fireplace. A picture frame lies broken on the floor, the glass shattered. I bend down. It is my framed wedding photograph, the one Krysia hid on the night that I first arrived. The Gestapo must have found it somehow. So my secret will not die with the Kommandant. After more than a year of concealment, it has been revealed twice in one day.

An acrid whiff of smoke fills my nostrils. This is not the usual smell of neighbors burning leaves and brush that sometimes wafts in through the windows. It is more intense and coming from inside the house. My head snaps around, searching for the source of the fire. It must be upstairs, I realize. "Krysia! Lukasz!" I call desperately, racing out of the parlor.

I climb the stairs to the second floor two at a time. "Oh, no!" I cry aloud. At the top of the stairs, Krysia lies sprawled on the floor, her eyes closed. Her arms are flung above her head and her legs are tangled in her skirt at strange angles. She does not move. I drop to her side, lifting her head. "Krysia!" I shake her gently but she does not respond. There is a large welt by her temple, as though she had hit it when she had fallen or been knocked down. Her skin is waxy and cool. I lower my face to hers, feeling for some sign of breath, but there is none. Don't leave me, Krysia, I plead silently. Not now, not when I need you to tell me what I should do. I open her mouth and place my lips over hers, trying to blow air into her lungs. A moment later, I stop, feeling for a pulse in her neck and finding none. It is too late, I realize; she is gone. "Oh, Krysia," I cry. I hold her close, rocking her back and forth as she had when she'd tried to comfort me.

Suddenly I hear a crackling sound behind me. The fire, I remember, looking around. I place Krysia's head back on the ground gently and I stand up. The smoke seems to be coming from several directions and I cannot discern the source of the blaze. For a moment, I consider trying to put out the fire. But even if I could stop it, the smoke will attract attention. I have to find the child and then we must get out of here.

I race to Lukasz's bedroom. The smoke here is nearly too thick for me to see. "Lukasz!" I call, covering my mouth and crouching low. He is not in his crib or on the floor. "Lukasz!" I shout again, running to Krysia's room, and finally my own. Even through the smoke, I can tell that the Gestapo had searched the house thoroughly—every room is in shambles, clothes strewn from the dressers, mirrors smashed. But there is no sign of Lukasz. Did they do something with him? I wonder.

Perhaps he ran outside, I think, starting back down the stairs. Then I hear a creaking noise coming from overhead. The attic! I remember Krysia telling me how, after Lukasz's mother had been shot, relatives had hidden him in their attic for several days. He must have been frightened when the Gestapo had come and gone there to hide.

I race into Krysia's room and throw open the closet door. Pushing aside Krysia's clothes, I climb up the ladder. "Lukasz," I call through the opening. There is silence. I cannot make out anything in the darkness. "Lukasz, it's Anna. It's all right, come to me."

I hear shuffling in the dark, then a tiny warm hand finds mine. *"Na,"* I hear him say. I grab his arm and pull his small, trembling body to me. "It's okay," I say, holding him close and climbing back down the stairs. The smoke has grown thicker now. We have to get out fast. I grab a rag from Krysia's dresser and place it over Lukasz's mouth. As we start to leave the room, I see a flash of blue out of the corner of my eye. It is the sweater Krysia made for Lukasz. I grab it to take with us.

As we cross the hallway to where Krysia lies, I cover Lukasz's eyes so he will not see her. He has already seen too much death. I climb over Krysia and start down the stairs, then turn back. Krysia. My heart wrenches. She had been everything to us. Saved us. Cared for us as if we were her own. So you became a mother, after all, I think. I wish that we could take her with us. She deserves a proper burial. A funeral where the hundreds who loved and admired her could come to pay their respects. But there is no time. "Thank you," I whisper, looking at her one last time. I blow her a kiss, and run out with Lukasz into the cold morning air.

O utside, it is nearly dawn and the farmers of Chelmska are just beginning their day. They feed their livestock and sweep their front porches as if it is any other morning. Some look up and nod as we pass, others do not acknowledge us at all as we walk up the road into the forest. If they think it strange that I am walking toward the woods carrying a soot-covered child, instead of to the bus stop at the roundabout for work as I normally would, they give no indication. They have not yet seen the smoke that will surely pour out of Krysia's house within minutes.

As we climb the road that winds upward into the forest, the houses grow fewer and farther apart. Ahead the trees are dense, their dark cover a promise. Soon the road ends, trickling into a narrow forest path. I pause and turn to look at the neighborhood below. The roofs of the houses look sleepy, unperturbed.

Enough, I think. There is no point in dwelling on what must be left behind. I look down at the ground beneath me. There is a thin layer of frost that I had not noticed previously. I am suddenly aware of my circumstances: the cold, the heaviness of the child, how far we have to go. The fact that we have nothing.

A sense of urgency overtakes me. We must keep going. Shifting Lukasz to my left hip, I begin to walk again. Safely enveloped by the trees and out of the eyesight of the neighbors, I quicken my pace now, nearly running, my gait awkward with the girth of my stomach and the weight of the child. The path grows uneven and steep. My legs begin to ache and my shoes become caked with damp spring mud. Suddenly, my foot catches on a rock and I lurch forward, tripping. As I fall, I cling fiercely to the child, hitting the ground first and rolling to break his fall. A wave of pain shoots through my shoulder.

I lay dazed for a few seconds, trying to catch my breath. "Lukasz…" I sit up and pull the child onto my lap. Quickly, I check him for injury, but he seems fine, except for some dirt on his already-blackened forehead. "Are you okay?" He nods silently and makes the face that I know means he is hungry. My stomach twists. He should be having breakfast now, safe and warm at Krysia's table. I wish that I at least had some milk to give him. I should have remembered to take the rations Krysia had prepared for our travels. The rabbi's reproachful face flashes in my mind. What kind of caretaker will I make without Krysia? Will I be able to care for my own child when he or she is born? I reach into my coat pocket and find an old square of chocolate from a bar the Kommandant had given me once. I pull back the paper and dust it off before handing it to Lukasz. "Here." He takes it and puts it in his mouth hurriedly, as though afraid it will disappear. A wide smile appears on his face. Chocolate for breakfast.

Still trying to catch my breath, I study his face as he eats. Not an hour after the trauma of the Gestapo and the fire and leaving Krysia's, his eyes are clear and calm. So you are coming with me after all, I think. "Come, darling," I say, standing up. Remembering the blue sweater, I take it from inside my coat and pull it over his head. It fits snugly, almost too small for him. He has gotten so big in the year that he has been with us. Despite all of the tragedy and tension, he has thrived, growing from a toddler to a child when none of us were looking. My child. I cannot think of him as anything else, though I still wonder if someday the rabbi or some other relative will come looking for him, and claim him for their own. For now, though, he is here. I squeeze his solid fingers in mine, as if to be sure. He looks up and smiles, as if to reassure me that everything will be okay.

"Safe," I say aloud. Then I realize that this is far from true. We are hundreds of long, dangerous kilometers from safe. No, not safe, but free. I have no idea where we are going or how, and I don't know if we will make it. Still, the word has an undeniable ring to it. "Free." I will not have to be someone else again.

"Fee?" Lukasz reaches up to me as he tries to repeat the word. I look down at him. There is chocolate on his fingers. I reach into my pocket to find a tissue to wipe them. My hand brushes against something in my pocket. The rings and the certificate, I remember suddenly. Marta had handed them to me on the bridge. Once again I consider whether I should get rid of them, bury them in the ground. Then I realize that, for better or for worse, the charade is over. I take the rings from my pocket and put them on my fingers once more.

As we make our way through the woods, I think of those we have left behind. Krysia and Alek are gone, my mother, too. I will grieve for them all in time, I know, each in a different way. And then there's the Kommandant. I see his face before me suddenly, and stop, my breath catching. "Don't," I tell myself aloud, but even as I say the word, I know that it is no use. The face I see in my mind is not that of the Nazi who lorded over the city from high atop Wawel, or who held a gun to my chest on the bridge. No, he is gone. Instead, I see the man who walked into Krysia's the night of the dinner party, who caught my eyes and didn't let go, who brought me to new places in my body and held me afterward as I slept. The man who asked forgiveness as he lay dying on the railway bridge. I realize then that it was not only he who died in that moment. The Kommandant brought Anna to life, and when he was gone, she was, too. Anna Lipowski, I think. The Kommandant's girl. I wonder if I will miss her.

"Enough," I say, and my words echo in the clearing of trees where we have paused. There will be time to try to make sense of it all later. For now we have to keep going. I force Lukasz, who has dropped to the dirt, to stand up and start walking again.

Shaking thoughts of the Kommandant, I think instead of the others we left behind. My father. He is still alive, or was a few hours ago. I picture the burning light in his eyes through the hole in the ghetto wall. Perhaps he will somehow survive whatever lies ahead.

Marta is alive, too, I remind myself. I remember her sitting on the bridge, clasping the gun, gravely wounded but unafraid.

She saved my life. I wish that our last words before that night had not been spoken in anger, that she had not thought ill of me for sleeping with the Kommandant. Most of all I wish our friendship had not been tainted by her feelings for my husband. My mind flashes back to the moment she appeared on the bridge, gun in hand. She could have killed me and had Jacob for herself, I realize, but she had not. Our friendship meant more to her than her feelings for him.

Perhaps by some miracle Marta managed to escape from the bridge before the Nazis arrived, despite her wounds. Maybe she and my father will survive the war, I mused, and we will somehow be reunited: me, Jacob, my father, Marta and Lukasz.

I drop my hand to my stomach, thinking of my unborn child, who will also be a part of this eclectic family of survivors. As I look around the deserted forest, a wave of despair washes over me: how can I bring a child into a world such as this? Even if I find Jacob and we manage to escape, we will have nothing to give our child, not even a home. A cool breeze blows by me then and I look up through the tree branches, which are just beginning to bud, at the early morning sky. It will be fine, a voice whispers. The child will be strong. I know in that moment that the child will be a boy and that we will name him Alek.

An hour later, we reach the far edge of the forest, where the trees abruptly give way to the sloping, cleared fields of Czernichow. I pause, loosening my grip on Lukasz's hand and scanning the panorama below us. Off to the right, not a kilometer away, I spot the blue roof of the Kowalczyk farm. Squinting, I can just make out a tiny hut behind it. I imagine Jacob standing on the porch, his face breaking into a wide smile when he sees us coming. Then I laugh aloud. I have spent so much time daydreaming, imagined our reunion for so long, that it has become second nature. Now there is nothing stopping me, yet I am still standing here thinking about it instead of going to him. I take a deep breath and step forward.

Away from the shelter of the trees, the sun shines warmly now, more spring than winter at last. Birds circle over the fields before us, calling out merrily to one another. "Come, *kochana*," I beckon to Lukasz, tugging on his arm gently. Jacob is waiting. Together, the child and I descend from the forest, his small, strong legs quickening their pace to match my own. Though a long, difficult journey surely lies ahead, the first part of it, at least, is over. We have left Krysia's as we had come, with only the clothes on our backs. But this time, we are going together, finding our way without anyone else to guide us.

Read all about it...

MORE ABOUT THIS BOOK

2 Questions for your reading group

3 Inspiration for writing
   Kommandant's Girl

5 Further recommended reading

MORE ABOUT THE AUTHOR

7 Author biography

9 Q&A on writing

13 Books I Love

14 A day in the life

QUESTIONS FOR YOUR READING GROUP

1. Did you agree with Emma's choices in the book? Did you find them believable? Why or why not?

2. Do you think the ends that Emma was seeking justified the means of her choices and actions?

3. How did Emma's character change/evolve throughout the story?

4. What was the most difficult challenge faced by Emma in the book?

5. What role does Krysia play in the story? Lukasz?

6. Do you agree with Emma's decision to keep the paternity of her unborn child a secret from her husband? Why or why not?

7. Emma kept secrets from both of the men in her life—the Kommandant and Jacob. Do you think real intimacy is possible in such circumstances?

8. What is it that you think Emma really wanted?

9. How do you think Marta felt about Emma?

10. Where do you think Emma winds up one month after the end of the book? One year? Five years?

11. Who is your favourite character in the book and why?

12. What is the central theme of the book? Did it resonate with you?

PAM JENOFF ON WRITING
Kommandant's Girl

I lived in Krakow, Poland from 1996-1998
while working as a diplomat for the State
Department. Just a few years after Communism
ended in Eastern Europe, it was a tremendously
exciting time to explore Jewish issues: the local
Jewish community was truly free for the first
time since before World War II, Poland as a
whole was beginning to embrace its Jewish
history and heritage, and widespread contacts
were being developed for the first time between
Jewish scholars and artists in the East and West.
As a result, there was something of a Jewish
cultural renaissance, which defied all that the
Nazis and Communists had tried to do, and
served as a testimony to the human spirit. Also
during this period, many painful issues of the
Holocaust, such as preservation of Auschwitz
and the other camps, property restitution,
anti-Semitism and the role of the local Polish
community during the Holocaust were
beginning to be openly explored. I was profoundly affected by my experiences in Poland,
and by the many close relationships I developed
with both Jewish and Gentile Poles.

For several years after my return to the United
States, I had wanted to write a novel that
reflected these experiences. I was captivated
for some time by the vision of a young woman
nervously guiding a child across Krakow's
market square during the Nazi occupation. But
it was not until early 2002 when I had the good
fortune to ride a train from Washington, DC to
Philadelphia with an elderly couple who were
both Holocaust survivors that I learned for the
first time the extraordinary story of the Krakow
resistance, one that I had never known during

my years of living there. And with that historical foundation, *Kommandant's Girl* was born.

People often ask me how I researched the historical background for *Kommandant's Girl.* Part of it was intrinsic—I had spent so much time walking the streets of Krakow and the Jewish Quarter (Kazimierz) that I knew the setting by heart. But to learn more about the history, I had to "start over." I read memoirs and other accounts of resistance activities. And I went back to Krakow, where good friends of mine drove me around to all of the sites: where the ghetto had been, the café that had been bombed. I was amazed that I had walked among these sites every day for years without knowing what had taken place.

Kommandant's Girl and its characters are entirely fictitious. But the historical events and ideas that inspired me to write it—the war, the Holocaust, the resistance fighters who bombed a café and undertook many other brave actions, the non-Jews who risked their lives to help —are based on actuality. Though I have had to bend timelines and geography for the sake of storytelling, I have endeavoured to remain true to the spirit of those who lived and died during World War II and the Holocaust, and to realistically depict the full range of human strengths, frailties and emotions brought out by this tragic and remarkable era. To me this book is a love poem to the Jewish communities of Poland, and all of Central and Eastern Europe, past, present and future: their courageous struggle is an inspiration to us all.

FURTHER RECOMMENDED READING

There are many wonderful resources available on Poland and the Holocaust, if you are interested in learning more. A few of the sources I have enjoyed include:

Books:

- *Justyna's Narrative* by Gusta Davidson Draenger. A memoir chronicling the Krakow resistance.

- *Polyn: Jewish Life in the Old Country* by Alter Kacyzne. A pictorial history of pre-war Jewish Poland.

- *Poland's Jewish Heritage* by Joram Kagan. Documents Jewish sites of historical significance throughout Poland.

- *Schindler's Ark* by Thomas Kenneally. Story of Oskar Schindler containing interesting historical details.

There are also some books related to the Holocaust for young people which I adore, including:

- *I am Rosemarie* by Marietta Moskin

- *The Endless Steppe* by Esther Hautzig.

Websites:

- *United States Holocaust Memorial Museum* (www.ushmm.org)—Museum website containing many useful resources on the Holocaust.

- *Auschwitz Jewish Center Foundation* (www.ajcf.org)—Website for the foundation, which has created a museum in Oswiecim (the town where Auschwitz is located) commemorating pre-war Jewish life.

- *City of Krakow* (www. krakow.pl)—Official website of the city of Krakow, contains webcam, photographs and other information.

- *Jewish Community in Warsaw* http://warszawa.jewish.org.pl/engindex.html) —Website of Poland's Jewish community, contains information about community activities.

- *Auschwitz-Birkenau Museum* (www.auschwitz-muzeum.oswiecim.pl/html/ eng/start/index.php)—Official website of the concentration camp museum, containing many useful resources on the Holocaust.

- *Ronald S Lauder Foundation* (www.rslfoundation.org)—Information on the foundation's work to support Jewish life in Central and Eastern Europe.

- *US Commission for the Preservation of America's Heritage Abroad* (www.heritage abroad.gov)—Website of independent government agency committed to preserving cemeteries, synagogues and other sites significant to America's heritage overseas.

- *Jewish Cultural Festival in Krakow* (www.jewishfestival.pl)—Official website of the Krakow Jewish Cultural Festival.

Please note that these are Pam Jenoff's personal recommendations. Inclusion on this list does not indicate recommendation by the publisher, or any representation as to the content of these sources. Nor does it indicate that any of these entities have endorsed *Kommandant's Girl* or use of their listings here.

AUTHOR BIOGRAPHY

Pam was born in Maryland and raised in southern New Jersey and now lives just outside of Philadelphia, Pennsylvania. She attended George Washington University in Washington DC, where she received a Bachelor's Degree magna cum laude in International Affairs, with minors in History and Japanese.

Upon graduation, Pam received a scholarship to Jesus College, Cambridge University. She spent the next two years at Cambridge, earning a Master's Degree in History, travelling throughout Europe, coxing for the men's rowing team and making the friendships and having the experiences of a lifetime.

After Cambridge, Pam accepted an appointment as Special Assistant to the Secretary of the Army. The position provided a unique opportunity to witness and participate in operations at the most senior levels of government, including helping the families of the Pan Am Flight 103 victims secure their memorial at Arlington National Cemetery, observing recovery efforts at the site of the Oklahoma City bombings, and attending ceremonies to commemorate the 50th anniversary of World War II at sites such as Bastogne, Belgium and Corregidor in the Philippines.

Pam went from the Pentagon to the State Department and was assigned to the US Consulate in Krakow, Poland. There she worked on consular issues such as adjudicating visa applications of Poles wishing to visit the US and helping American citizens abroad. She also reported on political issues, including women's and minority rights.

It was during this period that Pam developed her expertise in Polish-Jewish relations and the Holocaust, working on matters such as preservation of Auschwitz and the other former concentration camp sites, and the restitution of Jewish property in Poland. She also developed close relations with the surviving Jewish community in Poland. Pam remains involved in Polish-Jewish issues by writing articles and participating in a number of organisations. She has been honoured by the US Commission for the Preservation of America's Heritage Abroad, served on the Board of Directors of the Jewish Community Relations Council of Southern New Jersey, been appointed as a fellow to the Salzburg Seminar (Social and Economic Dimensions of Human Rights), advised the Auschwitz Jewish Center and is a member of the Polish Institute of Arts and Sciences in America.

Pam left the Foreign Service in 1998 to attend law school, receiving her Juris Doctor degree cum laude from the University of Pennsylvania. Since 2001, Pam has worked as an associate in the Labor and Employment Practice Group of Morgan, Lewis & Bockius LLP in Philadelphia. When not writing novels or practising law, Pam enjoys spending time with her family and friends, going to the beach, cheering on her Philadelphia Eagles, reading, travelling and participating in running and other sports (she is a second-degree black belt in karate). She is also involved with pro bono and civic work through her law firm, focusing on at-risk youth, hunger relief and homelessness.

PAM JENOFF ON WRITING

What do you love most about being a writer?

I'm not sure yet what I love most: being a first-time author, I'm still experiencing lots of new things! But it is wonderful to have these ideas that I've created and refined for so long be shared with editors and others who are excited about them and committed to sharing your work with the widest audience possible.

I also love walking around "normal" day-to-day life with this whole alternative world in my head. That, and when I'm writing a scene and everything is clicking and I can hardly type fast enough to keep up with the ideas. Then I look up and think "Wow! I've created something and it's only six-thirty in the morning."

Where do you go for inspiration?

To sleep! I'm joking, but only partially. I find that stepping back from my work and clearing my head is the best way to generate ideas, either by resting, or working out or having a good belly laugh with family or friends. A surprising number of my ideas actually come together in the shower.

Of course spending time in idyllic places, such as at the beach or in the mountains or in the foreign settings that appear in my work, is inspirational, too. I've had tremendous writing experiences while in residence at the Banff Center for the Arts in the Canadian Rockies, and writing in Salzburg in a beautiful old library in the Alpine palace where *The Sound of Music* was filmed. But those are luxuries that aren't always available in daily life. So I sometimes turn to the internet; for example, there's a webcam that looks out on the Market Square in Krakow that completely takes me back there.

Where do your characters come from, and do they ever surprise you as they write?

I'm honestly not sure where the characters come from—don't do many character sketches, so the characters develop through the plot and being put in various situations. For *Kommandant's Girl*, the plot came first and Emma was the character who appeared because it was her story and couldn't have been anyone else's. For my current project, the main character, Marta Nedermann, has already been developed from *Kommandant's Girl*, so she has been telling me her story and introducing me to the others along the way.

Characters surprise me all of the time, what they do, what they tell me. Sometimes I don't even have to be writing—a really good character will wake you up at night and haunt you during the day to tell you what's important. For example, I had no intention of writing my second book as a continuation of *Kommandant's Girl* until Marta came to me and demanded that her story be told.

Do you have a favourite character that you've created and what is it you like about that character?

I like Krysia Smok, Jacob's aunt. She's not Jewish but she risks everything to protect Jews and support the resistance because she believes it is the right thing to do. She's also a strong woman who defies convention and stereotypes.

When did you start writing?

I started writing by the age of five or six, sending in articles to children's magazines, binding my stories into little books and showing them to anyone who would read them.

My first serious attempt at a novel came when

I was living in Poland. I lived alone in the countryside and had a tremendous amount of solitude, which helped me be creative and productive. But those were pre-internet days, and the lack of English-speaking support and communication stopped me from taking it as far as I liked. I still hope to rewrite and publish that project in the future.

For several years after I returned to the United States, I couldn't write much of anything. Then 9/11 happened and it really made me re-evaluate what was important to me. I decided that if I was going to be a writer, I had to start then and there. Soon after, I took an evening class on novel writing and began working on *Kommandant's Girl*.

What one piece of advice would you give a writer wanting to start a career?

Don't quit your day job! Just kidding. Seriously, I have the utmost respect for those writers who are willing to struggle until they make it in order to write full-time. For me, becoming an author (I call it my "rock star dream") has always had to coexist with my demanding career as an attorney. It's busy, but I like the contrast: the solitude of writing, the social interaction of my job. But it is a long haul from starting a book to publication. (Almost five years for me, and that may be on the shorter side of average.) So you need to have a life and support system to get you through the highs and lows of getting to publication.

I would also say that getting published is not a question of talent, because I've met dozens of writers over the years whose work was far better than mine who haven't yet "made it." I believe

"…*I decided if I was going to be a writer I had to start then and there…*"

there are three factors that make a difference. First, you have to be tenacious. For a long time, it didn't look like *Kommandant's Girl* was going to get picked up. But with the help of my agent, I developed the attitude that, if this one doesn't sell, the next one will. You just have to keep on knocking at the door until it opens.

Second, you have to be disciplined. Writing takes a lot of time, and I'm not just talking about the first draft. There are the revisions, and then there's the business-marketing side of it. You have to make choices in order to consistently carve out the time for your writing, if it is going to be important to you.

Finally, the single biggest skill that has helped me as a writer is having the ability to revise. *Kommandant's Girl* went through a dozen rewrites from first draft to publication. Many times I had to take broad, conceptual suggestions from my agent or editor and incorporate them into the work. Often I wasn't sure if I liked or agreed with the changes. Sometimes I would take the leap of faith and see if the changes worked (they almost always did). Other times, I would go back to whoever was making the suggestion and say, "Whoa, let's slow down here and revisit" in order to negotiate changes that made the story better without destroying my gut-level instinct about the spirit of the book. But ultimately, the collective input resulted in a richer, more complete creation, and I truly believe my ability to take those changes and integrate them made all the difference.

"...You just have to keep knocking at the door until it opens..."

BOOKS I LOVE

Individual books are difficult for me to name.
I tend to find favourite authors and read
everything they've written. So I would say
(in no particular order):

Anything by Tracy Chevalier
(Girl With A Pearl Earring)
Anything by Anita Shreve *(The Pilot's Wife)*
Anything by Pat Conroy *(Beach Music)*
Anything by Anne Tyler *(The Amateur
Marriage)*
Anything by Barbara Kingsolver
(The Poisonwood Bible)

Some single-book favourites include:
Air and Angels by Susan Hill (some of the most
beautiful prose I've ever read)
A Soldier of the Great War by Mark Helperin
(I remember being stuck during a rail strike in a
train station in Lille, France, completely oblivious because I was lost in this wonderful tale.)

*"...I tend
to find
favourite
authors and
read
everything
they've
written..."*

Two wonderful books for writers:
Writing Down the Bones by Natalie Goldberg
How to Write Killer Fiction by Carolyn Wheat

I'd also note that there are a number of
authors of historical fiction who have inspired
me, including Herman Wouk *(Winds of War)*,
Leon Uris *(Mila 18)* and John Jakes *(North
and South)*.

A DAY IN THE LIFE

I try to wake up at 5:00 am (or as close to that as I can manage!), in part, because I have to—I work full-time as an attorney, so most days I only get to work on the book until about 7:00 am or so. Then, I have to stop and get ready to go to the office. Also, I'm a morning person, so writing needs to happen before noon if it is going to get done.

On the weekends, it's a more relaxed pace, up by 6:00 or 7:00 am I write for a few hours, then off on errands or to the gym. And I live for the guilty pleasure of my Sunday afternoon nap —no catnaps for me, a good hour to two hours is ideal!

In the evenings, I exercise (gym or running), spend time with family or friends, and watch some television. I usually take some time to think about what I'll be writing the next morning and jot down some planning notes. Then it's off to bed by about 10:00 pm (a little later on the weekends)—I'm the first to admit I'm not a party animal, but I need at least seven hours' sleep, or I'm too tired to get up and write in the mornings.

"... The chance to get away and have a period of time to write in such a beautiful setting was invaluable..."

I generally write at the computer with a cup of coffee. All of my notes and planning are done long-hand, though, in a spiral notebook designated just for that project. No music when I'm working; I need lots of quiet.

Speaking of quiet, I recently had the opportunity to undertake a writing residence at the Leighton Studios, which are at the Banff Center for the Arts in Banff National Park in the Canadian Rockies. The chance to get away and have a dedicated period of time to write in such a beautiful setting was invaluable and I highly recommend it.

Turn the page to read an extract for
Pam Jenoff's stunning prequel to *Kommandant's Girl*,

THE AMBASSADOR'S DAUGHTER

THE AMBASSADOR'S DAUGHTER

The sun has dropped low beneath the crumbling arches of Lehrter Bahnhof as I make my way across the station. A sharp, late-autumn breeze sends the pigeons fluttering from the rafters and I draw my coat closer against the chill. The crowds are sparse this Tuesday evening, the platforms bereft of the usual commuter trains and their disembarking passengers. A lone carriage sits on the track farthest to the right, silent and dark.

I had been surprised by the telegram announcing Stefan's return by rail. There were hardly any trains since the Allies had bombed the lines. At least that's what the newspapers write—the defunct trains and the British naval blockade are the excuses given for everything, from the lack of new pipes to start the water running again—a problem that has forced us back outside as though it were a century ago—to the impossibility of getting fresh milk. Looking around the desolate station now, I almost believe the excuse.

Stefan's face appears in my mind. It was more than four years ago on this very platform that we said goodbye, the garland of asters I'd picked hung freshly around his neck. "Don't go," I pleaded a final time. Stefan was not cut out to fight— he had a round, gentle face, wide brown eyes that said he could never hurt anybody. But it was too late—he had gone down to the enlistment center two weeks earlier, ahead of any conscription, and come home with papers ordering him to report. The war was going to be quick, everyone said. The horse-mounted Serbs, with their swords, were no match for the Kaiser's tanks and planes. The fighting would be over in weeks, and all of the boys wanted a piece of the glory before it was gone.

I peer back over my shoulder past the closing kiosk, which gives off the smell of stale ersatz coffee, at the station doors, creaking open and closed with the wind. Someone more important than me should have been here to meet Stefan. He is a soldier, wounded in battle. More to the point, he is the only young man from our Jewish enclave in Berlin who had gone off to fight and come back at all. I don't know what I expected, not a marching band and reporters exactly, but perhaps a small delegation from the local war council. The once-proud veterans' group had been disbanded, though. No one wanted to be identified as a soldier now, to face the glares of reproach and the questions about why they had not gotten the job done.

Fifteen minutes pass, then twenty. I clutch tighter the fine leather gloves that I've managed to twist into a damp, wrinkled ball. Fighting the urge to pace, I start toward the station office to inquire if there is news of the next arrival. I navigate around a luggage trolley, which has been upended and abandoned midstation. My skirt catches on something and I pause, turning to free the hem. It is not a nail or board, but a filthy, long-haired man sitting on the ground, a fetid mass of bandages where his right leg had once been.

"Bitte…" a voice rasps as I jump backward. "I'm sorry to startle you." He is a soldier, too, or was, his tattered uniform barely recognizable. I fish a coin from my purse, trying not to recoil from the hand that reaches out for it. But inwardly, I blanch. Will Stefan look like this sorry creature?

I lift my head as a horn sounds long and low from the darkness beyond the edge of the station. A moment later a train appears, threading its way onto one of the tracks. It moves so slowly that it seems to have no engine at all, nudged instead by some slight tilt of the earth. Great clouds of steam billow from its funnel, filling the station. As I walk toward the platform, straining to see through the mist, my heart begins to pound.

The train grinds to a halt. The doors open with painstaking slowness and a few men spill out, some in uniform and others street clothes. I search those walking toward me for Stefan, knowing that he will not be among them.

When the platform has nearly cleared, a nurse pushes a wheelchair from one of the train carriages. I step forward, and then stop again. The chair does not contain Stefan, but an elderly man, hunched over so only the top of his bald head shows. The nurse struggles with the chair and as its rear wheels catch on the door, I hasten to help her.

The man in the chair uncurls, straightening slightly as I near. It is Stefan, I realize, biting my lip so hard I taste blood. A giant slash across the right side of his face from temple to chin combines with the lack of hair to make him almost un-recognizable. But the worst part is his arms, skeletal and shaky. My mind races as I try to fathom the horrors that could age a man decades in a few years.

Stefan gazes up with vacant, watery eyes, not speaking. "Hello, darling," I manage, bending to brush my lips against his papery cheek.

He reaches for me with a quivering hand. "Let's go home," he croaks, and as his fingers close around my wrist like cold death, I let out the cry I can hold back no longer.

My eyes fly open and I sit up in the darkness, still screaming.